Physics

for the IB Diploma
Exam Preparation Guide

K. A. Tsokos

WELLINGTON COLLEGE
PHYSICS DEPARTMENT

Cambridge University Press's mission is to advance knowledge and research worldwide.

Our IB Diploma resources aim to:
- encourage learners to explore concepts, ideas and topics that have local and global significance
- help students develop a positive attitude to learning in preparation for higher education
- assist students in approaching complex questions, applying critical-thinking skills and forming reasoned answers.

CAMBRIDGE
UNIVERSITY PRESS

CAMBRIDGE
UNIVERSITY PRESS

University Printing House, Cambridge CB2 8BS, United Kingdom

Cambridge University Press is part of the University of Cambridge.

It furthers the University's mission by disseminating knowledge in the pursuit of education, learning and research at the highest international levels of excellence.

www.cambridge.org
Information on this title: www.cambridge.org/9781107602618

First published 2012
3rd printing 2013

Printed in India by Replika Press Pvt. Ltd

A catalogue record for this publication is available from the British Library

ISBN 978-1-107-60261-8 Paperback

....

This material has been developed independently by the publisher and the content is in no way connected with nor endorsed by the International Baccalaureate Organization.

ACKNOWLEDGEMENTS

Thanks to the International Baccalaureate Organization for permission to reproduce its intellectual property.

Cover image © Michael Dunning/Science Photo Library

The author would like to thank Anne Trevillion for her enormous help during the preparation of this book.

Contents

Contents

This volume contains brief, concise and to the point coverage of the IB syllabus for Physics. This guide follows the syllabus exactly for the core material and all the option topics. It is intended as a review in the last few weeks before the IB exams. The book assumes that the student has undertaken a regular two year course in IB Physics and is about to take the exam. It is not intended to replace a course textbook during the two year course – it is however complete and can be used along with a textbook as a quick reference to the various parts of the syllabus. For a more detailed and in depth coverage of the topics in this book the reader is referred to the textbook *Physics for the IB Diploma, Fifth edition*, Cambridge University Press.

Using this book

Each topic includes Test yourself questions of a type similar to IB exam questions, with full answers and explanations at the back of the book.

➡ **Before you answer**
Many of these examples have a **Before you answer** comment. It is intended to give you a hint about how to proceed by alerting you to the relevant law, principle or line of approach.

On many occasions, there are comments about common mistakes that students make in solving various problems and advice about how to avoid these pitfalls. These are in blue **Helpful hint** boxes.

Examiner tips are provided in pale green boxes.

Exam-style questions are included in a section at the end of the book. Answers are available at: ibdiploma.cambridge.org.

Preparing for the examination

In preparing for the examination, make sure that you have seen as many past papers and mark schemes as possible. It is important that you see mark schemes as well, so that you can understand how the examiners will mark your paper. Past papers and mark schemes are not confidential information and should be made readily available to you by your school.

Sitting the examination

During the examination itself, you must pay attention to the following points for each of the three papers you will be examined on. For a start, make sure you have a ruler with you! It is a vital tool and will make life easier for you.

Paper 1
- It is very important to really read the question carefully! Some of the questions are tricky and play on the meaning of words.

- On many occasions most, if not all, of the four possible answers may be correct statements. But you must choose the option that answers the question and not one that is merely a correct statement. When compressing a gas, the molecules collide more frequently with each other, but that does not explain why the pressure goes up.

- Do not spend too much time on any one question. Remember that these are supposed to be questions that you can answer quickly. Long algebraic or arithmetical calculations are unnecessary in this paper and if you cannot get the answer quickly, the chances are that you will not get it even if you spend a long time on the question.

- If you cannot choose the correct answer, see if you can eliminate those that are obviously wrong.

- Sometimes you can choose the correct answer just by checking the units of the answer. If you are looking for a force, your chosen answer must have units of force!

- Do not leave any blank answers. Guess if necessary!

Papers 2 and 3

- Read the questions carefully and answer what is being asked. Perfect answers to questions that are not being asked do not gain you any points.

- Pay attention to the action verbs. This determines the amount of detail required in the answer. If the question says 'state', a simple sentence will do. An essay type answer is not required. If the question says 'explain' or 'discuss', a lot of detail is required. Feel free to answer the question in your own way and in your own words. But don't overdo it by including extra and irrelevant information. The examiner may deduct points if you say something that is incorrect or contradictory to things mentioned elsewhere.

- Pay attention to the number of lines allotted to each question, which also determines to a large extent the quantity to be provided in the answer.

- Watch your significant figures (round numbers at the very end and not in the intermediate stages of a calculation) and don't forget to include units for your final answer.

- Know your calculator well. The examination room is not the place to learn how to use a calculator.

- Know the definitions of key terms well. If you have to use an equation in lieu of a definition, do so, but remember to define all the symbols appearing in the equation.

- The A1 question is a data-based question. Remember that a 'line' of best fit is not necessarily a straight line.

- For all three papers, pay special attention to the axes of any graphs. Often, the units for a quantity are expressed with a power of 10. Thus if the x co-ordinate of a point is 2.0 but the axis is labelled $/ \times 10^{-3}$ m the value you use is $x = 2.0 \times 10^{-3}$ m.

- This only applies to Paper 3. Do not plan to go to the exam hoping to answer questions on an option that you not studied or one that you have studied by yourself outside the classroom. Statistics shows that these attempts are disastrous. Do the best you can with the option studied in your school even if you do not find it interesting and you would have preferred to have studied something else.

K. A. Tsokos

Athens, December 2010

Units

Fundamental units

It is a fascinating fact that all physical quantities have units that can be expressed in terms of those for just seven **fundamental** quantities (the IB syllabus uses only the first six). The seven fundamental quantities in the SI system and their units are:

1	time	second (s)
2	length	metre (m)
3	mass	kilogram (kg)
4	temperature	kelvin (K)
5	quantity of matter	mole (mol)
6	electric current	ampere (A)
7	luminous intensity	candela (cd)

Derived units

All other quantities have **derived** units, i.e. combinations of the fundamental units. For example, the derived unit for force (the newton) is obtained using $F = ma$ to be $kg\,m\,s^{-2}$ and that for electric potential difference (the volt) is obtained using $W = qV$ to be $\dfrac{J}{C} = \dfrac{N\,m}{A\,s} = \dfrac{kg\,m\,s^{-2}\,m}{A\,s} = kg\,m^2\,s^{-3}\,A^{-1}$.

Significant figures

There is a difference in stating that the measured mass of a body is 283.63 g rather than 283.6 g. The uncertainty in the first measurement is expected to be ±0.01 g and that in the second ±0.1 g, i.e. the first measurement is more precise – it has more **significant figures** (s.f.). When we do operations with numbers (multiplication, division, powers and roots) we must express the result to as many s.f. as those in the least precisely known number in the operation.

Number		Number of s.f.	Scientific notation
34		2	3.4×10^1
3.4		2	3.4×10^0 or just 3.4
0.0340	zeros in front do not count but zeros at the end **in a decimal** do count	3	3.40×10^{-2}
340	zeros at the end **in an integer** do not count	2	3.4×10^2

Thus the kinetic energy of a mass of 2.4 kg (2 s.f.) moving at $14.6\,m\,s^{-1}$ (3 s.f.) is $E_k = \dfrac{1}{2} \times 2.4 \times 14.6^2$
$= 255.792\,J \approx 260 = 2.6 \times 10^2\,J$. Similarly, the acceleration of a body of mass 1200 kg (2 s.f.) acted upon by a net force of 5250 N (3 s.f.) is $\dfrac{5250}{1200} = 4.375 \approx 4.4\,m\,s^{-2}$.

Test yourself 1

The force of resistance from a fluid on a sphere of radius r is given by $F = 6\pi\eta rv$ where v is the speed of the sphere and η is a constant. What are the units of η?

Test yourself 2

The radius R of the fireball t seconds after the explosion of a nuclear weapon depends only on the energy E released in the explosion, the density ρ of air and the time t. Show that the quantity $\dfrac{Et^2}{\rho}$ has units of m^5 and hence that $R \approx \left(\dfrac{Et^2}{\rho}\right)^{\frac{1}{5}}$. Calculate the energy released if the radius of the fireball is 140 m after 0.025 s. (Take $\rho = 1.0\,kg\,m^{-3}$.)

Uncertainties

Definitions

Random uncertainties   Uncertainties due to the inexperience of the experimenter and the difficulty of reading instruments. They can be reduced by repeated measurements and taking an average of the measurements.

Systematic uncertainties   Uncertainties mainly due to incorrectly calibrated instruments. They cannot be reduced by repeated measurements.

Accurate measurements   Measurements that have a small systematic error.

Precise measurements   Measurements that have a small random error.

We measure the length of the side of a cube to be 25 ± 1 mm. The 25 mm represents the **measured value** of the length and the ± 1 mm represents the **absolute uncertainty** in the measured value. The ratio $\frac{1}{25} = 0.04$ is the **fractional uncertainty** in the length and $\frac{1}{25} \times 100\% = 4\%$ is the **percentage uncertainty** in the length.

In general for a quantity Q we have $Q = \underset{\text{measured value}}{Q_0} \pm \underset{\text{absolute uncertainty}}{\Delta Q}$, $\frac{\Delta Q}{Q_0}$ = fractional uncertainty, $\frac{\Delta Q}{Q_0} \times 100\%$ = percentage uncertainty.

Suppose quantities a, b and c have been measured with uncertainties, respectively, Δa, Δb and Δc. If we use these quantities to calculate another quantity Q, these uncertainties will cause uncertainties in Q. You need to know these (approximate) rules for calculating the uncertainty in Q.

If $Q = a \pm b \pm c$, then $\Delta Q = \Delta a + \Delta b + \Delta c$

I.e. for **both** addition and subtraction, **add absolute** uncertainties.

If $Q = \frac{ab}{c}$, then $\frac{\Delta Q}{Q} = \frac{\Delta a}{a} + \frac{\Delta b}{b} + \frac{\Delta c}{c}$

I.e for multiplication and/or division, **add fractional** or **percentage** uncertainties to get the fractional or percentage uncertainty in the result.

If $Q = \frac{a^n}{b^m}$, then $\frac{\Delta Q}{Q} = n\frac{\Delta a}{a} + m\frac{\Delta b}{b}$

I.e. for powers, **add fractional** or **percentage** uncertainties, multiplied by their individual power.

If $Q = \sqrt{ab}$ or $Q = \sqrt{\frac{a}{b}}$, then $\frac{\Delta Q}{Q} = \frac{1}{2}\frac{\Delta a}{a} + \frac{1}{2}\frac{\Delta b}{b}$

I.e. for square roots and other roots, **add fractional** or **percentage** uncertainties and then divide by the power of the root. This is a special case of the rule for powers.

Test yourself 3
The resistance of a lamp is given by $R = \frac{V}{I}$. The uncertainty in the voltage is 4% and that in the current is 6%. What is the absolute uncertainty in a calculated resistance value of $24\,\Omega$?

Test yourself 4
Each side of a cube is measured with a fractional uncertainty of 0.02. Estimate the percentage uncertainty in the volume of the cube.

Test yourself 5
The period of oscillation of a mass m at the end of a spring of spring constant k is given by $T = 2\pi\sqrt{\frac{m}{k}}$. What is the percentage uncertainty of the period if m is measured with a percentage uncertainty 4% and the k with a percentage uncertainty 6%?

Graphical analysis

Error bars

Suppose that we want to plot the point $(3.0 \pm 0.1, 5.0 \pm 0.2)$ on a set of x- and y-axes. First we plot the point with coordinates $(3.0, 5.0)$ and then show the uncertainties as error bars. The horizontal error bar will have length $2 \times 0.1 = 0.2$ and the vertical error bar will have length $2 \times 0.2 = 0.4$.

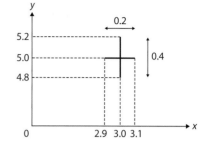

Definition

Line of best fit The curve or straight line that goes through all the error bars.

According to the IB, a 'line' may be straight or curved and you must remember that. Do **not** assume a 'line' to mean a straight line.

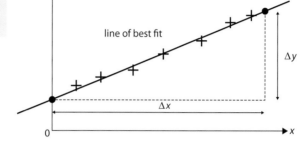

line of best fit

Finding slopes (gradients)

To find the slope of a curve at a particular point draw the tangent to the curve at that point. Choose two points **on the tangent** that are as far apart as possible to form the 'triangle'.

$$\text{slope} = \frac{1.2 - 6.0}{2.0 \times 10^{-2} - 0.0} \frac{\text{volt}}{\text{m}}$$

$$= -2.4 \times 10^2 \,\text{V m}^{-1}$$

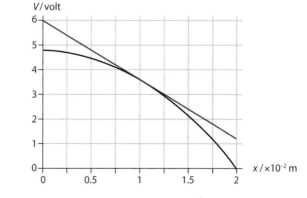

Notice that the units on the horizontal axis in the graph are in terms of 10^{-2}. Make sure you get the right sign of the slope. Make sure you state its correct units.

Estimating areas under curves

To estimate the area under the curve in the graph on the right, draw the straight line from the point $(0, 6)$ to the point $(4, 1.5)$. Each small square has area $0.5 \times 0.5 = 0.25$ square units.

It is easy to find the area of the trapezium formed as $\frac{(6 + 1.5)}{2} \times 4 = 15$.
Now count squares in between the straight line and the curve and subtract. The number of squares in between is about 11 and so the required area is about $15 - (11 \times 0.25) = 12$ square units.

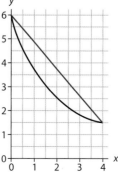

Use common sense – break up the area in order to reduce the counting of squares whenever possible.

Getting straight-line graphs

If we know the relationship between two variables we can usually arrange to plot the data in such a way that we get a straight line. We must always bear in mind that the standard equation of a straight line is

$$y = \underset{\text{gradient}}{m} \quad x \quad + \quad \underset{\text{vertical intercept}}{c}$$

where we plot the variable y on the vertical axis and the variable x on the horizontal.

Consider the relationship $T = 2\pi\sqrt{\dfrac{m}{k}}$ for the period T of a mass m undergoing oscillations at the end of a spring of spring constant k. Compare this relationship with $y = mx + c$.

> We say that y is proportional to x if $c = 0$, i.e. if the straight line goes through the origin. If the line of best fit is not straight or does not go through the origin, then **either** reason is sufficient to claim that y is **not** proportional to x.

$$T = \frac{2\pi}{\sqrt{k}} \times \sqrt{m}$$
$$\downarrow \qquad\qquad \downarrow$$
$$y = \underset{\text{constants}}{\frac{2\pi}{\sqrt{k}}} \times \ x$$

By identifying $T \leftrightarrow y$ and $\sqrt{m} \leftrightarrow x$ we get the equation of a straight line $y = \dfrac{2\pi}{\sqrt{k}}x$. So we must plot T on the vertical axis and $\sqrt{m}$ on the horizontal axis to get a straight line whose gradient will be $\dfrac{2\pi}{\sqrt{k}}$. Alternatively we may write

$$T^2 = \frac{4\pi^2}{k} \times m$$
$$\downarrow \qquad\quad \downarrow$$
$$y = \underset{\text{constants}}{\frac{4\pi^2}{k}} \times x$$

By identifying $T^2 \leftrightarrow y$ and $m \leftrightarrow x$ we get the equation of a straight line $y = \dfrac{4\pi^2}{k}x$. So we must plot T^2 on the vertical axis and m on the horizontal axis to get a straight line whose gradient will be $\dfrac{4\pi^2}{k}$.

A different procedure must be followed if the variables are related through a power relation, such as $F = kr^n$ where the constants k and n are unknown. Taking natural logs (or logs with any base) we have

$$\ln F = \ln k + n \times \ln r$$
$$\downarrow \qquad\qquad\qquad \downarrow$$
$$y = \ln k + n \times \ x$$

and so plotting $\ln F$ against $\ln r$ gives a straight line with gradient n and vertical intercept $\ln k$.

A variation of this is used for an exponential equation, such as $A = A_0 e^{-\lambda t}$ where A_0 and λ are constants. Here we must take logs to get $\ln A = \ln A_0 - \lambda t$ and so

$$\ln A = \ln A_0 - \lambda \times \ t$$
$$\downarrow \qquad\qquad\qquad \downarrow$$
$$y = \ln A_0 - \lambda \times \ x$$

> Plot $\ln A$ on the vertical axis and t on the horizontal so that we get a straight line with gradient $-\lambda$ and vertical intercept $\ln A_0$.

Test yourself **6**

Copy and complete this table.

Equation	Constants	Variables to plot to give straight line	Gradient	Vertical intercept
$P = kT$	k			
$v = u + at$	u, a			
$v^2 = 2as$	a			
$F = \dfrac{kq_1 q_2}{r^2}$	k, q_1, q_2			
$a = -\omega^2 x$	ω^2			
$V = \dfrac{kq}{r}$	k, q			
$T^2 = \dfrac{4\pi^2}{GM} R^3$	G, M			
$I = I_0 e^{-aT}$	I_0, a			
$\lambda = \dfrac{h}{\sqrt{2mqV}}$	h, m, q			
$F = av + bv^2$	a, b			
$E = \dfrac{1}{2} m\omega^2 \sqrt{A^2 - x^2}$	m, ω^2, A			
$\dfrac{1}{u} + \dfrac{1}{v} = \dfrac{1}{f}$	f			

Test yourself **7**

State what variables must be plotted so that we get a straight line for the relation $d = ch^{0.8}$ where c is a constant.

Estimating uncertainties in measured quantities

The general simple rule is:

For **analogue meters**, take half of the smallest scale division. For example, for an ordinary metre rule the smallest scale division is 1 mm and so the uncertainty is ±0.5 mm. (But bear in mind that if a metre rule is to be used to measure the length of say a rod, the uncertainty of ±0.5 mm applies to the measurement of each end of the rod for a total uncertainty of ±1 mm.)

Note that this is a conservative approach. Someone may claim to be able to read to better precision than this. See **Test yourself 8**.

For **digital meters**, take ± of the smallest division. For example, for a digital voltmeter that can read to the nearest hundredth of a volt, the uncertainty is ±0.1 V. For an ammeter that can read to the nearest tenth of an ampere take ±0.1 A.

Test yourself **8**

Estimate the reading and the uncertainty in each of the instruments in the diagrams.

a

b

Uncertainty in the measured value of a gradient (slope)

To find the uncertainty in the gradient of the (straight) line of best fit, draw the lines of maximum and minimum gradient. Calculate these two gradients, m_{max} and m_{min}. A simple estimate of the uncertainty in the gradient is then $\frac{m_{max} - m_{min}}{2}$.

Test yourself 9

Electrons that have been accelerated by a potential difference V enter a region of magnetic field where they are bent into a circular path of radius r. Theory suggests that $r^2 = \frac{2m}{qB^2}V$. The table shows values of the radius r and potential difference V obtained in an experiment.

Radius r/cm ±0.1 cm	Potential difference V/V	r^2/cm²
4.5	500	±
4.9	600	±
5.3	700	±
5.7	800	±
6.0	900	±

a Explain why a graph of r^2 against V will result in a straight line.

b State the slope of the straight line in **a** in terms of the symbols m, q and B.

c Copy the table and complete the right column by inserting values of the radius squared including the uncertainty.

The graph shows the data points plotted on a set of axes.

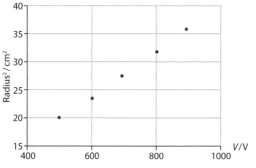

d Trace the graph and then draw error bars for the first and the last data points.

e Draw a line of best fit for these data points.

f Calculate the gradient of the line of best fit including its uncertainty.

The magnetic field used in this experiment was $B = 1.80 \times 10^{-3}$ T.

g Calculate the value of the charge to mass ratio $\left(\frac{q}{m}\right)$ for the electron that this experiment gives. Include the uncertainty in the calculated value.

Vectors

Definitions

Vectors   Physical quantities that have both **magnitude** and **direction**. They are represented by arrows and written in *bold italics*. The **length** of the arrow gives the magnitude of the vector. The **direction** of the arrow is the direction of the vector. (Vectors can be positive or negative.)

Scalars   Physical quantities with magnitude but **not** direction.

Vectors	Scalars
displacement	distance
velocity	time/mass
acceleration	energy/work/power
force	temperature
momentum/impulse	electric current/resistance
electric/gravitational/magnetic fields	electric/gravitational potential

Adding vectors   Have *a* and *b* start at the same point, O. Draw the parallelogram whose two sides are *a* and *b*. Draw the diagonal starting at O.

Subtracting vectors   Have *a* and *b* start at the same point, O. To find *b* − *a* draw the vector −*a* and then add *b* to −*a*.

Components of vectors

As the diagrams show, the component adjacent to the angle θ involves $\cos\theta$ and that opposite to θ involves $\sin\theta$. Follow the three stages: **draw the forces, add the axes, get the components**. Choose as one of your axes the direction in which the body moves or would move if it could.

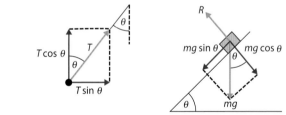

Test yourself **10**

A river is 16 m wide. The diagram shows a boat travelling at $4.0\,\mathrm{m\,s^{-1}}$ with respect to the water when the current has a speed of $3.0\,\mathrm{m\,s^{-1}}$ with respect to the shore and is directed to the right. The boat is rowed in such a way so as to arrive at the opposite shore directly across from where it started. Calculate the time taken for the trip.

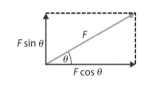

Order of magnitude estimates

The tables below give values for various distances, masses and times. You are not required to know these by heart but you must have a **general** idea of the size, mass and duration of various quantities and processes. Use the information in these tables to answer the questions which follow.

	Length / m
radius of the observable universe	10^{26}
distance to the Andromeda galaxy	10^{22}
diameter of the Milky Way galaxy	10^{21}
distance to Proxima Centauri (star)	10^{16}
diameter of solar system	10^{13}
distance to Sun	10^{11}
radius of the Earth	10^{7}
size of a cell	10^{-5}
size of a hydrogen atom	10^{-10}
size of an average nucleus	10^{-15}
Planck length	10^{-35}

	Mass / kg
the universe	10^{53}
the Milky Way galaxy	10^{41}
the Sun	10^{30}
the Earth	10^{24}
Boeing 747 (empty)	10^{5}
an apple	0.2
a raindrop	10^{-6}
a bacterium	10^{-15}
mass of smallest virus	10^{-21}
a hydrogen atom	10^{-27}
an electron	10^{-30}

	Time / s
age of the universe	10^{17}
time of travel by light to nearest star (Proxima Centauri)	10^{8}
one year	10^{7}
one day	10^{5}
period of a heartbeat	1
period of red light	10^{-15}
time of passage of light across an average nucleus	10^{-23}
Planck time	10^{-43}

Test yourself **11**
Estimate the weight of an apple.

Test yourself **12**
Estimate the number of seconds in a year.

Test yourself **13**
Estimate the time taken by light to travel across a nucleus.

Test yourself **14**
Estimate the time in between two of your heartbeats.

Test yourself **15**
Estimate how many grains of sand can fit into the volume of the Earth.

Test yourself **16**
Estimate the number of water molecules in a glass of water.

Test yourself **17**
If the temperature of the Sun were to increase by 2% and the distance between the Earth and the Sun were to decrease by 1%, by how much would the intensity of the radiation received on Earth change?

$$I \propto \frac{T^4}{d^2}$$

Kinematics

Definitions

Displacement   The vector $\mathbf{r}$ from some arbitrary fixed point to the position of a particle, i.e. the distance in a given direction.

Average velocity   The ratio of the change of the displacement to the time taken, $\frac{\Delta r}{\Delta t}$. This vector has the same direction as $\Delta \mathbf{r}$.

Average speed   The ratio of the **total** distance travelled d to the **total** time t taken, $\frac{d}{t}$.

> The average speed is not, in general, related to the magnitude of the average velocity.

Instantaneous velocity   The rate of change with time of the displacement vector, $v = \lim\limits_{\Delta t \to 0} \frac{\Delta r}{\Delta t}$. Instantaneous velocity is along the tangent to the path.

Instantaneous speed   The rate of change with time of the distance travelled: speed $= \lim\limits_{\Delta t \to 0} \frac{\Delta d}{\Delta t}$. It is equal to the magnitude of the instantaneous velocity vector.

Average acceleration   The ratio of the change of the velocity vector to the time taken, $\frac{\Delta v}{\Delta t}$. This vector is in the same direction as $\Delta \mathbf{v}$.

Instantaneous acceleration   The rate of change with time of the velocity vector, $a = \lim\limits_{\Delta t \to 0} \frac{\Delta v}{\Delta t}$.

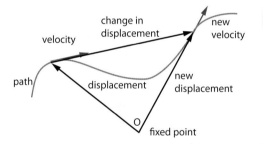

> The diagram shows the difference between displacement (blue curved line) and change in displacement. The direction of velocity (red arrows) is at a tangent to the path. The average speed is always **equal to** or **greater than** the magnitude of the average velocity.

Test yourself 1

The diagram shows a particle moving around a circle with constant speed. The displacement of the particle is measured from point O, the position of the particle at $t = 0$. Draw a graph to show how the magnitude r of the displacement vector varies with time for one complete revolution.

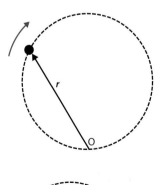

> **Before you answer**
> What is the displacement initially?
> Does it reach a maximum value?

Test yourself 2

The diagram shows a particle which takes 5.0 s to move along a semicircle of radius 5.0 m. Calculate the average velocity and average speed.

> **Before you answer**
> Make sure you understand the difference between average speed and average velocity.

Motion on a straight line – formulae and graphs

The basic formulae for motion on a straight line with constant acceleration are shown below. These formulae can **only** be used when we have **constant acceleration** and motion on a **straight line**.

If the acceleration is not constant we must rely on analysis of graphs.

The equations of motion

$v = u + at$ $\qquad$ u = initial velocity

$s = ut + \dfrac{1}{2}at^2$ $\qquad$ v = velocity after time t

$v^2 = u^2 + 2as$ $\qquad$ s = displacement

$s = \left(\dfrac{u + v}{2}\right)t$ $\qquad$ t = time elapsed

Graphs

- Slope of displacement–time graph gives the velocity.
- Slope of velocity–time graph gives the acceleration.
- Area under velocity–time graph gives the change in displacement.
- Area under acceleration–time graph gives the change in velocity.

Relative velocity

Imagine two objects, A and B, whose velocities as measured by the **same** observer are v_A and v_B. We define the relative velocity of B with respect to A as $v_{B|A} = v_B - v_A$.

The first diagram shows the velocities with respect to the ground of the bird and the cyclist.

The second diagram shows the relative velocity of the bird with respect to the cyclist is $v_{\text{bird|cyclist}} = v_{\text{bird}} - v_{\text{cyclist}}$.

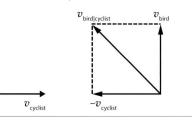

Test yourself 3

An object starts from rest and accelerates with constant acceleration. It covers a distance of 20 m in 5.0 s. The speed after 5.0 s is

A 2.0 m s⁻¹ $\quad$ **B** 4.0 m s⁻¹ $\quad$ **C** 8.0 m s⁻¹ $\quad$ **D** 10 m s⁻¹

➡ **Before you answer**
You need a formula without acceleration.

Test yourself 4

The graph shows the variation with time of the speed of a particle.
a Calculate the instantaneous acceleration at 2.0 s.
b Draw a sketch graph to show the variation with time of the acceleration of the particle.
c Estimate the displacement at 6.0 s (assume zero initial displacement).

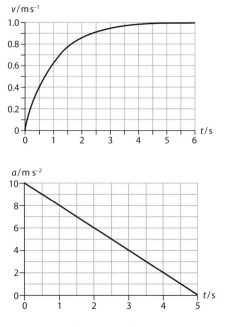

Test yourself 5

The graph shows the variation with time of the acceleration of a particle. The particle starts from rest. Determine its velocity after 5.0 s.

Forces and Newton's first law

Definitions

Force   An unbalanced force causes acceleration of the body on which the force acts. The SI unit of force is the newton.

Representation of forces   Forces, being vectors, are represented by arrows whose length is the magnitude of the force. The direction of the arrow gives the direction of the force.

Net (resultant) force   This is the single force whose effect is the same as the combined effect of all the individual forces on the body. This force is found by vector addition.

Maximum and minimum magnitude of net force   The resultant of two forces of magnitude say 5 N and 7 N can have a magnitude of at most 12 N if the forces are in the same direction and 2 N if they are opposite. In any other case the force is in between these extremes. The net force can never be less than 2 N nor greater than 12 N.

The first law of mechanics   When the net force on a body is zero the body moves with constant velocity. It is impossible to do an experiment that will determine what your velocity is if you are in a closed box moving at constant velocity. (You cannot look outside.)

Equilibrium   The situation when the net force on a body or system is zero.

Example

A block of weight 100 N is suspended by two strings of unequal length as shown in the diagram. Estimate the tension in each string. The arrow shown represents the tension in the vertical string.

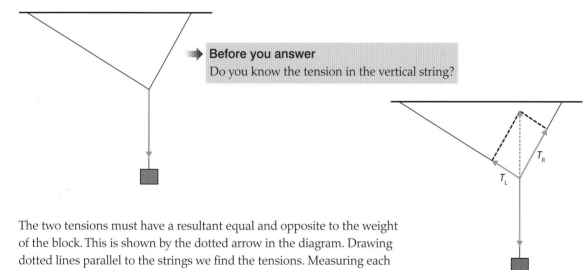

Before you answer
Do you know the tension in the vertical string?

The two tensions must have a resultant equal and opposite to the weight of the block. This is shown by the dotted arrow in the diagram. Drawing dotted lines parallel to the strings we find the tensions. Measuring each with a ruler and comparing to the length of the arrow representing the weight we find approximately $T_L \approx 50\,\text{N}$ and $T_R \approx 83\,\text{N}$.

Test yourself **6**

An elevator is moving downward at constant velocity. A person drops a ball from rest. Will the time it takes the ball to hit the elevator floor be less than, equal to, or larger than the time the ball would have taken in an elevator at rest?

Before you answer
You can solve the problem **either** by looking at things from the point of view of the observer inside the elevator **or** from the point of view of an observer outside. Choose one.

Newton's second law of motion

The net force on a body of constant mass is equal to the product of the mass and the acceleration of the mass, $F_{net} = ma$.

In all mechanics problems:
- Draw a diagram.
- Draw a free body diagram showing the forces on each body.
- For each body, find the net force in terms of the forces acting on each body.
- Use Newton's second law **separately** on each body or treat all bodies as one if convenient.

> It is important to realise that the force and the acceleration are in the same direction.

Test yourself **7**

The diagram shows a block of mass M is on a horizontal, frictionless table which is connected by a string to a smaller mass m that hangs from the string. If m is released, find the acceleration and the tension in the string.

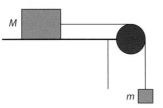

> ### Before you answer
> You can save time if you consider the two bodies as one of mass $M + m$.
> In this case what is the net force on the whole system?
> Is the tension relevant if you consider the two bodies as one?
> If you have to find the tension as in this example, find the acceleration first treating the bodies as one, and then treat them as separate.

Test yourself **8**

The diagram shows five identical blocks which are connected by four strings A, B, C and D. Force F acts on the front block. Friction is negligible.

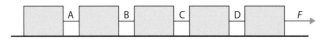

In which string is the tension the greatest?

Test yourself **9**

The diagram shows a force of 60 N being applied to the body of mass 12 kg. A string joins this body to another body of mass 8.0 kg. Calculate **a** the acceleration and **b** the tension in the string. (Friction is to be ignored.) **c** How would your answers to **a** and **b** change (if at all) if the order of the blocks was reversed?

There are now frictional forces between both blocks and the ground. The frictional force on the 8.0 kg block is 24 N. The pulling force of 60 N cannot get the blocks to move. Calculate **d** the tension in the string and **e** the frictional force on the 12 kg block.

Newton's third law of motion

If a body A exerts a force on body B, then B will exert on A an equal and opposite force.

- A tennis racket comes into contact with a tennis ball and exerts a force on the ball. The ball will exert an equal and opposite force on the racket.
- The weight of a body is the force that the Earth exerts on the body. The force is directed vertically downwards. Therefore the body exerts at the centre of the Earth an equal and opposite force, i.e. a force of the same magnitude upwards.
- A rocket exerts a force on the exhaust gases pushing them backward. The gases exert an equal force on the rocket pushing it forward.
- A helicopter rotor exerts a force on air pushing air downwards. The air exerts an equal, upward force on the rotor.

> This is often remembered as 'for every action there is an equal and opposite reaction' but you should **not** quote this in an exam!

Test yourself **10**

A girl stands on a weighing scale inside an elevator that accelerates vertically upwards. The forces on the girl are her weight W and the reaction force from the scale R. The reading of the scale is

A $R + W$ **B** W **C** R **D** $R - W$

> ➡ **Before you answer**
> The scale reads the force exerted on it.

> Two forces that are equal and opposite are **not necessarily** the 'action–reaction' pair of the law.
> The forces mentioned in Newton's third law act on **different** bodies.

Test yourself **11**

The diagram shows a block on a wedge of angle θ to the horizontal.

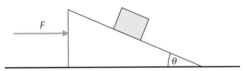

A horizontal force F is applied to the wedge accelerating it forward. The block does not move relative to the wedge. Show that $\tan\theta = \dfrac{F}{W}$ where W is the combined weight of the wedge and the block. (There is no friction between the block and the wedge or the wedge and the ground.)

Test yourself **12**

The diagram shows a body of mass m on the floor of an elevator that is accelerating upwards with acceleration a. Derive an expression for the reaction force from the floor on the block in terms of m, g and a.

> ➡ **Before you answer**
> Is the reaction force equal to the weight?

> Assume that the body is actually resting on a scale. Then R is the force that the scale exerts on the body. By Newton's third law the force the body exerts on the scale is also R in magnitude. But the scale reads the force acting on it, i.e. R. So if the elevator is accelerating, the scale does **not** read the weight of the body.

Momentum, momentum conservation and impulse

Definitions

Momentum   The product of the mass and the velocity of a body, $p = mv$. It is a vector with the same direction as that of velocity.

Impulse   The product $F\Delta t$, i.e. the average force on the body multiplied by the time for which the force was acting. Impulse is the area under the curve in a graph of F against t.

> Impulse equals **the change in momentum** of a body. Impulse is a vector.

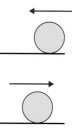

The second law in terms of momentum $F_{net} = \dfrac{\Delta p}{\Delta t}$. The usefulness of this formula is that it can be applied when the mass varies. In those cases where the mass of a body (or system) is constant this law becomes the usual $F_{net} = ma$, since $F_{net} = \dfrac{\Delta p}{\Delta t} = m\dfrac{\Delta v}{\Delta t} = ma$.

Conservation of momentum   When the resultant (net) external force on a system is zero, the total momentum of the system stays constant.

Proof of momentum conservation

Let a system have total momentum p. Then by Newton's second law, $F_{net} = \dfrac{\Delta p}{\Delta t}$ where F_{net} is the net external force on the system. If $F_{net} = 0$, it follows that $\Delta p = 0$, i.e. the total momentum stays constant.

Test yourself **13**

A ball of mass 0.20 kg moving at 4.0 m s⁻¹ collides with a vertical wall. It rebounds with a speed of 2.5 m s⁻¹. The ball was in contact with the wall for 0.14 s. Calculate **a** the magnitude and direction of the change in momentum of the ball, **b** the magnitude of the average force on the ball and **c** discuss whether the law of momentum conservation applies to this situation. **d** The same ball now falls vertically on the floor. The impact and rebound speeds are the same. State and explain whether the reaction force from the floor on the ball is different from the answer in **b**.

> **Before you answer**
> Is the velocity before collision 4.0 m s⁻¹ or −4.0 m s⁻¹?
> Momentum is a **vector**. There is a very common error that is made at this point.

Test yourself **14**

A rocket of mass 120 kg contains an additional 80 kg of fuel. Gases from the burned fuel leave the rocket with a speed of 3.0×10^2 m s⁻¹, **relative to the rocket**, at a rate of 2.2 kg s⁻¹. The rocket is initially at rest in outer space.
a Calculate the force exerted on the gases. **b** Explain why the rocket accelerates.
c Calculate the **initial** acceleration of the rocket.

> **Before you answer**
> What is the force exerted on the gases?

Test yourself **15**

A projectile moving horizontally collides elastically with a vertical steel plate. During contact with the plate the force on the projectile varies with time as shown on the graph. Calculate **a** the duration of the contact, **b** the impulse delivered to the ball, **c** the average force on the projectile. **d** Given that the speed of the projectile before and after the collision was 18 m s⁻¹, calculate its mass.

> **Before you answer**
> What does the area under the curve tell you?

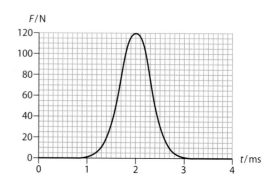

Work, energy and power

For motion along a straight line and a constant force, the work done by a force is the product of the magnitude of the force and the distance travelled in the direction of the force, $W = Fd\cos\theta$, where θ is the angle between the force and the direction of motion. Work is a scalar quantity.

> If the force is **not constant** you **cannot** use this formula. The work is then the area under the force–distance graph. Make sure you understand **which force** you want to find the work of. Some questions ask for work done without specifying the force, so you must be careful.

Definitions

Energy   The ability to work. Energy is a scalar quantity. In mechanics we deal with the following forms of **mechanical energy**.

Kinetic energy $E_K = \frac{1}{2}mv^2$ (another formula for kinetic energy using momentum is $E_K = \frac{p^2}{2m}$)

Gravitational potential energy $E_P = mgh$, where the height may be measured from any horizontal level.

Elastic potential energy of a spring $E_E = \frac{1}{2}kx^2$ (k is the spring constant.)

Total mechanical energy   The sum of all forms of mechanical energy: $E_T = E_K + E_P + E_E = \frac{1}{2}mv^2 + mgh + \frac{1}{2}kx^2$

Conservation of energy   Total energy, mechanical and otherwise, cannot be created or destroyed. It only gets transformed from one form into another. In a system where no resistance/frictional/dissipative forces act the total mechanical energy stays the same. If such forces do act, then the mechanical energy gets **transformed** into other forms of non-mechanical energy, for example **thermal** energy. The work done by these forces is the change in the total mechanical energy of the system.

Elastic collisions   Collisions in which the total kinetic energy before and after the collision is the same.

Power   Power is the rate at which a force does work (or rate at which energy is being consumed), i.e.
$P = \frac{\Delta W}{\Delta t}$. Power is measured in joules per second, i.e. in watt (W). If a constant force $\boldsymbol{F}$ acting on a body moves the body at speed v along a straight line then the instantaneous power developed is $P = \frac{\Delta W}{\Delta t} = \frac{F \times \Delta s}{\Delta t} = Fv$.

> You must know how to derive $P = Fv$ in an exam.

The work kinetic energy relation   The work done by the net force on a body is equal to the change in the body's kinetic energy, $W_{net} = \Delta E_K$

Test yourself 16
A force of magnitude 20 N pushes a body along a horizontal circle of radius 5.0 m at constant speed. The **direction of the force is tangent to the circle**. Calculate the work done by this force after completing one full circle.

> **Before you answer**
> What angle does the force make with the direction of motion? Does the definition of work involve distance or displacement?

Test yourself 17
The work done in extending a spring from its natural length to an extension e is W. The work done in extending the same spring from an extension e to an extension $2e$ is

A W **B** $2W$ **C** $3W$ **D** $4W$

> **Before you answer**
> How does the work done depend on extension?

Test yourself 18
A body of mass 5.0 kg and speed 3.0 m s^{-1} collides head on with a stationary block of mass 7.0 kg. The two blocks stick together. Calculate the common speed of the two blocks after the collision. Why is this collision not elastic?

> **Before you answer**
> Collision $\Rightarrow$ momentum conservation.

Test yourself 19
A body of initial kinetic energy 48 J moves on a horizontal straight line. It is brought to rest by a constant frictional force of 6.0 N. Calculate the distance travelled until the body stops.

Uniform circular motion

It is convenient to measure displacement from the centre of the circle.

The displacement at P and that at Q have the same magnitude but their directions are different.

The velocity at P and that at Q have the same magnitude but their directions are different.

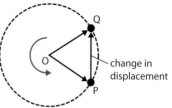

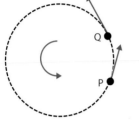

Therefore we have acceleration. The direction of acceleration is the same as the direction of the **change** in velocity.

> The particle is going around a circle with constant speed. Even though the speed is constant, the direction of the velocity is always changing so we have acceleration.

The acceleration has magnitude $\frac{v^2}{r}$ and is directed towards the centre of the circle. This means that the **net** force on the particle must be directed towards the centre of the circle. This is the centripetal force that provides the centripetal acceleration.

Examples of circular motion:
- A car taking a circular bend (the force is provided by friction between the road and the tyres)
- The Earth revolving around the Sun (the force is provided by the gravitational attraction between the Earth and the Sun)

An alternative formula for the centripetal acceleration
In circular motion the time for a complete revolution is called the period T. The inverse of the period is the frequency f.

Then $v = \frac{2\pi r}{T}$ and so $a = \frac{v^2}{r} = \frac{\left(\frac{2\pi r}{T}\right)^2}{r} = \frac{4\pi^2 r}{T^2} = 4\pi^2 r f^2$

Test yourself **20**
The diagram shows a block of mass m held horizontal at the end of a string of length L. The block is released. What is the tension in the string as it moves past the vertical position?

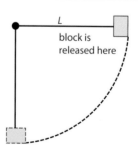

> ➡ Before you answer
> Is the block in equilibrium as it moves past the vertical position?
> Is the block moving in a straight line or a circle? You must use
> Newton's second law (since you are looking for a force) but you will
> also need conservation of energy.

Thermal concepts

Definitions

The absolute temperature scale   A temperature in which the lowest possible temperature is zero degrees. The Kelvin (absolute) and Celsius scales are related by $T(\mathrm{K}) = t(°\mathrm{C}) + 273$.

Absolute temperature and random kinetic energy of molecules   The average random kinetic energy of the molecules of a substance is proportional to the absolute temperature of the substance. Thus, at zero absolute temperature the random kinetic energy of the molecules becomes zero (in classical, i.e. non-quantum, physics).

Internal energy, U   The sum of the total random kinetic energy of the molecules and their intermolecular potential energy. (Internal energy also includes chemical energy and nuclear energy but we do not consider these in this topic.) It is customary to call the part of the internal energy dealing with total random kinetic energy of the molecules and the intermolecular potential energy the **thermal** part of the internal energy, or just thermal energy.

Intermolecular forces   There are forces (electromagnetic in origin) between any two molecules in any substance whether solid, liquid or vapour. The forces are strongest in the solid phase and weakest in the vapour. Because of the intermolecular forces, increasing the separation of molecules demands work to be done. This work increases the intermolecular potential energy, and hence the internal energy of the substance.

> In the case of an ideal gas these forces are zero and so internal energy only consists of random kinetic energy.

Heat, Q, is 'energy in transit'   Energy that is transferred from one body to another due to a difference in temperature.

> We cannot speak of the 'heat content' of a body.

Direction of energy flow   Thermal energy, on its own, always gets transferred from a high temperature region to a lower temperature region. When two bodies are at the same temperature they are said to be in thermal equilibrium and no further net energy gets transferred between them.

The mole   The SI unit for quantity. One mole of any substance contains the same number of molecules. This number is known as **Avogadro's number** and equals $N_A = 6.02 \times 10^{23}$. The **mass in grams** of one mole of a substance is known as the **molar mass**.

> The mass number of an element is its **approximate** molar mass (in grams).

Thus for $^{238}_{92}\mathrm{U}$ the molar mass is 238 g and for $^{4}_{2}\mathrm{He}$ it is 4 g. To find the molar mass of a compound we need to know the chemical formula for that compound. Thus, for water we have the formula H_2O. The molar mass of hydrogen ($^{1}_{1}\mathrm{H}$) is 1 g and that of oxygen ($^{16}_{8}\mathrm{O}$) is 16 g. Hence the molar mass of water is $2 \times 1 + 16 = 18$ g.

Test yourself **1**
The molar mass of lead is $207\,\mathrm{g\,mol^{-1}}$ and its density is $1.13 \times 10^4\,\mathrm{kg\,m^{-3}}$. Estimate the average separation of lead atoms.

> ➡ **Before you answer**
> Try to understand and justify the diagram. Each dotted square represents a cube with one lead atom at its centre.

Test yourself **2**
The temperature of a liquid changes from $22\,°\mathrm{C}$ to $32\,°\mathrm{C}$. What is the change in temperature of the liquid and what is its final temperature in kelvin?

Calorimetry

Definitions

Specific heat capacity, c The energy required to change the temperature of a unit mass by one degree.

Thermal capacity, C The energy required to change the temperature of a body by one degree. Its units are JK^{-1}. Thermal capacity of a body of mass m is related to specific heat capacity through: $C = mc$.

Change of phase Substances undergo **phase changes** at specific, **constant** temperatures. For example, ice will melt into water at $0\,^{\circ}C$ (melting point) and water will boil into steam at $100\,^{\circ}C$ (boiling point).

Specific latent heat The energy required to change the phase of a **unit mass** at **constant temperature**. When a quantity Q of energy is supplied to a body of mass m at its melting or boiling point: $Q = mL$. Here the constant L is the specific latent heat of fusion (if melting) or vaporisation (if boiling).

> Note that you must mention that temperature is constant in this definition.

When a quantity Q of heat is supplied to a body of mass m and there is no change of phase, the body's temperature will increase by $\Delta\theta$. $Q = mc\Delta\theta$. Here the constant c is the specific heat capacity.

For water, $c = 4200\,J\,kg^{-1}\,K^{-1}$. So to change the temperature of 2.0 kg of water by $15\,^{\circ}C$ we require $Q = 2.0 \times 4200 \times 15 \approx 126\,kJ$.

Energy changes during a phase change

A solid can melt into a liquid and a liquid can boil into vapour. The reverse processes are a liquid freezing into a solid and vapour condensing into a liquid. These are phase changes and occur at a **constant temperature**.

Let us calculate the energy required to change 2.0 kg of ice at $-15\,^{\circ}C$ to liquid water at $+15\,^{\circ}C$.

To increase temperature of ice from $-15\,^{\circ}C$ to $0\,^{\circ}C$ ($c_{ice} = 2100\,J\,kg^{-1}\,K^{-1}$)	$Q = mc\Delta\theta$ $= 2.0 \times 2100 \times 15 \approx 63\,kJ$
To melt 2.0 kg of ice at $0\,^{\circ}C$ to liquid water at $0\,^{\circ}C$ (the specific latent heat of fusion of ice: $L = 334\,kJ\,kg^{-1}$)	$Q = mL$ $= 2.0 \times 334 \approx 670\,kJ$
To increase temperature of melted ice (which is now liquid water) from $0\,^{\circ}C$ to $15\,^{\circ}C$	$Q = mc\Delta\theta$ $= 2.0 \times 4200 \times 15 \approx 126\,kJ$
	Thus we require a total of about 860 kJ.

Test yourself 3

A 80 g piece of aluminium ($c = 900\,J\,kg^{-1}\,K^{-1}$) at $250\,^{\circ}C$ is dropped into 0.75 kg water ($c = 4200\,J\,kg^{-1}\,K^{-1}$) at $15\,^{\circ}C$ in a calorimeter. The thermal capacity of the calorimeter is $C = 180\,J\,K^{-1}$. Estimate the final temperature of the water.

> ➡ **Before you answer**
> Give a symbol to represent the final temperature. What loses energy and what gains energy?

Test yourself 4

A sample of 120 g of solid paraffin initially at $20\,^{\circ}C$ is being heated by a heater of constant power. The specific heat capacity of solid paraffin is $2500\,J\,kg^{-1}\,K^{-1}$. The temperature of paraffin varies with time as shown.

Use the graph to determine **a** the power of the heater, **b** the melting temperature of paraffin, **c** the specific latent heat of fusion of paraffin and **d** the specific heat capacity of paraffin in the liquid phase. **e** Explain why the temperature of paraffin stays constant during melting.

> ➡ **Before you answer**
> What does internal energy consist of?

The kinetic model of gases

Pressure

A gas is a very large collection of molecules with distances between molecules that, on average, are about 10 times as large as in the solid and liquid phase. An ideal gas is an idealised form of gas that obeys the assumptions:

- Molecules are hard spheres of negligible radius and volume.
- Collisions (between molecules and between molecules and walls) are elastic.
- Duration of collisions is short.
- There are no forces between molecules except during contact.
- Molecules move randomly with a range of speeds.
- Molecules obey the laws of mechanics.

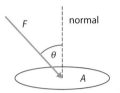

A force of magnitude F is acting on a region of area A. The force makes an angle θ with the normal to the area.

Pressure is defined as the normal force per unit area acting on a surface: $P = \dfrac{F\cos\theta}{A}$. The unit of pressure is $\mathrm{N\,m^{-2}}$ and this is known as the pascal, Pa.

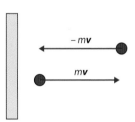

There is a force on the molecule because its **momentum** has changed from $-mv$ to mv, i.e. it has changed by $2mv$ (in magnitude). Therefore there is also a force on the wall. Pressure develops as result of the force from the very many molecules colliding with the walls.

Two factors affect the pressure of a gas: the average speed of the molecules and the frequency with which the molecules collide with the walls.

Evaporation

Whereas a liquid boils at a specific temperature, a liquid can evaporate (i.e. turn into a vapour) at **any temperature**. Unlike boiling, the evaporation process involves **surface molecules only**. In boiling, molecules from anywhere in the liquid can leave the liquid.

Evaporation in a liquid is followed by a drop in the temperature of the liquid. This is because it is the faster molecules that will escape, leaving behind the slower ones. Thus the average speed, and hence the average kinetic energy of the molecules left behind, decreases. Since temperature is a measure of the average kinetic energy of the molecules, the temperature also decreases.

The rate of evaporation increases with increasing temperature and surface area of the liquid.

Test yourself **5**

A gas is compressed at constant temperature. Explain why the pressure increases.

> **Before you answer**
> What does the constant temperature tell you? What does a smaller volume imply?

Test yourself **6**

A gas is heated at constant volume. Explain why the pressure will increase.

> **Before you answer**
> Does the temperature stay constant?

Simple harmonic motion (SHM)

In SHM the acceleration (or the net force) is **proportional to and opposite to the displacement from equilibrium**.

Mathematically this means that $a = -\omega^2 x$ where ω is a constant called the angular frequency.

SHM consists of **periodic oscillations** with a period that is **independent** of the **amplitude**. The period is given by $T = \dfrac{2\pi}{\omega}$.

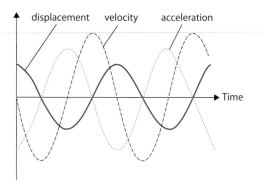

You must be in a position to draw graphs showing the variation with time of the displacement, velocity and acceleration for SHM. You must be careful to show the relative positioning of these three graphs.

$$x = x_0 \cos(\omega t) \text{ thus } v = -\omega x_0 \sin(\omega t)$$

The data booklet has $v = v_0 \sin(\omega t)$. You must remember that $v_0 = -\omega x_0$.

$$a = -\omega^2 x_0 \cos(\omega t) = -\omega^2 x$$

Energy in SHM

The kinetic energy of a mass m that undergoes SHM is given by $E_K = \frac{1}{2}mv^2$ which can also be written as $E_K = \frac{1}{2}m\omega^2 x_0^2 \sin^2(\omega t)$.

The maximum kinetic energy is therefore $E_{max} = \frac{1}{2}m\omega^2 x_0^2$ and this is also the total energy of the system.

The potential energy is $E_P = \frac{1}{2}m\omega^2 x^2$.

The speed in SHM is given by $v = \pm\omega\sqrt{x_0^2 - x^2}$.

At the extremes of the oscillation, $x = \pm x_0$ and so $v = 0$.

In SHM, kinetic energy gets transformed to potential energy and vice versa.

As the mass goes past the equilibrium position, $x = 0$ and so $v = \pm\omega x_0$.

Test yourself **1**

The acceleration is related to displacement according to **a** $a = -4x$, **b** $a = 4x$ **c** $a = -4x^2$.
In which cases do we have SHM?

Test yourself **2**

The graph on the right shows the variation with displacement of the acceleration of a particle oscillating between $x = \pm15$ cm. **a** Use the graph to explain why the oscillations are SHM. Calculate **b** the period of the motion and **c** the maximum velocity.

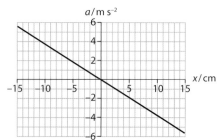

Test yourself **3**

The graph shows the kinetic energy of a mass of 0.25 kg undergoing SHM as a function of the displacement. Calculate **a** the period of the motion and **b** the maximum speed and the maximum acceleration. **c** Copy the graph and draw on another graph to show the variation with displacement of the potential energy. **d** Estimate the displacement when the potential energy of the mass is equal to its kinetic energy.

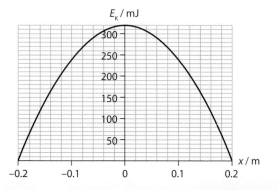

Oscillations with damping

Damped oscillations are oscillations in which the mechanical energy is reduced as time goes on. This implies that the amplitude is decreasing.

In **a** the degree of damping is light. It will take a long time before the oscillations die out.

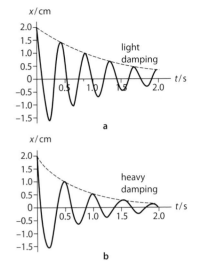

The initial amplitude is 2.0 cm. The amplitude after one full oscillation is 1.4 cm. The energy has been reduced by $\left(\frac{1.4}{2.0}\right)^2 \approx 0.5$. After one more oscillation it is reduced by $\left(\frac{1.0}{1.4}\right)^2 \approx 0.5$, i.e. by the **same** fraction.

In **b** the damping is greater. The oscillations die out faster than in **a**. After one full oscillation the energy has been decreased to $\left(\frac{1.0}{2.0}\right)^2 \approx 0.25$ of its original value.

> For light damping the frequency (and hence period) of oscillations is the same as with no damping (but the frequency **decreases** a bit in the case of heavy damping).

Critical damping

Critical damping means that the system returns to its equilibrium position as fast as possible but without performing oscillations.

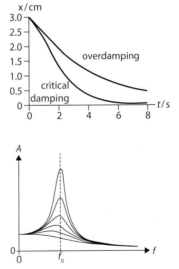

In the overdamped case, the system returns to equilibrium without oscillations in a time longer than that in the critically damped case.

Driven (forced) oscillations

This refers to oscillations in which an external force acts on the system with a specific frequency f_D.

The graph shows the amplitude versus driving frequency for driven oscillations with various degrees of damping.

For small damping (top curve) the amplitude is largest (we say we have **resonance**) when the driving frequency is equal to the natural frequency f_0.

> For heavy damping (lower curves) the frequency at which resonance takes place is slightly less than the natural frequency.

Test yourself 4

A car travels on a horizontal road that has bumps 5.0 m apart. The driver observes that at a speed of 12 m s⁻¹ the car oscillates vertically with large amplitude. If the speed is reduced or increased, the amplitude of oscillations becomes smaller.

a Explain these observations.

b Calculate the angular frequency ω of the vertical oscillations of the car.

What is a wave?

A wave is the organised (as opposed to random) propagation of a **disturbance** through a medium. As the wave passes through the medium the molecules of the medium are **displaced** from their equilibrium positions.

It is important to realise that in wave motion the molecules of the medium undergo small displacements whereas the wave itself can move very large distances. A good example is the 'wave' in football games. The people move up and down just a bit but the wave they create can travel the entire circumference of a stadium.

A wave transfers energy and momentum.

Mechanical waves	Electromagnetic waves
Water, sound, string waves, earthquake waves etc.	Light, radio, X-rays, infrared, ultraviolet etc.
Require a medium, cannot propagate in vacuum.	Can propagate in vacuum as well as in various media.
The speed of mechanical waves is determined by the properties of the medium.	In vacuum, electromagnetic waves have the same speed $c = 3 \times 10^8 \, \mathrm{m\,s^{-1}}$.
The disturbance is the change of a property of the medium from its equilibrium value when there is no wave.	The disturbance is an oscillating electric and magnetic field as they propagate together.

Electromagnetic spectrum

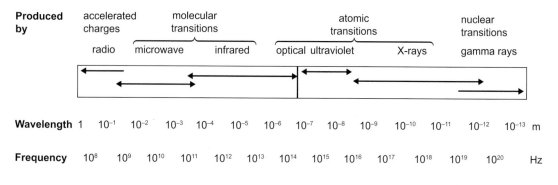

Wave characteristics

Definitions

Displacement, y   The vector to the position of a point in the medium from the equilibrium position of that point.

You must know these definitions well!

Amplitude, A   The maximum displacement.

Crest   A point of maximum displacement.

Trough   A point of maximum negative displacement.

Wavelength, λ   The length of a full wave. It may be found from a displacement–distance graph.

Frequency, f   The number of full waves produced by a source in one second. It is measured in hertz (Hz). The frequency is the inverse of the period, $f = \frac{1}{T}$.

Period, T   The time taken to produce one full wave. It may be found from a displacement–time graph.

Wave speed, v   The speed at which a crest moves past an observer at rest in the medium or the rate of energy transfer, $v = f\lambda$.

Intensity, I   This is the power transferred by the wave per unit area. It is proportional to the square of the amplitude, $I \propto A^2$. For a point source emitting uniformly in all directions the intensity a distance d from the source is proportional to $\frac{1}{d^2}$.

Transverse waves

These are waves where the displacement of the medium is at right angles to the direction of energy transfer.

The displacement–distance graph is a 'photograph' of what the medium looks like at a particular instant of time, here $t = 0$ s.

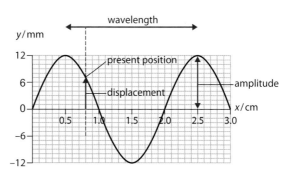

The red arrow at $x = 0.8$ cm is the **displacement** (not the velocity) of that point in the medium at a particular time. From a displacement–distance graph we can determine the amplitude (here 12 mm) and the wavelength (here 2.0 cm).

But we may want to concentrate at a **particular point** in the medium. For example the point at $x = 0.5$ cm has displacement 12 mm at $t = 0$ s. At other times the displacement of this specific point is given by the displacement–time graph. We can also determine the amplitude (here 12 mm) and the period (here 4.0 ms.) from the displacement–time graph.

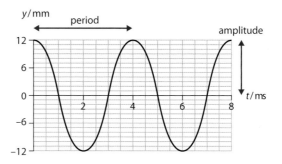

Every point in the medium undergoes SHM with the same frequency and amplitude as the wave.

The solid line shows a **transverse** wave on a string at $t = 0$ that moves towards the right. The dotted line shows the wave at time $t = 1$ ms later. In a time of $t = 1$ ms the crest moved forward a distance of 0.30 m and so the speed of the wave is
$v = \dfrac{0.30}{1 \times 10^{-3}} = 300 \, \text{m s}^{-1}$. The wavelength is 2.0 m.
The frequency is therefore $f = \dfrac{v}{\lambda} = \dfrac{300}{2} = 150 \, \text{Hz}$.

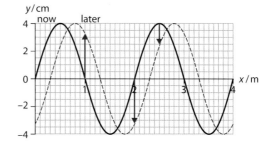

We see that the crests have changed positions – this is what is expected of a **travelling wave**.

By drawing the waves at present and at a bit later we can see how the points on the string move. We see e.g. that the point at $x = 1.0$ m moved upwards whereas the points at $x = 2.0$ m and $x = 2.5$ m moved downwards.

Test yourself **5**
For the wave in the first two diagrams above, calculate the speed of a point in the medium at $x = 0.8$ cm when $t = 0$.

Longitudinal waves

These are waves in which the displacement of the medium is **parallel** to the direction of energy transfer. **Sound** is the best example of a longitudinal wave. Shown is the displacement–distance graph for a longitudinal wave.

The red small arrows represent the **displacement** (not the velocity) of the medium at a particular time.

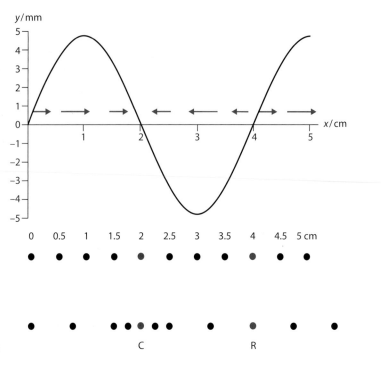

The 11 dots in the first row represent air molecules at their equilibrium positions, here shown every 0.5 cm. The dots in the second row show the new positions of these molecules at the time at which the displacement of the medium is given by the graph above (whose amplitude is 5.0 mm, i.e. 0.50 cm).

The molecules at x = 0, 2.0 and 4.0 cm have stayed at the same position (y = 0), those between x = 0 and 2.0 cm and x = 4.0 and 5.0 cm have moved to the right ($y > 0$) and those between x = 2.0 and 4.0 cm have moved to the left ($y < 0$).

This means that the molecule at x = 2.0 cm is at the centre of a **compression** (C) and the molecule at x = 4.0 cm is at the centre of a **rarefaction** (R).

> Looking at graphs of displacement–distance (or time) does **not** allow us to tell if the wave is transverse or longitudinal. The graphs look the same for both types.

Wavefronts and rays

We call the direction of energy transfer of a wave a ray. Surfaces at right angles to rays are called wavefronts. (All the points on a wavefront have the same phase.) By convention we usually draw wavefronts through crests so that two neighbouring wavefronts are separated by one wavelength.

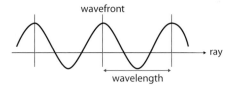

The diagram on the right shows circular wavefronts. We would create such wavefronts if, for example, we dropped a small stone in a lake.

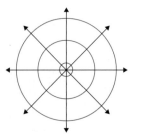

Wave phenomena

Reflection

A wave will reflect off a surface that is sufficiently smooth. The law of reflection states that the angle of incidence (angle between ray and normal) is equal to the angle of reflection (angle between reflected ray and normal) and, further, the incident and reflected rays and the normal are on the same plane.

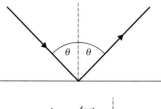

Refraction

A wave will, in general, change speed (but **not** frequency) as it moves from one medium into another. This means that the wavelength will also change. Referring to the diagram the angles of incidence and refraction are related through: $\frac{\sin\theta_1}{v_1} = \frac{\sin\theta_2}{v_2}$ (Snell's law) where v_1 and v_2 are the speeds of the wave in the two media.

For light only, we may rewrite this equation as $n_1\sin\theta_1 = n_2\sin\theta_2$ where $n = \frac{c}{v}$ is the refractive index of the medium and c is the speed of light in vacuum. The ray in the diagram enters a medium in which the speed is slow and so bends **towards** the normal.

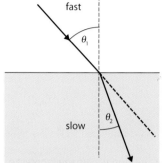

Water waves refract when they move from deep to shallow water. The speed in shallow water is decreased (we know this because the distance between the wavefronts in shallow water is smaller) and so we have refraction.

For the wave shown in the diagram, the ratio of the speeds in the deep and shallow parts is about 1.7, found from measuring the distances between wavefronts.

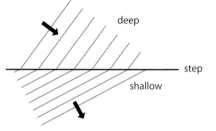

Diffraction

Diffraction is the spreading of a wave as it goes through an aperture (opening) or past an obstacle.

Diffraction applies to all waves but it is important to realise that the degree to which a wave diffracts depends crucially on the size of the wavelength compared to the size of the aperture or the obstacle.

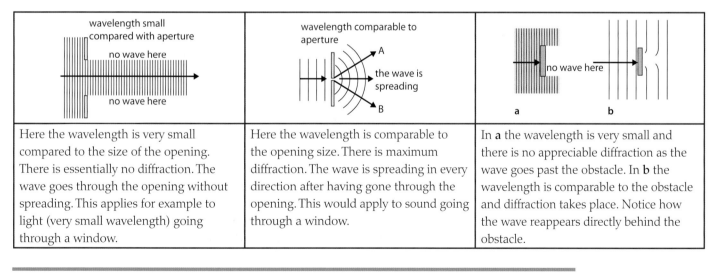

wavelength small compared with aperture	wavelength comparable to aperture	
Here the wavelength is very small compared to the size of the opening. There is essentially no diffraction. The wave goes through the opening without spreading. This applies for example to light (very small wavelength) going through a window.	Here the wavelength is comparable to the opening size. There is maximum diffraction. The wave is spreading in every direction after having gone through the opening. This would apply to sound going through a window.	In **a** the wavelength is very small and there is no appreciable diffraction as the wave goes past the obstacle. In **b** the wavelength is comparable to the obstacle and diffraction takes place. Notice how the wave reappears directly behind the obstacle.

Test yourself 6

A ray of light in air of wavelength 540 nm enters water ($n = 1.33$) making an angle of 50° with the water surface. Calculate **a** the speed of light in water, **b** the wavelength of light in water and **c** the angle of the ray with the normal in water.

➡ **Before you answer**
Watch what angles you need.

TOPIC 4: **Oscillations and waves – Core**

Superposition and interference

When two waves meet the resultant displacement is the sum of the individual displacements.

Two waves (green line and red dotted line) meet. The sum of the two displacements is shown by the blue heavy line.

If the two waves meet crest to crest (here one wave is shown slightly displaced for clarity), the result is a wave with double the amplitude of the individual waves. This is **constructive interference**.

If the two waves meet crest to trough, the result is that the two cancel each other out. The resulting wave has zero amplitude, i.e. we do not have a wave! This is **destructive interference**.

Notice that if the waves have different amplitude then they will never completely cancel out. Here the two waves (green line and red dotted line) meet crest to trough but the amplitudes are different. There is a non-zero resultant wave here even though we still have destructive interference.

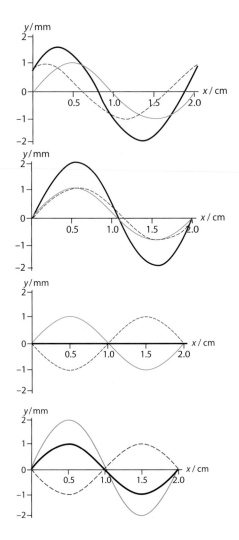

Two-source interference

In this case **identical** waves from two **coherent** sources (i.e. the phase difference between the sources is constant) arrive at the same point in space. What is the wave at that point, i.e. how do we know if the waves will interfere constructively or destructively? It all depends on how much **extra distance** one wave has to travel to get to the point. We call the extra distance **path difference** = $S_2P - S_1P$ (see diagram).

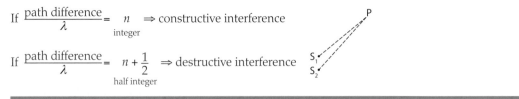

If $\dfrac{\text{path difference}}{\lambda} = \underset{\text{integer}}{n} \Rightarrow$ constructive interference

If $\dfrac{\text{path difference}}{\lambda} = \underset{\text{half integer}}{n + \dfrac{1}{2}} \Rightarrow$ destructive interference

---

Test yourself **7**

Two sources S_1 and S_2 emit waves of wavelength $\lambda = 0.30\,\text{m}$. Point P is such that $S_1P = 3.40\,\text{m}$ and $S_2P = 4.0\,\text{m}$ and point Q is such that $S_1Q = 3.20\,\text{m}$ and $S_2Q = 3.65\,\text{m}$. Determine what is observed at P and at Q.

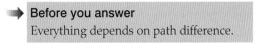

Before you answer
Everything depends on path difference.

Key ideas

In a **conductor**, such as a metal, there are 'free' electrons. Free electrons are dispersed throughout the metal volume and are not attached to any one particular atom. The higher the temperature, the higher the average kinetic energy of the free electrons. The atoms also have kinetic energy, vibrating about their equilibrium positions. The charge on one electron is -1.6×10^{-19} C.

In an **insulator** there are very few such free electrons.

When an **electric field** (see Topic 6) is established **within** the conductor, the free electrons will get a small drift velocity opposite to the electric field.

(**Caution**: The diagram is way out of scale; the drift velocity is very much smaller than the random velocity of the electrons. Typically, $v_{drift} = 10^{-3}$ m s^{-1} whereas $v_{random} = 10^5$ m s^{-1}.)

This means that, unlike before, the electrons now have a net motion in a specific direction, namely opposite to the electric field. This means that electric charge gets transferred in a direction opposite to the electric field. This is called **electric current**.

Definitions

Electric current   The charge that moves through the cross-sectional area of a conductor per unit time, $I = \frac{\Delta Q}{\Delta t}$. The unit of current is the ampere, 1A = 1C s^{-1}. (The **definition** of the ampere is given in terms of the magnetic force between parallel currents – see Topic 6.)

Potential difference   The work done per unit charge in moving charge between two points: $V = \frac{W}{q}$. The unit of potential difference is the volt, V, and 1V = 1J C^{-1}.

Important: This means that the work done to move a charge q through a potential difference V is $W = qV$.

The electronvolt   This formula allows for the definition of a new unit of energy (to be used extensively in Topics 7 and 13) called the electronvolt, eV. 1 eV is the energy required to move a charge of 1 e through a potential difference of 1 V. Thus an electron moved through a potential difference of 6 V requires 6 eV and an alpha particle (charge 2 e) requires 12 eV. In SI units: 1 eV = 1.6×10^{-19} C $\times$ 1 V = 1.6×10^{-19} J.

Electric resistance   The resistance of a device is defined as the ratio of the potential difference **across it** to the current **through it**, $R = \frac{V}{I}$. The unit of resistance is the ohm, 1Ω = VA^{-1}.

Omitting the words in **bold** will not get you points in an exam.

A current of 2.0 A in a resistor of 25 Ω implies a potential difference across the resistor of $V = RI = 50$ V.

Avoid thinking about resistance in terms of the 'resistance experienced by electrons as they move in a metal'. Also, resistance is **not** defined in terms of the slope of a V–I graph.

Test yourself 1

The current in a conductor varies with applied voltage as shown in the graph. Calculate the resistance of the conductor when the voltage is 0.30 V.

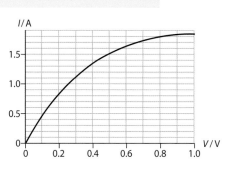

Power

Power is the rate at which energy is dissipated.

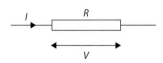

The amount of charge that gets transferred across the resistor in time t is $Q = It$.
The work required to move a charge Q across a potential difference V is
$QV = (It)V$. The work per unit time is the power and so $P = \dfrac{ItV}{t}$, i.e. $P = VI$.

Using the definition of resistance $R = \dfrac{V}{I}$ we have the equivalent forms: $P = VI = RI^2 = \dfrac{V^2}{R}$.

For a conductor of uniform cross-sectional area: $R = \rho\dfrac{L}{A}$ where L is the length and
A the cross-sectional area. The constant ρ is called the resistivity and depends on the
temperature and the kind of material from which the conductor is made.

Ohm's law

At constant temperature, many metallic conductors have the property that the current through them is
proportional to the potential difference across them, i.e. $I \propto V$. This is known as Ohm's law. Ohm's law
implies that the resistance is constant. For a conductor that obeys Ohm's law a graph of current through,
versus voltage across, gives a **straight line through the origin**.

The graph below shows the I–V characteristics of
two conductors of different resistance, each obeying
Ohm's law.

This graph shows the I–V characteristics of a
conductor that does **not** obey Ohm's law. As V
increases the resistance increases.

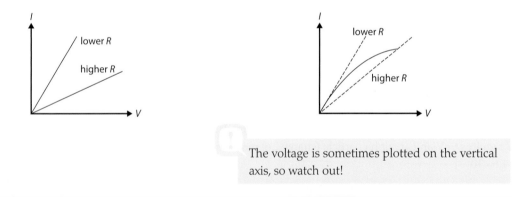

The voltage is sometimes plotted on the vertical
axis, so watch out!

Test yourself **2**
Determine the resistance of a lamp rated as 60 W at 240 V. Assuming the resistance stays constant,
determine what the power of the lamp would be if connected to a source of 120 V.

Test yourself **3**
a The length and radius of a cylindrical conductor of resistance R are both doubled at constant temperature.
Calculate the new resistance of the conductor.
b A cylindrical conductor has cross-sectional area A and length L. The conductor is cut into two equal parts
of length L each. The two parts are connected in parallel. Calculate the resistance of the combination.

Emf and series circuits

Work must be done in order to move an amount of charge Q completely around a circuit. The total work done per unit charge is called the emf of the source, i.e. of the battery in the circuit shown.

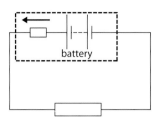

$$\text{emf, } \mathcal{E} = \frac{\text{work to move charge } Q \text{ around the circuit}}{\text{charge } Q}$$

(Emf is associated with conversions of various forms of energy into electrical energy. In the case of a battery it is chemical energy that gets converted into electrical energy.)

Emf is measured in joules per coulomb and this combination is called the **volt**.

> You may use either one of these statements to define emf.

If this work is done in time t then emf, $\mathcal{E} = \dfrac{\text{work to move charge } Q \text{ around the circuit } / t}{\text{charge } Q / t}$

$$\mathcal{E} = \frac{\text{total power}}{\text{total current}}$$

The total power delivered by the battery is therefore $\mathcal{E}I$.

The battery has internal resistance r.

Power used in R is VI. Power used in r is rI^2.

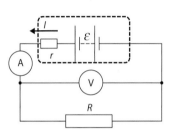

Hence $\mathcal{E}I = rI^2 + VI \Rightarrow V = \mathcal{E} - Ir$ (energy conservation)

So the potential difference across the battery is equal to the emf when the **current in the circuit is zero**.

Two important facts about a series circuit

In many cases we can assume that the internal resistance of the battery or power supply is negligible.

In the circuit shown we have that:

Total power delivered by battery is $\mathcal{E}I$.

Power used in R_1 is R_1I^2. Power used in R_2 is R_2I^2.

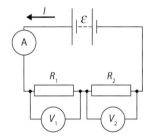

Hence, $\mathcal{E}I = R_1I^2 + R_2I^2 \Rightarrow I = \dfrac{\mathcal{E}}{R_1 + R_2}$

i.e. the effective (total) resistance of two resistors in series is the sum of the two.

For the same reason as above we also have that $\mathcal{E}I = V_1I + V_2I \Rightarrow \mathcal{E} = V_1 + V_2$

i.e. the sum of the potential differences across resistors in series is equal to the emf of the battery.

In the circuit shown, if $\mathcal{E} = 12\,V$ and $R_1 = 10\,k\Omega$ and $R_2 = 50\,k\Omega$ we must have that: $V_1 + V_2 = 12$ and $V_2 = 5V_1$ (since both have same current and R_2 is 5 times R_1). We therefore find $V_1 = 2.0\,V$ and $V_2 = 10\,V$.

Test yourself **4**

A battery of internal resistance $0.80\,\Omega$ sends a current of $1.4\,A$ through an external resistance. The work required to push one electron through the external resistor is $7.2 \times 10^{-19}\,J$. Calculate the emf of the battery.

Parallel circuits

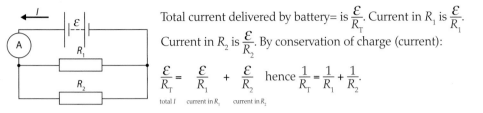

Total current delivered by battery= is $\frac{\mathcal{E}}{R_T}$. Current in R_1 is $\frac{\mathcal{E}}{R_1}$.

Current in R_2 is $\frac{\mathcal{E}}{R_2}$. By conservation of charge (current):

$$\underset{\text{total } I}{\frac{\mathcal{E}}{R_T}} = \underset{\text{current in } R_1}{\frac{\mathcal{E}}{R_1}} + \underset{\text{current in } R_2}{\frac{\mathcal{E}}{R_2}} \quad \text{hence} \quad \frac{1}{R_T} = \frac{1}{R_1} + \frac{1}{R_2}.$$

Test yourself 5

a Calculate the total resistance between A and B. Each resistor shown has a resistance of 60 Ω. **b** The resistance between A and B is measured and found to be 120 Ω. Which resistor is faulty and how?

Test yourself 6

In the circuit the battery has negligible internal resistance and emf 12 V.

Calculate the value of **a** resistance R_2 and **b** resistance R_1.

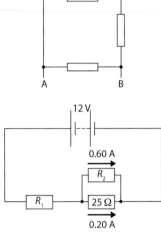

Test yourself 7

A battery of emf 12 V and internal resistance $r = 2.0$ Ω is connected to three resistors of resistance $R = 6.0$ Ω. **a** Calculate the total current in the circuit. **b** The bottom 6.0 Ω resistor burns out (i.e. its resistance becomes infinite). Calculate the total resistance of the circuit.

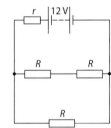

Test yourself 8

a Two lamps, A and B, are connected in series with a battery of negligible internal resistance. Lamp A is brighter than lamp B. Determine which lamp has the greater resistance.

> **Before you answer**
> Brightness is related to power. Which form of the power formula is convenient here?

b The lamps are now connected to the same battery in parallel. State and explain which lamp is the brighter of the two.

> **Before you answer**
> You now need a different version of the power formula.

Test yourself 9

In the circuit the battery has emf 12 V and negligible internal resistance. The voltmeter is ideal. Calculate the magnitude of the reading on the voltmeter.

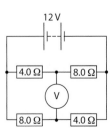

The potential divider

The circuit on the left is called a **potential divider circuit**. It looks complicated but is in fact equivalent to the conventional circuit to its right. The point where the slider S touches the resistor determines how the resistance R splits into R_1 and R_2.

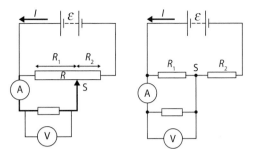

The next two pairs of circuit diagrams show two extreme positions of the slider and their equivalent conventional circuits.

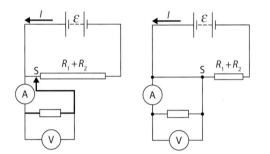
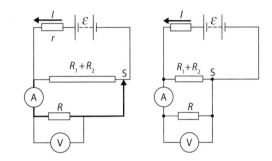

When the slider is at the far left the voltmeter will show 0 V (even if the battery has an internal resistance) because its ends are at the same potential.

When the slider is at the far right the voltmeter will show its greatest reading. This will be $\mathcal{E}$ if the battery has zero internal resistance. It will be $V = \mathcal{E} - Ir$ otherwise.

Test yourself **10**
Calculate the maximum reading of the voltmeter in the potential divider circuits if $\mathcal{E} = 12\,\text{V}$, $R_1 + R_2 = 100\,\Omega$, $R = 5.0\,\Omega$ and $r = 2.0\,\Omega$.

Definitions
Thermistor   Resistor in which the resistance decreases as the temperature increases.

LDR (light-dependent resistor)   Resistor in which the resistance decreases as the incident intensity of light increases.

Test yourself **11**
The diagram shows a potential divider circuit. The battery has negligible internal resistance and AC is a wire whose resistance increases uniformly with length.

The lamp is rated as 12 W at 6.0 V at normal operation. The lamp operates normally when the moveable contact is attached to point B such that the length AB is double that of BC. Calculate **a** the resistance of the light bulb, **b** the current through the light bulb and **c** the resistance R of the wire AC.

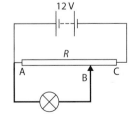

Test yourself **12**
a The thermistor T in the circuit shown has resistance R at room temperature. What will happen to the potential difference across T when the temperature is increased? Assume zero internal resistance.
b The thermistor is now replaced by an LDR. What will happen to the voltage across it if the light intensity is increased?

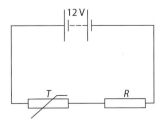

Comparing gravity and electricity

There are great similarities but also differences between gravity and electricity. The two topics are presented side by side to emphasise this relationship. You may want to study one column first and then the other or both at the same time.

Gravity	Electricity
Newton's law of gravitation Two **point** masses m_1, m_2 separated by a distance r **attract** each other with a force that equals $F = G\dfrac{m_1 m_2}{r^2}$	**Coulomb's electrostatic law** Two **point** charges q_1, q_2 separated by a distance r exert a force on each other that equals $F = k\dfrac{q_1 q_2}{r^2}$
This formula can also be used for two uniform spherical masses, in which case the separation r is the centre-to-centre separation.	Because there are two types of charge the electric force is attractive between charges of opposite sign but repulsive for charges of the same sign.
G is the universal gravitational constant $G = 6.67 \times 10^{-11}\,\mathrm{N\,m^2\,kg^{-2}}$.	k is the Coulomb constant $k = 8.99 \times 10^9\,\mathrm{N\,m^2\,C^{-2}}$.

Notice the mathematical connection between the two laws: they are both inverse square laws but the gravitational force is always attractive whereas the electrical can be attractive or repulsive.

Test yourself **1**
The weight of a body on a planet is 20 N on the planet surface. What is the weight at a height from the surface equal to the planet's radius?

⮕ **Before you answer**
Weight means the gravitational force.

Test yourself **2**
The Earth orbits the Sun in a circular orbit of radius 1.5×10^{11} m. Calculate the mass of the Sun.

Test yourself **3**
An electrically neutral conducting sphere is suspended vertically from an insulating thread. A point charge of magnitude Q is brought near the sphere. The electric force between the point charge and the sphere

A depends on whether Q is positive or negative.
B is always zero.
C is always repulsive.
D is always attractive.

⮕ **Before you answer**
The sphere is conducting and so charge in it can separate.

© IB Organization 2006

The concept of a field

How does the force propagate from one body to another? To ask the question anthropomorphically, how does a mass 'know' that another mass is attracting it? In other words if the Sun were to magically disappear, after how much time would its force on Earth become zero?

In an attempt to answer this question physicists introduced the idea of a **field**.

We say that a mass M creates around it a **gravitational field**. Other **masses** respond to this field by having a gravitational force act on them.

Similarly, an electric charge Q creates in the space around it an **electric field**. Other **charges** respond to this field by having an electric force act on them.

To 'feel' the gravitational field you must have mass and to 'feel' the electric field you must have charge.

A **field** exists in a region of space and exerts a force on a particle (a mass or electric charge) that is present in that region of space. The field is a property of the mass or the charge creating the field (the 'source') and (usually) distance (from the source).

Gravitational field, *g* (a vector quantity)	Electric field, *E* (a vector quantity)
This is defined as the vector gravitational force per unit mass exerted on a small, point mass m, i.e. $g = \dfrac{F}{m} \Leftrightarrow F = mg$	This is defined as the vector electric force per unit charge exerted on a small, positive point charge q, i.e. $E = \dfrac{F}{q} \Leftrightarrow F = qE$
Recall that the field is a property of the mass creating it. In the definition above it appears that the mass m also enters the definition. If the definition is correct the dependence on m must cancel out. So consider the gravitational field created by a spherical mass M. A point mass m placed a distance r from the centre of M will experience a force $F = G\dfrac{Mm}{r^2}$ and so the gravitational field is $g = \dfrac{F}{m} = \dfrac{GMm/r^2}{m} = \dfrac{GM}{r^2}$	Recall that the field is a property of the charge creating it. In the definition above it appears that the charge q also enters the definition. If the definition is correct the dependence on q must cancel out. So consider the electric field created by a spherical charge Q. A positive point charge q placed a distance r from the centre of Q will experience a force $F = k\dfrac{Qq}{r^2}$ and so the electric field is $E = \dfrac{F}{q} = \dfrac{kQq/r^2}{q} = \dfrac{kQ}{r^2}$

Test yourself 4

The gravitational field strength at the surface of Earth is g. The gravitational field strength at the surface of a planet of mass and radius double that of the Earth is

A $\dfrac{g}{8}$ **B** $\dfrac{g}{4}$ **C** $\dfrac{g}{2}$ **D** g

Test yourself 5

Four point charges of equal magnitude are held at the corners of a square as shown.

Which arrow shows the direction of the resultant electric field strength at the centre of the square due to the four point charges?

A ↑ **B** ← **C** → **D** ↓

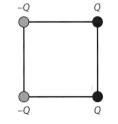

Before you answer
Imagine a positive charge at the centre of the square and find the direction of the force on this charge from each of the four charges separately. Then use vector addition.

© IB Organization 2005

Field patterns

Gravitational and electric fields

The gravitational field of a **point mass** (here, at the origin of the axes) is radial.

The exact same pattern also holds for a **negative** electric point charge. The pattern for a positive charge would have the arrows going outwards.

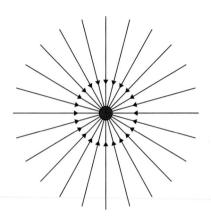

These diagrams show electric field patterns. On the left: two opposite but unequal charges. The charge on the right is three times larger. On the right: two equal positive charges.

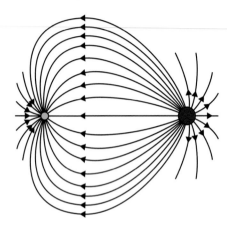

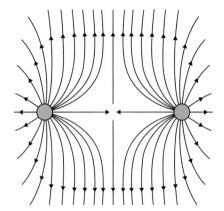

Magnetic fields

Electric current in wires of various shapes will produce a **magnetic field**.

The diagrams on the right show the magnetic field around a **long straight** wire at varying distances. The arrows show magnetic compass needles. The magnetic field lines are obtained by joining the compass needles smoothly with curves, forming circles around the wire. The magnetic field itself is tangential to these circles in a direction found from the right hand grip rule.

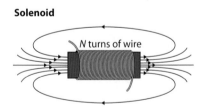

The magnetic field lines are also shown for a current loop, permanent magnet and solenoid.

Current loop

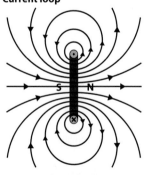

Permanent magnet

Solenoid

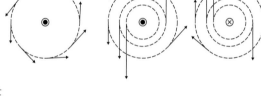

N turns of wire

Test yourself **6**
Draw the electric field around a negatively charged conducting sphere.

Before you answer
What is the direction of the field? At what angle do the field lines meet the surface of the sphere? What is the electric field inside a conductor?

Motion of charged particle in electric and magnetic fields

Magnetic forces

The presence of a magnetic field is detected by its effects on permanent magnets such as magnetic compass needles, or its effects on moving charged particles and other electric currents. A magnetic field B exerts a force on moving charges given by $F = qvB \sin \theta$ and a force on electric currents given by $F = BIL \sin \theta$.

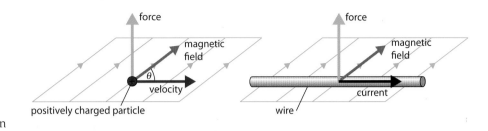

Definitions

Ampere (A)   Two parallel conductors 1m apart have a current of 1A in them if the force on 1m of their length is exactly 2×10^{-7}N.

Magnetic field strength   The strength of a magnetic field is said to be 1 tesla (1T) when it exerts a force of 1N on a 1m length of a wire carrying a current of 1A at right angles to the direction of the field.

A charged particle of mass m and charge q that enters a region of magnetic field B at right angles to the magnetic field will move in a circular path of radius R given by

$$\underset{\text{centripetal force}}{m\frac{v^2}{R}} = \underset{\text{magnetic force}}{qvB} \Rightarrow R = \frac{mv}{qB}$$

> The magnetic force does zero work on the charged particle because the force is at right angles to the velocity. Therefore the magnetic force cannot change the speed of the particle (only the direction of the velocity).

Crossed electric and magnetic fields

An electron enters a region of electric and magnetic fields as shown.

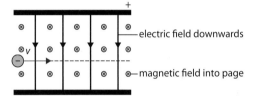

The electron is negatively charged so the electric force is opposite to the electric field, i.e. upwards. The right hand rule for the magnetic force direction gives a downward force for the negative electron.

The path of the electron is undeflected. This means that the electric force on the electron upwards is cancelled by the force due to the magnetic field downwards, i.e. $qE = qvB$, so $E = vB$.

> A positively charged particle, for example a proton or an alpha particle, would also be undeflected if it enters with the same velocity. Think about how the electric and magnetic forces on these particles change in direction and magnitude compared to what they were on the electron.

Work done

A very large number of problems are solved using the result from the topic of **electricity** that the work done in moving a charge q across a potential difference ΔV is $W = q\Delta V$.

Combining this with the result from the topic of **mechanics** that the work done is also the change in kinetic energy $W = \Delta E_K$ gives: $q\Delta V = \Delta E_K$.

Test yourself **7**

Two wires, X and Y, carry equal currents into the page as shown in the diagram.
Point Z is at the same distance from X and Y. The direction of the magnetic field at Z is

A ↓   **B** →   **C** ↑   **D** ←

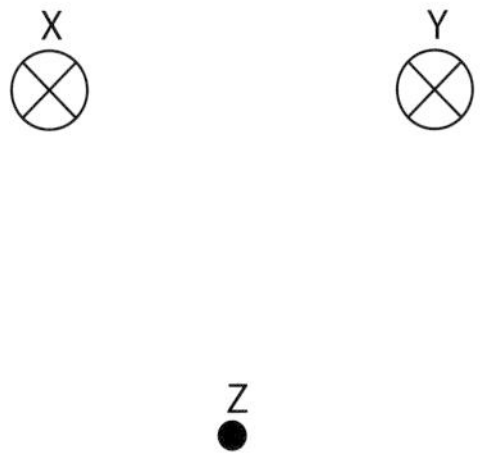

X   Y

$\otimes$ $\otimes$

Z
●

> ➡ **Before you answer**
> You must find the magnetic field at Z from each wire **separately** and then use vector addition.

Atomic structure

The Rutherford, Marsden, Geiger experiment

Alpha particles (massive positively charged particles) from a radium source are directed at a thin gold foil. The expectation was that the particles would suffer **very small angle** deflections due to the **electrical repulsion** between the positive charge on the alpha particles and the positive charge in the atom.

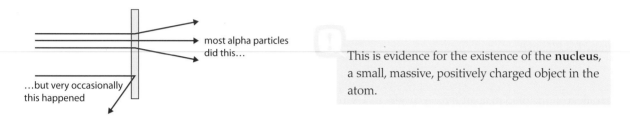

most alpha particles did this…

…but very occasionally this happened

This is evidence for the existence of the **nucleus**, a small, massive, positively charged object in the atom.

The fact that a few of the particles deflect by very **large angles** implies that the force deflecting them is very large. This can happen only if the alpha particles come very close to the positive charge of the atom. In the model of the atom available at the time of the experiment, the closest the alpha particles could come to the positive charge of the atom was 10^{-10} m, but to produce the large deflections the closest distance should have been about 10^{-15} m.

The diagrams below show Thomson's old model of the atom and the new model suggested by Rutherford to explain alpha particle scattering.

The positive charge of the atom must be concentrated in a very small volume, i.e. the **nucleus**.

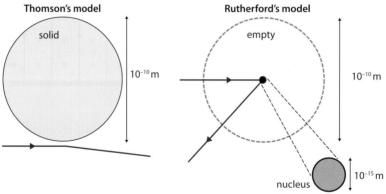

But the new model has a problem: The orbiting electrons have centripetal acceleration and so should radiate, losing energy and spiralling into the nucleus.

Resolution: Electrons in atoms show **quantum behaviour** that dictates that they can exist in discrete energy levels. No radiation is emitted except when the electrons make transitions from high energy levels to lower energy levels.

Test yourself **1**

Explain why in the Rutherford experiment **a** the alpha particle beam must be very narrow and **b** the foil must be very thin.

Test yourself **2**

Describe the Rutherford experiment and state what conclusions may be reached from it about the distribution of matter in an atom.

Atomic energy levels and nuclear structure

The emission spectrum
Gases emit light when heated to a high temperature or when exposed to a high electric field. The light emitted consists of **specific** wavelengths. The set of wavelengths emitted is characteristic of the gas.

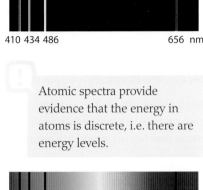

Light is emitted in bundles of energy called photons and each photon has an energy given by $E = hf$ where h is a constant.

The wavelength and frequency of a photon are related by $c = \lambda f$ where c is the speed of light.

The photon carries away an energy equal to the **difference** ΔE in energy of the levels involved in the transition.

> Atomic spectra provide evidence that the energy in atoms is discrete, i.e. there are energy levels.

The absorption spectrum
If white light is transmitted through hydrogen gas, various wavelengths will be missing in the transmitted light. These wavelengths correspond exactly to the emission line wavelengths. This is because electrons in the atoms of hydrogen absorbed these photons and made a transition to a higher energy state.

Nuclear structure
The approximate mass of a nucleus of mass number A is A atomic mass units (u).

$1u = 1.66 \times 10^{-27}$ kg. The u is $\frac{1}{12}$ of the mass of the neutral atom of the carbon isotope $^{12}_{6}C$.

Nuclei contain **nucleons**, i.e. protons and neutrons. A particular nucleus with Z protons and N neutrons is denoted by $^{N+Z}_{Z}X$ or $^{A}_{Z}X$ where A is the **nucleon number**, Z is the **proton number** and X is the chemical name of the element. Thus $^{4}_{2}He$ represents the nucleus of helium with 2 protons and $4-2 = 2$ neutrons.

A nucleus with a specific number of protons and a specific number of neutrons is called a **nuclide**. Nuclei with same proton number but different nucleon number are called **isotopes** of each other. Thus $^{3}_{2}He$, $^{4}_{2}He$, ..., $^{10}_{2}He$ are the eight isotopes of helium. Isotopes have the same **chemical** (same number of electrons) but different **physical** properties (e.g. different mass, nuclear radii, specific heat capacity).

Forces in the nucleus
The dominant forces acting within a nucleus are:

1. the electrical repulsion force between the **protons**.
2. the strong nuclear force acting between nucleons (**protons and neutrons**) which is (mostly) attractive.

The presence of the strong nuclear force prevents the electrical force from ripping the nucleus apart.

> The gravitational force is negligible because the masses involved are so small.

> The strong force has a **short range**, which means that a nucleon attracts its immediate neighbours **only**, unlike the electrical force, which, with its infinite range, implies that any one proton repels all other protons in the nucleus.

Test yourself **3**
Calculate the wavelength of the photon emitted in a transition between two energy states that differ in energy by 1.9 eV.

Nuclear stability and radioactivity

Nuclear stability

Of some 2500 nuclides, less than about 300 are stable. The rest are **unstable** and **decay** by the emission of particles in a phenomenon called **radioactivity**, which is discussed below.

The instability of nuclei may be discussed in terms of the forces acting within the nucleus.

If a nucleus contains **too many protons** compared to neutrons, the nucleus will be unstable because the electrical repulsion force will overwhelm the strong nuclear force.

But a nucleus may also be unstable if it contains **too many neutrons** compared to protons. In that case, the nucleus can reduce its energy (and so become more stable) by a process known as beta decay (see below) in which a neutron is converted to a proton.

It appears that a nucleus should be stable if it contains about the same number of protons and neutrons. This is true for small nuclei. But large nuclei require **a few more** neutrons than protons to be stable. The neutrons contribute to binding without contributing to the repulsive electric force.

> A small stable nucleus has about the same number of protons and neutrons and a large stable nucleus has more (but not many more) neutrons than protons.

Radioactivity

Most nuclei are unstable and try to become more stable by **decaying**, i.e. by emitting one or more of three types of particles or radiation: **alpha**, **beta** or **gamma**.

- Alpha particles are helium-4 nuclei, ^4_2He or $^4_2\alpha$.
- Beta particles are fast electrons, $^0_{-1}\text{e}$.
- Gamma particles are photons, $^0_0\gamma$.

These particles are **ionising**, i.e. they knock electrons off the atoms they collide with, creating ions and radicals.

The process of radioactive decay is:

- **random** – it cannot be predicted **which** nucleus will decay or **when** it will decay
- **spontaneous** – it cannot be induced to happen or prevented from happening.

> For the same energy, alpha radiation is the least penetrating and the most ionising, while gamma radiation is the most penetrating and the least ionising.

The biological effect of radiation

Alpha, beta and gamma radiation are all damaging to living organisms. The damage is caused because the **ions and radicals** formed by ionisation may disrupt the ordinary function of cells. In addition, if too many molecules in a cell are ionised the cell may die or become defective. A defective cell may reproduce into more defective cells, leading to various forms of cancer.

Examples of alpha decay

$^{242}_{94}\text{Pu} \rightarrow \,^4_2\alpha + \,^{238}_{92}\text{U}$

$^{238}_{92}\text{U} \rightarrow \,^4_2\alpha + \,^{234}_{90}\text{Th}$

$^{218}_{84}\text{Po} \rightarrow \,^4_2\alpha + \,^{214}_{82}\text{Pb}$

$^{211}_{83}\text{Bi} \rightarrow \,^4_2\alpha + \,^{209}_{81}\text{Tl}$

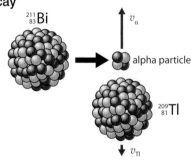

In alpha decay a nucleus decays by emitting an alpha particle.

The diagram shows decay of a $^{211}_{83}\text{Bi}$ nucleus at rest. The products have equal and opposite momenta.

Test yourself **4**

Calculate the ratio of kinetic energies $\text{KE}_\alpha : \text{KE}_{\text{Pb}}$ in the alpha decay $^{218}_{84}\text{Po} \rightarrow \,^4_2\alpha + \,^{214}_{82}\text{Pb}$ when the Po nucleus is at rest.

➡ **Before you answer**
Remember that momentum is conserved.

Examples of beta decay

$$^{14}_{6}C \rightarrow ^{0}_{-1}e + ^{14}_{7}N + ^{0}_{0}\bar{\nu}$$

$$^{40}_{19}K \rightarrow ^{0}_{-1}e + ^{40}_{20}Ca + ^{0}_{0}\bar{\nu}$$

$$^{60}_{27}Co \rightarrow ^{0}_{-1}e + ^{60}_{28}Ni + ^{0}_{0}\bar{\nu}$$

In beta decay a nucleus decays by emitting an electron as well as an antineutrino.

The electron and the proton are created during the decay. Do not think of a neutron as consisting of an electron and a proton.

Examples of gamma decay

$$^{60}_{28}Ni \rightarrow ^{0}_{0}\gamma + ^{60}_{28}Ni$$

$$^{24}_{12}Mg \rightarrow ^{0}_{0}\gamma + ^{24}_{12}Mg$$

$$^{238}_{92}U \rightarrow ^{0}_{0}\gamma + ^{238}_{92}U$$

In gamma decay a nucleus decays by emitting a gamma particle, i.e. a photon.

The nuclei to the left and right of the reaction arrow differ only in the amount of energy they have.

The energies of the alpha and gamma particles are **discrete** whereas those of the electrons in beta decay are **continuous**.

The radioactive decay law

Despite the random nature of radioactive decay we can still formulate a **radioactive decay law** which states that (when we have a very large number of unstable nuclei) the **activity**, i.e. the **rate of decay**, is proportional to the number of nuclei present: $\frac{dN}{dt} \propto N$.

The unit of activity is the becquerel: $1\,Bq = 1$ decay per second.

The time interval after which the activity of a sample is reduced by a factor of 2 is called the **half-life**, $T_{\frac{1}{2}}$.

The chance any nucleus will decay within any interval equal to the half-life is 50%.

The radioactive decay law implies an exponential decrease in activity as time passes.

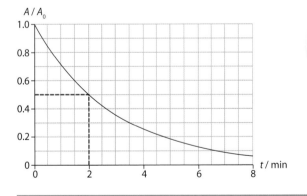

In a graph of activity against time the half-life is determined by finding the time at which the activity is half of the initial activity. For this isotope the half-life is 2.0 min.

Test yourself 5
The half-life of an isotope is 4.0 days. Calculate the fraction of the original activity of the isotope left 12 days after it was prepared.

Test yourself 6
An isotope X has a half-life of 2.0 minutes. It decays into isotope Y that is stable. Initially no quantity of isotope Y is present. After how much time will the ratio of Y atoms to X atoms be equal to 7 : 1?

Test yourself 7
A radioactive isotope has a half-life of 2.0 minutes. A particular nucleus has not decayed within a 2.0 min time interval. A correct statement about the next 2.0 min interval is that this nucleus

A has a lower than 50% chance of decaying.
B will certainly decay.
C has a 50% chance of decaying.
D has a better than 50% chance of decaying.

➡ **Before you answer**
Remember the definition of half-life.

Mass defect and binding energy

A nucleus consisting of Z protons and N neutrons has a mass that is **less** than the mass of the protons and neutrons making it up. The difference is the **mass defect** δ of the nucleus.

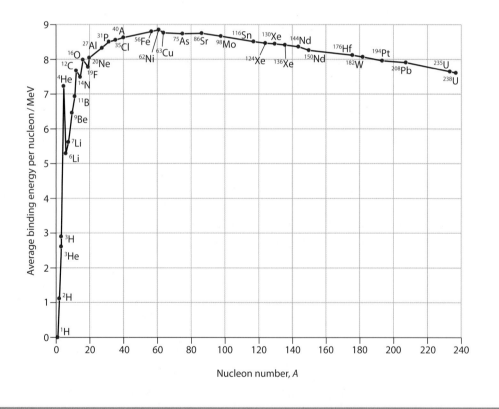

Mass defect:

$$\delta = \underbrace{Zm_p + Nm_n}_{\text{total mass of nucleons}} - \underbrace{M}_{\text{mass of nucleus}}$$

The product of mass defect multiplied by the square of the speed of light is called **binding energy**, B.E. The binding energy is the **minimum** energy needed to completely separate the nucleons of a nucleus.

A graph of the binding energy per nucleon against nucleon number A shows a peak at the nucleus Ni-62. This makes this nucleus the most stable nucleus.

It also shows that most nuclei have approximately the same binding energy per nucleon, roughly 8.5 MeV.

> The similarity in binding energy per nucleon is a consequence of the short range of the strong nuclear force: in a large nucleus any one nucleon is surrounded by the **same** number of nucleons and so it takes the **same** energy to remove it.

Test yourself 8

a Express the energy released in the alpha decay $^{218}_{84}\text{Po} \rightarrow ^{4}_{2}\alpha + ^{214}_{82}\text{Pb}$ in terms of the binding energies of polonium, lead and helium. **b** Using the graph above, estimate the energy released.

Test yourself 9

The binding energy per nucleon of the nucleus $^{11}_{5}\text{B}$ is approximately 7 MeV. The energy needed to completely separate the nucleons of this nucleus is approximately

A 35 MeV **B** 42 MeV **C** 77 MeV **D** 112 MeV

> **Before you answer**
> How many nucleons are there in the nucleus of $^{11}_{5}\text{B}$?

Fission and fusion

Definitions

Fission   A large nucleus splits (fissions) into two smaller nuclei plus a few neutrons plus energy (and usually photons). For example: $^{235}_{92}U + ^{1}_{0}n \rightarrow ^{98}_{40}Zr + ^{135}_{52}Te + 3^{1}_{0}n$.

Fusion   Two light nuclei join (fuse) into a heavier nucleus plus energy. For example: $^{2}_{1}H + ^{2}_{1}H \rightarrow ^{3}_{2}He + ^{1}_{0}n$.

Artificial transmutation   An element is induced to change nature.

Energy calculations in fission and fusion

The energy produced by a fission or fusion reaction is calculated using the mass defect. A mass of 1 u is equivalent to 931.5 MeV.

The fission reaction used as an example above is:

$$^{235}_{92}U + ^{1}_{0}n \rightarrow ^{98}_{40}Zr + ^{135}_{52}Te + 3^{1}_{0}n$$

The masses are: U-235 = 235.0439 u, Zr-98 = 97.9128 u, Te-135 = 134.9165 u and the mass of the neutron is 1.0087 u.

The difference in mass (the mass defect, found from the mass on the left of the reaction minus the mass on the right) is:

$$(235.0349 + 1.0087) - (97.9128 + 134.9615 + 3 \times 1.0087) = 0.1972\,u$$

This is positive and so energy is released. This energy is $Q = 0.1972 \times 931.5 = 184$ MeV.

The fusion reaction between two deuterium nuclei (used as an example above) is:

$$^{2}_{1}H + ^{2}_{1}H \rightarrow ^{3}_{2}He + ^{1}_{0}n$$

The masses are: deuterium = 2.0141 u, helium = 3.0160 u and that of the neutron is 1.0087 u. The difference in masses is (left minus right)

$$2 \times 2.0141 - (3.0160 + 1.0087) = 0.0035\,u$$

The energy released is then $0.0035 \times 931.5 = 3.26$ MeV.

It is important that you realise that the energy released, Q, in both the fission and the fusion processes can also be calculated by adding the binding energies of the products to the **right** of the reaction and subtracting the total binding energy on the **left**.

For example, a nucleus with mass number 200 has a binding energy (see the binding energy curve on page 40) of approximately $200 \times 8 = 1600$ MeV. If it fissions into two nuclei of mass number 100, the total binding energy is approximately $2 \times 100 \times 8.6 = 1720$ MeV. Then $Q = 1720 - 1600 = 120$ MeV.

Fusion in stars

Stars produce their energy by nuclear fusion in the core of the star where the temperature and the pressure are both high.

Temperature must be high for the nuclei to overcome their electrical repulsion.

Pressure must be high to ensure a high probability of collisions and hence fusion.

Test yourself **10**

In 1919, Rutherford observed the following **artificial transmutation** reaction: $^{4}_{2}He + ^{14}_{7}N \rightarrow ^{17}_{8}O + ^{1}_{1}H$.

The masses (in u) are: He: 4.002 60, N: 14.003 07, O: 16.999 13 and H: 1.007 83. Explain why the reaction cannot occur unless the alpha particle supplies sufficient kinetic energy.

Energy sources

Non-renewable sources of energy Finite sources, which are being depleted much faster than they can be produced, and so will run out. They include fossil fuels (e.g. oil, natural gas and coal) and nuclear fuels (e.g. uranium). Worldwide, about 86% of our energy comes from fossil fuels and about 7% from nuclear. Fossil fuels have been created over millions of years when buried animal and plant matter decomposed under the combined action of bacteria and the high pressure of the material on top.

Renewable sources of energy Include solar energy (and the other forms indirectly dependent on solar energy such as wind energy, wave energy, bio-fuels) and tidal energy. At present, about 7% of our energy comes from these sources.

Energy density of fuels The amount of energy that can be obtained from a unit mass of the fuel. It is measured in $J\,kg^{-1}$.

Degradation of energy Energy, while being always conserved, becomes less useful, i.e. it cannot be used to perform mechanical work – this is called **energy degradation**. The thermal energy that comes out of the exhaust of a car is degraded energy. It cannot be used further.

Fossil fuels

Typical engine efficiencies

diesel/oil/gasoline engines	30–40%
coal power plants	30%
natural gas power plants	45%

Advantages of fossil fuels	Disadvantages of fossil fuels
• high energy density • a variety of engines and devices use them directly and easily • an extensive distribution network is in place	• fossil fuels, especially oil, pose serious environmental problems due to leakages at various points along the production–distribution line • contribute to the greenhouse effect by releasing greenhouse gases in the atmosphere when burnt • need extensive storage facilities

Electricity production

Many of the energy sources that are available to us today are used to produce electricity.

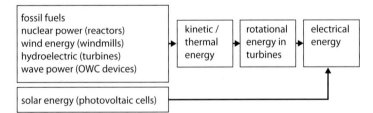

Nuclear power

Definitions

Nuclear reactors   Machines in which nuclear reactions take place, producing energy. The 'fuel' of a nuclear reactor is typically uranium-235. A typical energy-producing fission reaction is:

$$^{1}_{0}n + ^{235}_{92}U \rightarrow ^{140}_{54}Xe + ^{94}_{38}Sr + 2\,^{1}_{0}n$$

Chain reactions   The neutrons produced in a fission reaction can be used to collide with other nuclei of uranium-235 in the reactor (after they are first slowed down), producing more fission, energy and neutrons.

Critical mass   Critical mass is the minimum mass of uranium-235 for the chain reactions to sustain themselves; otherwise the neutrons escape without causing further reactions.

Uranium enrichment   The uranium commonly mined is uranium-238 which contains small traces (0.7%) of uranium-235. The process of increasing the concentration of the useful fuel uranium-235 in uranium samples is called enrichment. For nuclear power plants the concentration is increased up to 5%. Uranium used in nuclear weapons is enriched to much higher values, around 80%.

Heat exchanger   This is where the kinetic energy of the reaction products is converted into thermal energy (in the moderator) through collisions with the molecules of the moderator. A coolant (for example water) passing through the moderator can then extract this energy by, for example, turning the water in the coolant into steam at high temperature and pressure. The steam can then be used to turn the turbines of a power station, finally producing electricity.

Control rods   Control rods absorb excess neutrons whenever this is necessary in order to control the rate of energy production.

Moderator   The neutrons produced in the fission reactions must be slowed down if they are to be used to cause further fissions. This slowing down is achieved through collisions of neutrons with the moderator atoms.

Fuel rods   These are rods containing the fuel (e.g. uranium) in pellet or powder form. In the case of uranium, the fuel rods contain a mixture of fissionable ^{235}U and non-fissionable ^{238}U.

Types of reactors

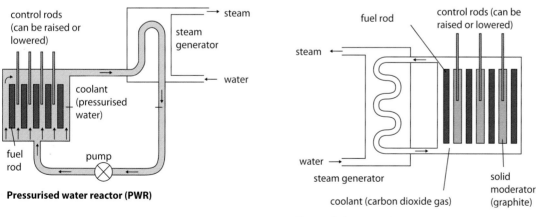

Pressurised water reactor (PWR)

Gas-cooled reactor

Problems with nuclear power

Plutonium production

The fast neutrons produced in a fission reaction may be used to bombard uranium-238 and produce plutonium-239:

$$_0^1n + {}_{92}^{238}U \rightarrow {}_{92}^{239}U \rightarrow {}_{93}^{239}Np + {}_{-1}^{0}e + \bar{v} \qquad {}_{93}^{239}Np \rightarrow {}_{94}^{239}Pu + {}_{-1}^{0}e + \bar{v}$$

The produced plutonium-239 can then be used in the production of nuclear weapons or as nuclear fuel in **fast breeder** reactors.

Radioactive waste

The spent fuel in a nuclear reactor, together with the products of the reactions, are all highly radioactive with long half-lives. It is difficult to dispose of this material safely.

Beta decay

Even if the reactor is shut down, production of thermal energy continues because of the beta decay of the product nuclei.

Uranium mining

Uranium mining is dangerous: uranium decays into radon gas, a known strong carcinogen. Inhalation of this gas as well as of radioactive dust particles is a major hazard in the uranium mining business.

Test yourself **1**

In a nuclear fission reaction involving uranium-235 approximately 200 MeV of energy is produced. How much mass of uranium is required per year in a nuclear reactor that produces 400 MW of electrical power with an overall efficiency of 40%?

➡ **Before you answer**
Recall the definition of efficiency.

Nuclear fusion

Nuclear fusion produces energy by joining together light nuclei, as for example in the reaction:

$$_1^2H + {}_1^3H \rightarrow {}_2^4He + {}_0^1n + 17.6\,\text{MeV}.$$

High temperatures (of order 10^7 K) are needed in order to bring together the nuclei which are both positively charged and so repel each other.

High pressures are needed to ensure a high probability of nuclei colliding and then fusing.

Containment is needed because the hot **plasma** (electrons disassociated from nuclei) required for fusion must be contained in such a way that temperature drops and contamination of the plasma are avoided. This is quite difficult to achieve.

Advantages of nuclear fission energy	Disadvantages of nuclear fission energy
• high power output/energy density • large reserves of nuclear fuels • no greenhouse gas emissions	• radioactive waste products difficult to dispose of • major public health hazard should 'something go wrong' • risk associated with production of nuclear weapons

Advantages of nuclear fusion energy	Disadvantages of nuclear fusion energy
• high power output/energy density • large reserves of nuclear fuels (hydrogen in water) • radioactive waste products minimal	• practically none except that the process has not been made to work commercially yet!

Solar power

Definitions

Solar constant (S) The Sun's total power output is $P = 3.9 \times 10^{26}$ W. The intensity of the radiation at the Earth's distance from the Sun is $\frac{P}{4\pi d^2} \approx 1400\,\text{W}\,\text{m}^{-2}$. This is called the solar constant S and so $S = 1400\,\text{W}\,\text{m}^{-2}$.

Insolation The **energy** per square metre that arrives at the surface of the Earth in the course of a day. Remember that some of the incident solar power is reflected and some is absorbed by the atmosphere.

Regional differences in insolation Insolation decreases as we move away from the equator and towards the poles. Light travels a greater distance in the atmosphere and is incident at an angle.

Seasonal differences in insolation In the winter the days are shorter and so less energy is received.

There are two different ways to extract energy from solar radiation.

Photovoltaic systems: solar to electric

These are cells made out of **semiconductors**. Sunlight incident on the cell produces a dc current and a dc voltage (by a process **similar** to the photoelectric effect). The currents and voltages are generally small so photovoltaic cells are of limited use if only a few of them are used.

Solar active devices: solar to thermal

These are commonly used in many countries to extract thermal energy from the sunlight and use it to heat water for domestic use. These simple collectors are cheap and are usually put on the roof of a house. Their disadvantage is that they tend to be bulky and cover too much space.

Advantages of solar power	Disadvantages of solar power
• 'free' • inexhaustible • clean	• works during the day only • affected by cloudy weather • low energy density • requires large areas • initial costs high (for photovoltaic systems)

Average intensity

The solar constant is $S = 1400\,\text{W}\,\text{m}^{-2}$. This is the power received per square metre on a surface perpendicular to the Sun's rays. The Earth presents to the Sun a disc of radius equal to the radius of the Earth. This disc therefore has area πR_E^2. The power incident on this disc may be thought to be spread over the entire Earth surface of area $4\pi R_E^2$, i.e. four times the area of the disc. So the average intensity on the entire upper atmosphere area is $\frac{S}{4} \approx \frac{1400}{4} = 350\,\text{W}\,\text{m}^{-2}$. About 30% is reflected, which means that the Earth's surface receives an **average** radiation intensity of $350 \times 0.70 \approx 250\,\text{W}\,\text{m}^{-2}$.

This is extremely important for examination purposes!

Test yourself **2**

A container holds 220 kg of water. When the container is hidden from sunlight, the temperature of the water decreases at a rate of $3.5 \times 10^{-3}\,\text{K}^{-1}\,\text{s}^{-1}$. During the day, the solar intensity is $640\,\text{W}\,\text{m}^{-2}$. The specific heat capacity of the water is $4.2\,\text{kJ}\,\text{kg}^{-1}\,\text{K}^{-1}$. Calculate the area of the water that must be exposed to sunlight so that the water temperature remains constant.

➡ **Before you answer**
If the temperature is constant, what does this imply about the rate of energy loss?

Hydroelectric power

Consider a mass m of water that is a height h from some horizontal level. When this mass of water descends a height h, its potential energy gets converted into kinetic energy. The power generated is $\frac{\Delta m}{\Delta t}gh$, where Δm is the change in mass in time Δt. The change in mass Δm is given by $\rho \Delta V$ where ρ is the density of water and ΔV the volume it occupies. Then $P = \frac{\Delta V}{\Delta t}\rho gh$.

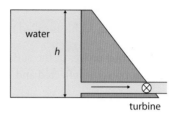
water

h

turbine

If the surface area of the dam is A, then, since $V = Ah$, $\frac{\Delta V}{\Delta t} = A\frac{\Delta h}{\Delta t}$ and so $P = \rho A\frac{\Delta h}{\Delta t}gh$, i.e. the power depends on the height of the water and the rate at which the height changes.

In a **pump storage system**, the water that flows to lower heights is again pumped back to its original height by using the generators of the plant as motors to pump the water. Obviously, to do this requires energy (more energy in fact that can be regained when the water is again allowed to flow to a lower height). This energy has to be supplied from other sources of electric energy. But this is the only way to **store** energy on a large scale. In other words, **excess** electricity from somewhere else can be provided to the plant to raise the water so that energy can be produced **later** when it is needed.

Energy conversions in a hydroelectric power plant include gravitational potential to kinetic to rotational energy of the turbines and finally to electric energy.

Advantages of hydroelectric energy	Disadvantages of hydroelectric energy
• 'free' • inexhaustible • clean	• very location dependent • requires drastic changes to environment • initial costs high

Wind power

Let us consider the amount of mass that can pass through a tube of cross-sectional area A with velocity v. Let ρ be the density of air. Then the mass enclosed in a tube of length $v\Delta t$ is $\rho Av\Delta t$. This is the mass that will exit the right end of the tube **within** a time interval equal to Δt. The kinetic energy of this mass of air is thus $\frac{1}{2}(\rho Av\Delta t)v^2 = \frac{1}{2}\rho A\Delta t v^3$. Therefore the power is $P = \frac{1}{2}\rho Av^3$.

You may be asked to reproduce this derivation.

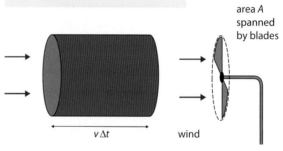

area A spanned by blades

$v\,\Delta t$ wind

Advantages of wind power	Disadvantages of wind power
• the source is the wind and so 'free' • for practical purposes it is inexhaustible • clean, without carbon emissions • ideal for remote island locations	• works only if there is wind! • aesthetically unpleasant (and noisy) • best locations far from large cities • maintenance costs high

Test yourself **3**
Calculate the number of windmills that are needed to supply power to a small village whose power needs are 5.0 MW. Each windmill has blade diameter 12 m, the density of air is 1.2 kg m^{-3} and the wind speed is 8.0 m s^{-1}. Comment on your answer.

Wave power

The simplified case of a square profile wave

The mass raised **above the undisturbed surface of the water** (the dotted line) is (density × volume) $\rho\frac{\lambda}{2}AL$ (ρ is the density of water). The centre of mass of this body of water is now at a height of $\frac{A}{2}$ above the undisturbed surface of the water. This mass of water used to be in a trough of the wave and so its centre of mass used to be a distance $\frac{A}{2}$ below the dotted line. The centre of mass is thus raised by a distance $h = A$ and so the potential energy of this body of water **increases** by:

$$\Delta E_P = mgh = \rho\frac{\lambda}{2}gA^2L$$

This is for one wave, but there are f waves per second where f is the frequency. The power carried is thus:

$$P = \Delta E_P f = \frac{1}{2}\rho gA^2 vL$$

The power per unit wavefront length is therefore:

$$\frac{P}{L} = \frac{1}{2}\rho gA^2 v$$

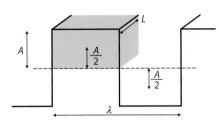

You may be asked to reproduce this derivation.

For a more realistic sine wave of the same speed and amplitude A, the power would be **less** since the height of the water is not always $\frac{A}{2}$ above or below the dotted line. We must then replace $\frac{A}{2}$ by its average value, which is $\sqrt{\frac{A^2}{2}}$.

The oscillating water column (OWC)

As a crest of the wave approaches the cavity in the device, the column of water in the cavity rises and so pushes the air above it upwards. The air passes through a turbine, turning it, and is then released in the atmosphere.

As a trough of the wave approaches the cavity, the water in the cavity falls and thus draws in air from the atmosphere, which again turns the turbine.

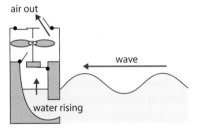

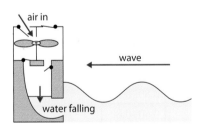

Advantages of wave power	Disadvantages of wave power
• the source is waves and so 'free' • reasonable energy density • for practical purposes, inexhaustible • clean, without carbon emissions	• works only in areas with large waves • wave patterns are irregular in wave speed, amplitude and direction – difficult to achieve reasonable efficiency over all the variables • maintenance and installation costs very high

Test yourself **4**

Consider a wave of amplitude 1.5 m and speed $v = 4.0\,\text{m s}^{-1}$. Calculate the power that can be extracted from a wavefront of length 5.0 m.

Radiation

Definitions

Black body   Theoretical body that absorbs **all** the energy that is incident on it, reflecting none.

Stefan–Boltzmann law   The power emitted per unit area of a **black body** at absolute temperature T is $\frac{P}{A} = \sigma T^4$ where $\sigma = 5.67 \times 10^{-8} \, \mathrm{W \, m^{-2} \, K^{-4}}$. Thus $P = \sigma A T^4$.

The graph shows the power radiated from $1 \, \mathrm{m^2}$ of the same surface as the temperature of the surface is varied. The vertical axis units are arbitrary.

The area under each curve represents the total power radiated from $1 \, \mathrm{m^2}$ of the same surface irrespective of wavelength and equals σT^4.

Most of the energy is radiated around a specific wavelength known as the **peak wavelength**.

The energy radiated by a body is electromagnetic radiation and is distributed over an infinite range of wavelengths.

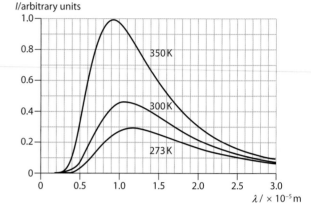

> ! For the temperatures shown in the graph, the peak wavelengths are in the infrared region of the electromagnetic spectrum.

Surfaces that are black and dull, as opposed to polished and shiny, are good approximations to the theoretical 'black body'. Everything else radiates according to $P = \varepsilon \sigma A T^4$.

The constant ε appearing in this formula is called the **emissivity** of the surface. It is a number that varies from 0 to 1. It may be defined as:

$$\frac{\text{power per unit area radiated at temp. } T}{\text{power per unit area radiated by black body at temp. } T}$$

Surface	Emissivity
black body	1.0
ocean water	0.80–0.90
ice	0.60–0.80
snow	0.05–0.60
dry land	0.70–0.80
forests	0.85–0.95
land with vegetation	0.75

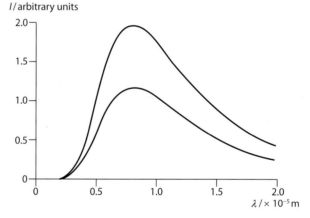

The graph shows the spectra for two bodies of the same surface area and temperature but different emissivities. At equilibrium, $P_{net} = 0$, i.e. the body loses as much energy as it gains and so the body's temperature stays constant and equals that of the surroundings: $T_1 = T_2$.

> ! A body of emissivity ε that is kept at some temperature T_1, will radiate power at $P_{out} = \varepsilon \sigma A T_1^4$ but will also **absorb** power at a rate $P_{in} = \varepsilon \sigma A T_2^4$, if its surroundings are kept at temperature T_2.
> Hence the net power lost by the body is:
>
> $P_{net} = P_{out} - P_{in} = \varepsilon \sigma A (T_1^4 - T_2^4)$.

The energy balance of the Earth and the greenhouse effect

Definitions

Power The rate (with time) at which energy is emitted or absorbed.

You must know these terms well!

Intensity This is the power received per unit area, $I = \frac{P}{A}$. If the source emits radially in all directions then at a distance d from the source the intensity is $I = \frac{P}{4\pi d^2}$.

Surface heat capacity, C_s This is the energy required to increase the temperature of $1\,m^2$ of the surface by 1 degree kelvin. The units of C_s are $J\,m^{-2}\,K^{-1}$. Thus for a surface of surface heat capacity C_s and area A, the amount of thermal energy needed to increase its temperature by ΔT is given by $Q = AC_s\Delta T$.

Albedo $\alpha = \frac{\text{reflected power}}{\text{total incident power}}$. The Earth as a whole has an average albedo of about 0.30 indicating that it reflects 30% of the radiation incident on it. The albedo is different for different parts of the Earth depending on type of soil, shallow or deep water, type of forestation and cloud cover.

Average intensity Recall the discussion on page 45 that the average intensity on the entire upper atmosphere area is $\frac{S}{4} \approx \frac{1400}{4} = 350\,W\,m^{-2}$ and since 30% is reflected, the Earth receives an average radiation intensity of $350 \times 0.70 \approx 250\,W\,m^{-2}$ everywhere on its surface.

Mechanisms for global warming

The greenhouse effect is a result of greenhouse gases in the atmosphere. Solar radiation mostly passes through the atmosphere and is absorbed by the Earth's surface. Some is then re-emitted by the Earth's surface as longer-wave IR radiation. Some of the IR radiation gets absorbed by the greenhouse gases in the atmosphere, and re-radiated in all directions including back to Earth. This causes warming of the Earth.

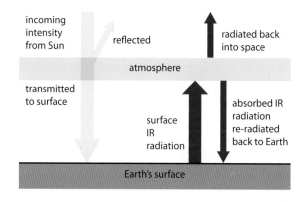

Test yourself 5

The surface heat capacity of a body of water is $C_s = 8.7 \times 10^7\,J\,m^{-2}\,K^{-1}$. Radiation of intensity $800\,W\,m^{-2}$ is incident on the body for a period of 8 hours every day for two months. The reflected intensity is 20% of the incident intensity. Estimate the change in temperature of the body, listing the assumptions you made.

Test yourself 6

Assume that the Earth's surface has a fixed temperature T and that it radiates as a black body. The averaged incoming solar radiation has intensity S. Take the albedo of the atmosphere to be $\alpha = 0.30$.
a Write down an equation expressing the fact that the power received by the Earth equals the power radiated by the Earth into space (an energy balance equation). **b** Solve the equation to calculate the constant Earth temperature. **c** Comment on your answer.

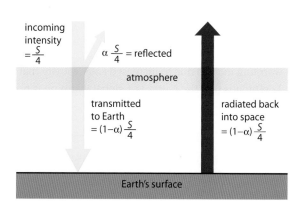

Greenhouse gases

Greenhouse gas	Natural sources	Anthropogenic (man-related) sources
H_2O (water vapour)	evaporation of water from oceans, rivers and lakes	
CO_2 (carbon dioxide)	forest fires, volcanic eruptions, evaporation of water from oceans	burning fossil fuels in power plants and cars, burning forests
CH_4 (methane)	wetlands, oceans, lakes and rivers	flooded rice fields, farm animals, termites, processing of coal, natural gas and oil, and burning biomass
N_2O (nitrous oxide)	forests, oceans, soil, grasslands	burning fossil fuels, manufacture of cement, fertilisers, deforestation (reduction of nitrogen fixation in plants)

The mechanism of photon absorption

Molecules exist in discrete energy states just like atoms. The difference in energy between molecular energy levels corresponds to infrared photon energies, so when infrared photons travel through a gas they will be absorbed, exciting the molecule to a higher energy state.

Transmittance curves

Consider infrared radiation passing through the atmosphere. The graph shows that the intensity of radiation after passing through the atmosphere is less than the incident intensity emitted because some of the radiation is absorbed. The amount of absorption depends on the concentration of the absorbing gas.

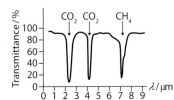

The enhanced greenhouse effect

Due to human activities the concentration of the greenhouse gases in the atmosphere is increasing, leading to additional warming of the Earth.

Long-term evidence for global warming

Samples of ice from in Antarctica have been thoroughly analysed to reveal a correlation between temperature changes and changes in carbon dioxide and methane concentrations.

The ice cores give a detailed account of global climatic conditions over a time period spanning some 420 000 years.

- Gas concentrations are studied by analysing the air trapped in the ice.
- Peaks in carbon dioxide concentrations match peaks in temperature.
- The temperature is studied by measuring concentrations of the isotope $^{18}_{8}O$ that are known to be temperature dependent.

Increased solar activity

One theory is that global warming may be due to increased solar activity that results in an increased solar power output. The general opinion is that the pattern of global warming is not consistent with changes in solar activity.

Volcanic activity

Other theories include increased concentrations of the greenhouse gases due to volcanic activity.

The Milankovitch cycles

There are changes in the Earth's orbit around the Sun and these are used to introduce variations in the received energy from the Sun. It is believed that these changes are not relevant for the climate changes on the 'short' time scale of, say, the last 200 years.

Sea-level changes and feedback mechanisms

One of the predictions of global warming is that increased temperatures will result in rising sea levels. This is because of water expanding in volume and ice melting.

Given a volume V_0 at a temperature θ_0, the volume after a temperature increase of $\Delta\theta$ will increase by $\Delta V = \gamma V_0 \Delta\theta$, where γ is a coefficient known as the volume coefficient of expansion. The coefficient of volume expansion is defined as the fractional change in volume per unit temperature change, $\gamma = \dfrac{\Delta V}{V_0 \Delta\theta}$.

We must distinguish between land ice (ice supported on land) and sea ice (ice floating in seawater). Sea ice, when melted, will not result in a change of sea level. By contrast, land ice will result in a rise in sea level.

Floating sea ice does **not** lead to a sea-level increase because of Archimedes' principle: a floating body of ice displaces water of weight equal to its own weight. So when it melts it occupies a volume equal to the displaced water volume, i.e. there is no change in the water level.

Definitions

Feedback mechanism   A change in one variable brings about a change in another variable whose effect is to increase the change in the original variable (positive feedback), or decrease it (negative feedback).

Negative feedback   Temperature increases, so more water evaporates. Evaporation causes cooling to take place reducing the temperature and so there is more cloud cover, reducing the temperature even further.

Positive feedback   Temperature increases and so ice melts. The albedo decreases which means that less radiation is reflected, so the temperature will increase even more.

Also, with higher temperatures, carbon solubility in the oceans decreases leaving more carbon dioxide in the atmosphere, increasing the temperature further.

Measures to reduce global warming
- Use fuel efficient cars – developing hybrid cars further
- Increase the efficiency of coal burning power plants
- Replace coal burning power plants with natural gas fired plants
- Consider methods of capturing and then storing (CCS) the carbon dioxide produced in power plants
- Increase the amounts of power produced by wind and solar generators
- Consider using nuclear power
- Be energy conscious – with buildings, appliances, transportation, industrial processes and entertainment
- Stop deforestation (trees absorb carbon dioxide)

International efforts
You must be aware of the following international initiatives:

- the Kyoto protocol (1997), an agreement aimed at reducing greenhouse gas emissions, and the more recent Copenhagen Conference
- the Asia–Pacific Partnership on Clean Development and Climate (AP6), that urged the signatory nations for voluntary reductions
- the Intergovernmental Panel on Climate Change (IPCC), an organisation that has undertaken a scientifically impartial analysis of global climate.

Test yourself **7**

The average depth of water in the oceans is about 3.7 km. Using a coefficient of volume expansion of water of $2 \times 10^{-4}\,\mathrm{K}^{-1}$, estimate the expected rise in sea level after a temperature increase of 2 K. Comment on your answer.

➡ **Before you answer**
What assumptions have been made in this calculation?

Motion in a uniform gravitational field

A projectile launched with speed u at any angle θ to the horizontal will follow a parabolic path in the absence of air resistance.

We treat the horizontal and vertical components of the motion independently.

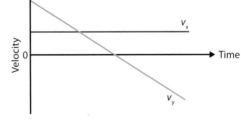

Horizontal motion	Vertical motion
There is no acceleration in this direction and so: $v_x = u\cos\theta \quad x = ut\cos\theta$	Here we have acceleration of magnitude g (free fall) in the vertically downward direction: $v_y = u\sin\theta - gt \quad y = ut\sin\theta - \frac{1}{2}gt^2$

The velocity–time graph shows how the components of the velocity change with time in a uniform gravitational field.

Energy considerations

Many problems in projectile motion can be solved faster using energy conservation rather than the full-blown kinematic equations. Consider this problem: a stone is thrown off the edge of a cliff with a speed $u = 12\,\text{ms}^{-1}$ at an angle 25° above the horizontal. The cliff is at a height $h = 30\,\text{m}$ above the sea. With what velocity does the stone hit the water? (Take $g = 9.8\,\text{ms}^{-2}$.)

At the point where the stone is thrown, the total energy of the stone is $E = \frac{1}{2}mu^2 + mgh$. As it hits the sea the total energy is $E = \frac{1}{2}mv^2$. Equating the two energies gives $\frac{1}{2}mv^2 = \frac{1}{2}mu^2 + mgh$, i.e. $v = \sqrt{u^2 + 2gh}$, which gives $v = 27.1 \approx 27\,\text{ms}^{-1}$. The horizontal component of velocity is $12 \times \cos 25° = 10.9\,\text{ms}^{-1}$ and since this remains constant this is also the horizontal component at impact. Hence the vertical component is $\sqrt{27.1^2 - 10.9^2} = 24.8 \approx 25\,\text{ms}^{-1}$. The angle of impact is then $\tan^{-1}\frac{24.8}{10.9} \approx 66°$.

Air resistance

The effect of air resistance (red circles) is to

- reduce the maximum height
- reduce the maximum range
- make the angle of descent steeper
- distort the shape away from parabolic.

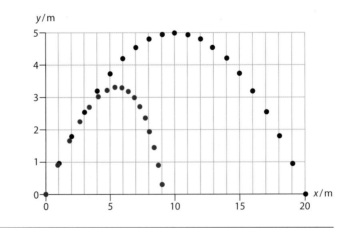

Test yourself 1

A projectile is launched horizontally from a height of 12 m with a speed of 15 ms⁻¹. Determine the horizontal distance travelled when the body lands.

Gravitational and electric potential

Gravitational potential	Electric potential
The work done per unit mass in moving a point mass m from infinity to a point near the mass M is $V = \dfrac{W}{m}$.	The work done per unit charge in moving a (positive) point charge q from infinity to a point near the charge Q is $V = \dfrac{W}{q}$.
The unit of gravitational potential is J kg^{-1}.	The unit of electric potential is the volt (V) and is equivalent to J C^{-1}.
The work done is independent of the path followed.	The work done is independent of the path followed.
The gravitational potential a distance r from a particle of mass M, $V = -\dfrac{GM}{r}$.	The electric potential a distance r from a particle of charge Q, $V = \dfrac{kQ}{r}$. **Note**: Unlike gravitation, where the sign is negative, the sign here is positive **but** the charge Q in this formula must be entered with its proper sign. Thus the electric potential a distance of 2.0×10^{-10} from an **electron** is $V = \dfrac{9 \times 10^9 \times (-1.6 \times 10^{-19})}{2.0 \times 10^{-10}} = -7.2$ V.
To find the gravitational/electric potential from more than one mass/charge, we find the potential from each mass/charge separately and add them together. This method is necessary because potential is a scalar quantity.	

Definition

Work done   To move a mass m from one point in a gravitational field to another requires work. The work done on the body **by an external agent** is given by $W = m\Delta V$ where $\Delta V = V_{final} - V_{initial}$ is the change in potential from the initial to the final position.

The work done **by the gravitational force** is $W = -m\Delta V$.

Test yourself 2
The diagram shows two unequal spherical masses. At which point is the gravitational potential greatest?

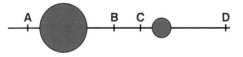

Test yourself 3
Two equal spherical masses M are a distance $2d$ apart. A small mass m is placed at the mid-point of the line joining the two masses. **a** What was the work done to bring m from infinity to this position? **b** The mass m is now moved a distance $\dfrac{d}{2}$ closer to the right mass. What is the work that must be done?

Test yourself 4
Four charges of equal magnitude are placed at the vertices of a square as shown. The origin of the axes is at the centre of the square.

The electric potential is zero

A at the origin only.   **B** along the x-axis only.
C along the y-axis only.   **D** along both the x- and y-axes.

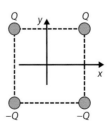

Equipotential surfaces

Equipotential surfaces are surfaces where the potential is the same.

The diagram on the right shows equipotential surfaces for two equal **masses or charges**.

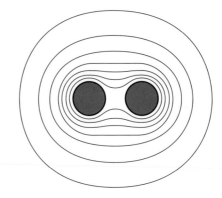

How are field lines related to equipotential surfaces? Copy the diagram and use it to draw the field lines.
Field lines are at right angles to the equipotentials.
Can equipotential surfaces cross?
No, because at the intersection point the potential would have two different values.
Can field lines cross?
No, because at the intersection point the field would have two different directions and would be infinite in magnitude.
In the case of electric charges, are the charges of the same or opposite sign in this diagram?
Opposite, because this is a case of an attractive force.

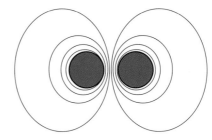

The diagram on the right shows equipotential surfaces for two equal and opposite **charges**.

Note that two masses can never give this arrangement of equipotential surfaces. Why?
At the midpoint of two masses the field would be zero – it is not zero in this arrangement.

The relation between field and potential
In both gravitational and electrical fields, the field strength is the negative gradient of the corresponding potential.

$$g = -\frac{dV}{dr}, \qquad E = -\frac{dV}{dr}$$

This means that in a graph of potential versus distance the gradient gives the (negative) field strength.

This means that field lines are always at right angles to equipotential surfaces.

For example, for a positive point charge Q the potential is $V = \frac{kQ}{r}$ and so $E = -\frac{d}{dr}\left(\frac{kQ}{r}\right) = \frac{kQ}{r^2}$ as we expect.

Test yourself **5**
Consider this electric field.

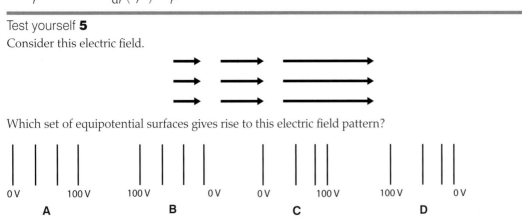

Which set of equipotential surfaces gives rise to this electric field pattern?

Gravitational and electric potential energy

Gravitational potential energy	Electric potential energy
The work done in moving a point mass m from infinity to a point near a mass M is $W = -\frac{GMm}{r}$. This work is now stored as **gravitational potential energy** between the two masses: 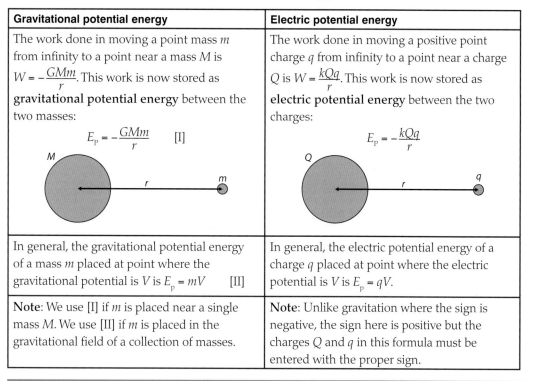	The work done in moving a positive point charge q from infinity to a point near a charge Q is $W = \frac{kQq}{r}$. This work is now stored as **electric potential energy** between the two charges: $$E_p = -\frac{kQq}{r}$$
In general, the gravitational potential energy of a mass m placed at point where the gravitational potential is V is $E_p = mV$ [II]	In general, the electric potential energy of a charge q placed at point where the electric potential is V is $E_p = qV$.
Note: We use [I] if m is placed near a single mass M. We use [II] if m is placed in the gravitational field of a collection of masses.	**Note:** Unlike gravitation where the sign is negative, the sign here is positive but the charges Q and q in this formula must be entered with the proper sign.

Test yourself **6**

Calculate the electric potential energy of an electron in orbit around a proton when the orbit radius is 2.0×10^{-10} m.

Test yourself **7**

A proton is kept on the surface of a positively charged metallic sphere. The radius of the sphere is 0.50 m and the potential at its surface is 180 V. The proton is now released. Calculate the speed of the proton **a** as it passes a point a distance of 1.0 m from the centre of the sphere, **b** after it has moved an infinite distance away from the sphere. **c** Sketch a graph to show the variation with distance from the centre of the sphere of the speed of the proton.

Test yourself **8**

Calculate the gravitational potential energy of a satellite of mass 3500 kg in orbit around the Earth at a height of 520 km above the surface of the Earth. (The Earth's radius is $R = 6.4 \times 10^6$ m and its mass is $M = 6.0 \times 10^{24}$ kg.)

Test yourself **9**

The graph shows the variation with the distance r from the centre of a planet of radius 5.0×10^5 m of the gravitational potential created by the planet.

a Calculate the gravitational field strength at a distance of 2.0×10^6 m from the centre.

b Calculate the work done to move a mass of 350 kg from the surface of the planet to a height of 2.0×10^6 m above the surface.

c Calculate the additional work to that in **b** that must be performed on the mass so that it is put in a circular orbit about the planet at a height of 2.0×10^6 m above the surface.

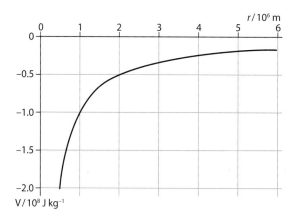

Motion in a gravitational field

Force considerations

A point mass m orbits a spherical mass M. The orbit radius is r and the orbital speed is v. The gravitational force provides the centripetal force on m and so

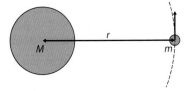

You must be able to quickly derive these formulae in an exam.

$$\frac{GMm}{r^2} = \frac{mv^2}{r} \Rightarrow v^2 = \frac{GM}{r}$$

The formula says that the closer m is to M the faster it moves.

For circular motion in general, we have $v = \frac{2\pi r}{T}$ where T is the period, the time for one full revolution.

Kepler's third law relates period to orbital radius. Taking M to be the mass of the Sun and m the mass of a planet we deduce, by combining the last two formulae, that $\left(\frac{2\pi r}{T}\right)^2 = \frac{GM}{r} \Rightarrow T^2 = \frac{4\pi^2}{GM}r^3$

Definitions

Orbital motion   A satellite orbits a spherical mass M. The kinetic energy of the orbiting satellite is $E_K = \frac{1}{2}mv^2$, and since $v^2 = \frac{GM}{r}$, we have that $E_K = \frac{1}{2}\frac{GMm}{r}$. The total energy is therefore

$$E_T = E_K + E_P = \frac{1}{2}\frac{GMm}{r} - \frac{GMm}{r} = -\frac{1}{2}\frac{GMm}{r}.$$

The total energy is negative. This means that the satellite finds itself in a **potential well**. Energy must be supplied if is to move away.

> For a satellite in orbit the total energy is the negative of the kinetic energy.

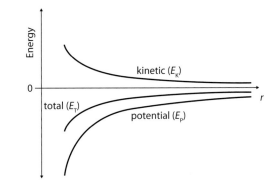

Escape speed   The **minimum** speed at launch at the surface of a planet so that the projectile can move far away and never return.

The total energy at launch at the surface of the planet is $E_T = E_K + E_P = \frac{1}{2}mv^2 - \frac{GMm}{R}$. For **minimum** escape speed the total energy at infinity will be **zero** and so by conservation of energy: $\frac{1}{2}mv^2 - \frac{GMm}{R} = 0 \Rightarrow v^2 = \frac{2GM}{R}$.

You can be asked to manipulate these equations to get $v^2 = \frac{2GMR}{R^2}$ $= 2gR$ or $v^2 = 2\left(-\frac{GM}{R}\right) = -2V$, where both the gravitational field g and the potential V are the values at the surface of the planet.

Test yourself **10**

A probe is launched from the surface of the Earth with a speed that is half the escape speed. How far away from the Earth does the probe get? (Give your answer in terms of the radius of the Earth.)

➡ **Before you answer**
Use conservation of energy.

Key ideas

Definition

Ideal gas A theoretical model of a gas in which there are no intermolecular forces and so no intermolecular potential energy in the internal energy of the gas. An **ideal gas** obeys the equation of state $PV = nRT$ at **all** pressures, volumes and temperatures.

> Real gases obey this law approximately and only for a limited range of pressures, volumes and temperatures.

The **state** of a gas is determined when we know the pressure, P, the volume, V, the temperature, T and the quantity of the gas, i.e. its number of moles, n.

The gas constant R is universal and has the value $R = 8.31\,\mathrm{J\,mol^{-1}\,K^{-1}}$.

From $PV = nRT$ we find $R = \dfrac{PV}{nT}$. Therefore, if the state of a gas is changed from (P_1, V_1, n_1, T_1) to (P_2, V_2, n_2, T_2) we must have $\dfrac{P_1 V_1}{n_1 T_1} = \dfrac{P_2 V_2}{n_2 T_2}$.

> Use this formula to find new values of P, V, n and T after a change in the state of a gas. Cross out what stays constant.

Work done

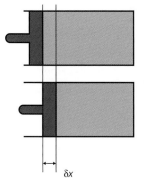

A gas in a container fitted with a movable piston exerts a force on the piston of area A. If the piston moves out as a result of this force by a very small amount, δx, the small amount of work done is $\delta W = F\delta x = (PA)\delta x = P\delta V$, since $A\delta x = \delta V$ gives the change in volume.

> If the pressure varies then we can only find the work done from the **area** under a P–V diagram.

If the pressure is constant then the total work done for a change in volume ΔV is $W = P\Delta V$.

Test yourself 1
Calculate the number of moles in a gas kept at temperature $300\,\mathrm{K}$, volume $4.0 \times 10^{-3}\,\mathrm{m^{-3}}$ and pressure $2.0 \times 10^5\,\mathrm{Pa}$.

Test yourself 2
A gas is heated at constant volume from a temperature of $27\,^{\circ}\mathrm{C}$ and pressure $3.0 \times 10^5\,\mathrm{Pa}$ to a temperature of $127\,^{\circ}\mathrm{C}$. No gas enters or leaves the container. Calculate the new pressure.

> **Before you answer**
> What units must temperature have?

Test yourself 3
An isolated container is divided into two equal volumes by a partition. In each part of the container there is an ideal gas. They have the same pressure P. The partition is removed. Which of the following is the final pressure?

A $\dfrac{P}{2}$ **B** P **C** $\dfrac{3P}{2}$ **D** $2P$

© IB Organization 2008

> **Before you answer**
> Use common sense! You must assume that the temperature in each half is the same and that it stays the same when the partition is removed.

Test yourself 4
Calculate the work done in the expansion from a volume of $2.0 \times 10^{-3}\,\mathrm{m^3}$ to a volume of $8.0 \times 10^{-3}\,\mathrm{m^3}$ represented by the graph shown.

Thermodynamic processes

We may distinguish the following processes.

It is crucial that you can define these processes!

Isobaric	Isochoric	Isothermal	Adiabatic
Pressure stays constant.	Volume stays constant.	Temperature and internal energy stay constant in an isothermal change. An isothermal change is usually slow so that the temperature always equalises.	No thermal energy enters or leaves the system in an adiabatic change. An adiabatic change is usually fast so there is not time for thermal energy to be exchanged.

An isothermal and an adiabatic **expansion** from the same state: the adiabatic is steeper.

An isothermal and an adiabatic **compression** from the same state: the adiabatic is steeper.

The first law of thermodynamics

The first law of thermodynamics states that the thermal energy Q supplied to a system will be used to change the internal energy, U, and/or perform work W: $Q = \Delta U + W$.

This law is a statement of the conservation of energy. There are conventions about **signs** that go along with this law that you must know: $W > 0$ means work is done by a gas, $Q > 0$ means heat is supplied to the system.

Test yourself 5
A gas expands at constant pressure 4.0×10^5 Pa and temperature 300 K from a volume of 2.0×10^{-3} m^{-3} to a volume of 5.0×10^{-3} m^{-3}. **a** Calculate the new temperature of the gas and the work done. **b** Has thermal energy been provided to the gas or has it been taken out?

Test yourself 6
For an ideal gas **a** define internal energy and **b** state and explain how the internal energy and the absolute temperature are related.

➡ **Before you answer**
The gas is ideal so does it have potential energy? What is absolute temperature related to?

Test yourself 7
A gas is compressed adiabatically. Explain, using the molecular model of a gas, why the temperature of the gas will increase.

Test yourself 8
The same amount of energy Q is supplied to two equal quantities of ideal gases. The first absorbs the thermal energy at constant volume whereas the second absorbs it at constant pressure. Which one has the larger temperature increase?

➡ **Before you answer**
To determine the temperature change we must see what happens to internal energy – why?

Cycles in *P–V* diagrams and the second law

The *P–V* diagrams in Test yourself **9–11** below show **cycles**, i.e. changes that start and end at the same point. Considering the diagram of Test yourself **10**, we see that the gas does work along AB. Work is done on the gas along CA. The **net** work (work done by the gas minus work done on the gas) is the shaded area of the loop.

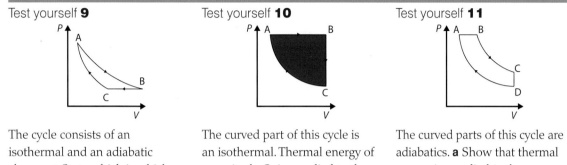

Test yourself **9**	Test yourself **10**	Test yourself **11**
The cycle consists of an isothermal and an adiabatic change. **a** State which is which. **b** Determine in which leg of the cycle thermal energy is extracted from the gas. **c** In which leg is the magnitude of the work done the greatest?	The curved part of this cycle is an isothermal. Thermal energy of magnitude Q_1 is supplied to the gas along AB and Q_2 is removed along BC and CA. Determine which is greater, Q_1 or Q_2.	The curved parts of this cycle are adiabatics. **a** Show that thermal energy is supplied to the gas along AB and taken out along CD. **b** Can it be determined in which leg, BC or DA the magnitude of ΔU is the greatest without any further information?

The second law of thermodynamics

This law deals with a complicated concept called entropy. We will take entropy to mean the same as the vague concept of 'disorder'. Observations such as

- thermal energy does not flow from cold to hot objects on its own
- thermal energy cannot be converted to mechanical energy in a cyclic process with 100% efficiency
- natural processes cannot be reversed (time does not go backwards)

and others like these have led to a law of thermodynamics that explains these observations.

A statement of the second law: The entropy of the universe always increases.

When thermal energy is **removed** from a system its entropy decreases. (The random energy of the molecules decreases and so we have a less disordered system.) According to the second law, some other place in the universe must have its entropy increase by a larger amount so that the overall entropy of the universe increases.

Even though this is not on the syllabus, it helps to know that there is a formula that can be used to calculate the entropy change ΔS when a quantity of thermal energy ΔQ is supplied or removed at temperature T:

$$\Delta S = \frac{\Delta Q}{T}$$

Test yourself **12**

A kilogram of ice at $0\,°C$ is placed in a warm room and melts to liquid water which eventually warms to the room temperature of $20\,°C$. Discuss the entropy changes taking place and explain how they are consistent with the second law of thermodynamics.

Standing waves

A standing wave is a wave formed when two identical travelling waves moving in opposite directions meet and superpose.

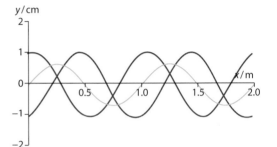

The diagrams show, at three different times:

- a **travelling** wave on a string, moving **towards the right** (blue line)
- a second **identical travelling** wave on the same string, moving **towards the left** (red line)
- the **superposition** of the two travelling waves (green line).

We see that the pattern (green line) stays the same, **only the amplitude changes**. This is why this is called a standing wave. The pattern does not move to the right or left.

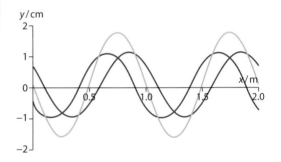

We also see that certain points on the string ($x = 0, 0.5, 1.0, 1.5$ and $2.0\,\text{m}$) always have zero displacement: these points are called **nodes**.

> It is very important to note that the distance between two consecutive nodes is half a wavelength.

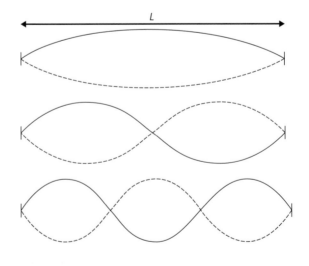

Waves on strings – fixed ends

Since the ends cannot move they must be **nodes** of the standing wave formed on the string.

First harmonic (fundamental)
The entire string length is occupied by 1 half wave.

$$L = 1 \times \frac{\lambda_1}{2} \Rightarrow \lambda_1 = 2L$$

Second harmonic
The entire string length is occupied by 2 half waves.

$$L = 2 \times \frac{\lambda_2}{2} \Rightarrow \lambda_2 = L$$

Third harmonic
The entire string length is occupied by 3 half waves.

$$L = 3 \times \frac{\lambda_3}{2} \Rightarrow \lambda_3 = \frac{2L}{3}$$

To create a particular harmonic then, we must shake the string (e.g. by attaching one end to an oscillator) with the frequency of the harmonic we want to create. This will create a travelling wave on the string, which, upon reflection from a fixed end, will create the second travelling wave moving in the opposite direction.

Test yourself **1**
A string has both ends fixed. Calculate the ratio of the frequency of the second harmonic to that of the first harmonic (fundamental).

Standing waves in pipes

Shown here is a pipe with the left end closed and the right open. We must have a node at the closed end since here the molecules cannot move. At the open end we must have an antinode. The diagrams on the left show the **mathematical** shape of the wave. It tell us how the molecules in the air in the pipe oscillate, shown by the arrows in the diagrams on the right.

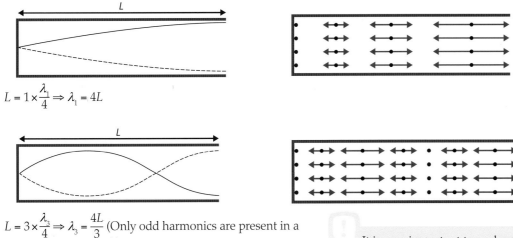

$$L = 1 \times \frac{\lambda_1}{4} \Rightarrow \lambda_1 = 4L$$

$$L = 3 \times \frac{\lambda_3}{4} \Rightarrow \lambda_3 = \frac{4L}{3}$$ (Only odd harmonics are present in a pipe open at one end.)

It is very important to understand that the graphs on the left imply the diagrams on the right.

Differences between travelling and standing waves
- Travelling waves transfer energy, standing waves do not. (Standing waves do have energy but do not transfer it.)
- Travelling waves have a constant amplitude, standing waves do not.
- In travelling waves, the phase changes as we move along the length of the medium. In standing waves all points in between two consecutive nodes (points in one loop) are in phase. Points in the next loop change phase by π with respect to points in between the next pair of nodes.

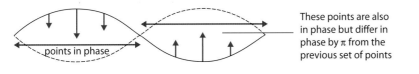

These points are also in phase but differ in phase by π from the previous set of points

---

Test yourself **2**

Two tubes have the same length. One (X) is open at both ends and the other (Y) is closed at one end and open at the other. Calculate the ratio of the fundamental frequencies $\frac{f_X}{f_Y}$.

Test yourself **3**

A tuning fork of frequency 560 Hz is sounded over a tube that is filled with water. The water is slowly removed and when the length of the air column is L_1 a loud sound is heard from the tube for the first time. The level of the water is slowly reduced further and the next time a loud sound is heard the length of the air column is L_2 with $L_2 - L_1 = x = 30$ cm. Calculate the speed of sound.

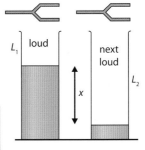

▸ **Before you answer**
The tuning fork is the same so the wavelength of sound is the same in both cases. So we must have the first harmonic in the first case and the next harmonic in the other with equal wavelengths. What is x in terms of λ?

The Doppler effect

This effect is the change in the observed frequency of a wave whenever there is **relative** motion between the emitter and the receiver.

> The effect is described in terms of frequency and not wavelength.

- The horn of an approaching car is heard at a higher frequency than that emitted.
- Light from a galaxy that moves away from Earth is measured to have a lower frequency (and so higher wavelength).

The Doppler effect has many applications. Two of the most common are to determine the speed of cars on a highway, or the speed of blood cells in an artery.

The equations below show how the observed frequency f_O depends on the speed of sound and the speeds of source and observer.

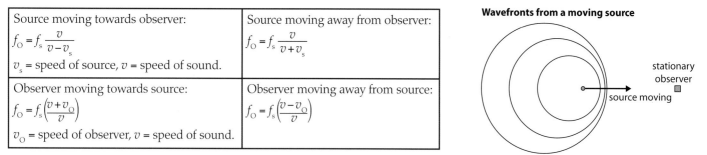

Source moving towards observer: $$f_O = f_s \frac{v}{v - v_s}$$ v_s = speed of source, v = speed of sound.	Source moving away from observer: $$f_O = f_s \frac{v}{v + v_s}$$
Observer moving towards source: $$f_O = f_s \left(\frac{v + v_O}{v} \right)$$ v_O = speed of observer, v = speed of sound.	Observer moving away from source: $$f_O = f_s \left(\frac{v - v_O}{v} \right)$$

Wavefronts from a moving source

stationary observer

source moving

The Doppler effect for light

Definitions

Redshift   The received light has a **longer** wavelength than that emitted.

Blueshift   The received light has a **shorter** wavelength than that emitted.

The Doppler effect for light is more complicated because the theory of special relativity must be used to analyse it. However, if the speed of the source is small compared to the speed of light we have the approximate formula $\Delta f = f_s \frac{v}{c}$ for the shift in frequency, where v is the speed of the source or the receiver and f_s is the emitted frequency at the source. The speed of light is c.

Note that this formula can also be used for sound if the speed of the source is much smaller than the speed of sound.

Test yourself **4**

A sound wave of frequency 300 Hz is emitted towards an approaching car. The wave is reflected from the car and is then received back at the emitter at a frequency of 315 Hz. What is the velocity of the car? (Take the speed of sound to be 340 m s⁻¹.)

➡ **Before you answer**
This is a double Doppler effect problem.

Test yourself **5**

A child on a carousel is sounding a whistle. The frequency measured by a stationary observer far away from the carousel varies between 510 Hz and 504 Hz. The speed of sound is 340 m s⁻¹. Use this information to calculate the speed of rotation of the carousel.

➡ **Before you answer**
Why do you think the frequency varies?

Test yourself **6**

Hydrogen atoms in a distant galaxy emit light of wavelength 658 nm. The light received on Earth is measured to have a wavelength of 720 nm. Calculate the speed of the galaxy and state whether the galaxy is approaching the Earth or moving away from it.

➡ **Before you answer**
Do we have a blueshift or a redshift?

Diffraction

This is the spreading of a wave as it goes through an opening (aperture) or past an obstacle.

Diffraction is the defining phenomenon for wave behaviour. **Anything** that diffracts may be called a wave.

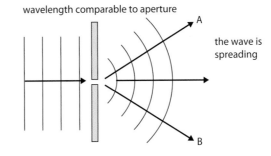

wavelength comparable to aperture

the wave is spreading

The single slit diffraction formula

Waves of wavelength λ moving from left to right encounter a slit of opening b.

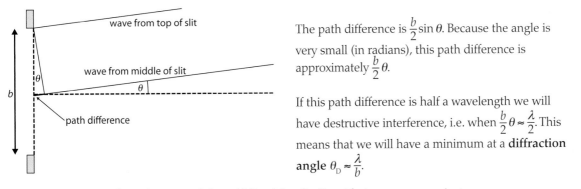

wave from top of slit

wave from middle of slit

path difference

The path difference is $\frac{b}{2}\sin\theta$. Because the angle is very small (in radians), this path difference is approximately $\frac{b}{2}\theta$.

If this path difference is half a wavelength we will have destructive interference, i.e. when $\frac{b}{2}\theta \approx \frac{\lambda}{2}$. This means that we will have a minimum at a **diffraction angle** $\theta_D \approx \frac{\lambda}{b}$.

This is for the waves from the top and the middle of the slit. Considering now waves just below the top and just below the middle of the slit we see that precisely the same condition applies. So we conclude that we will have a minimum in the diffraction pattern at an angle $\theta_D \approx \frac{\lambda}{b}$.

> You may be asked to prove this relation in an exam.

On the other hand, at the centre ($\theta = 0$) the waves arrive in phase and so we have constructive interference and a large intensity.

The intensity of the wave as a function of the angle θ is shown in the graph. We have a non-zero intensity even when $\theta \neq 0$, i.e. the wave spreads.

> This is the basic graph for single slit diffraction and you must know its features well.

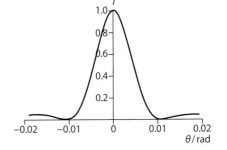

Circular apertures

A more detailed analysis for a circular aperture of diameter b shows that the first diffraction minimum is observed at a diffraction angle $\theta_D \approx 1.22\frac{\lambda}{b}$.

Test yourself **7**

The wavelength of the wave (light) in the intensity graph above is 4.80×10^{-7} m. Calculate the width of the slit assuming it is rectangular.

Resolution

Light from two point sources will diffract when it passes through an aperture. If the two sources are separated by a small angle the diffraction patterns will merge and the two sources will appear as one. Resolution is the ability to **see** as separate two objects that **are** separate.

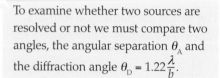

The two objects in the diagram are separated by a distance s and are a distance d from the observer (O). Their angular separation is $\theta_A \approx \dfrac{s}{d}$.

Rayleigh criterion

The Rayleigh criterion states that two sources are **just resolved** if the central maximum of the diffraction pattern of one source falls on the **first minimum of the other**.

Mathematically this means that the angular separation θ_A of the sources satisfies $\theta_A \approx \theta_D = 1.22\dfrac{\lambda}{b}$. Here b is the diameter of the circular aperture used to collect light from the sources.

> To examine whether two sources are resolved or not we must compare two angles, the angular separation θ_A and the diffraction angle $\theta_D = 1.22\dfrac{\lambda}{b}$.

	Individual patterns shown	Combined pattern shown
$\theta_A \approx \theta_D$ i.e. $\theta_A \approx 1.22\dfrac{\lambda}{b}$	Two sources that are **just resolved**. The central maximum of one coincides with the first minimum of the other.	Sources **just resolved**. We just barely see two separate peaks and so two sources.
$\theta_A > \theta_D$ i.e. $\theta_A > 1.22\dfrac{\lambda}{b}$	Sources **well resolved**.	Sources **well resolved**. The angular separation is large.
$\theta_A < \theta_D$ i.e. $\theta_A < 1.22\dfrac{\lambda}{b}$	Sources **not resolved**.	Sources **not resolved**.

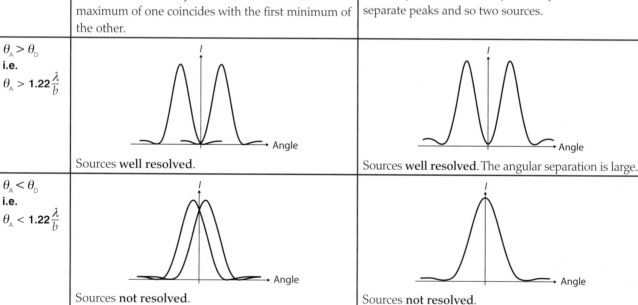

Test yourself 8

Mars has a diameter of 7×10^6 m and is 7×10^{10} m from Earth. It reflects light of wavelength 650 nm. Does the naked human eye with pupil diameter 3 mm see the planet as a point source of light or as an extended disc?

➡ **Before you answer**
To see the planet as a disc you must be able to resolve two points a diameter apart.

Polarisation

Polarisation is a property of transverse waves **only**.

Light is a transverse wave in which a pair of electric and magnetic fields, at right angles to each other, oscillate. The fields are at right angles to the direction of energy transfer.

When the electric field direction and the direction of energy propagation form a fixed plane (the plane of vibration) we say the light is polarised.

The diagram shows polarised light moving into the page. The dotted arrow shows the direction of energy transfer and the red arrows show the electric field (the magnetic field is not shown). On the left, the plane of vibration is vertical, in the middle it is horizontal, and on the right it is at about 15° to the vertical.

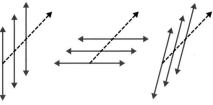

When the plane of vibration changes as the wave moves, the light is said to be unpolarised. This is shown in the diagram on the right.

We usually denote unpolarised light as in the diagram on the right. Light from light bulbs or from the Sun is unpolarised.

A **polariser** is a piece of plastic with a specific transmission axis. It only allows the transmission of the component of the electric field parallel to the transmission axis. In the diagram, unpolarised light is transmitted through a polariser with a vertical transmission axis. The transmitted light is therefore vertically polarised.

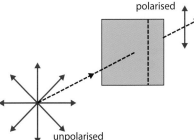

For unpolarised light passing through a polariser, the transmitted intensity is half of the incident intensity, $I = \frac{I_0}{2}$.

This is a result that you must know.

Polarised light is blocked by a polariser whose transmission axis is at right angles to the direction of the electric field.

The diagram shows two polarisers with their transmission axes at right angles. Only the vertical components of the electric field are transmitted through the first polariser. The axis of the second polariser is horizontal, so no light emerges.

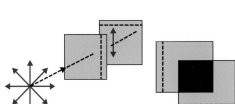

Malus' law

Consider vertically polarised light that is directed towards a polariser with a vertical transmission axis. The polariser is then rotated about the direction of the ray by an angle θ. The incident light has its electric field vertical. We know that only the component parallel to the transmission axis gets through. The component of the electric field along an axis parallel to the transmission axis is $E_0 \cos\theta$.

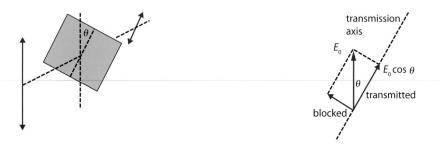

The transmitted intensity is, therefore, $I = I_0 \cos^2\theta$ – a result known as Malus' law. The graph below shows the transmitted intensity as the polariser is rotated from 0 to 180°.

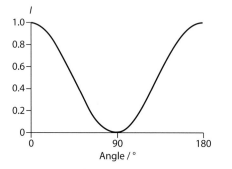

You will very likely be asked to reproduce this graph in an exam. Be sure to include numbers on the horizontal axis.

Polarisation by reflection

Light will reflect off a surface. It turns out that the reflection coefficients for light with an electric field parallel to the plane of incidence and one perpendicular to it are different. This results in reflected light that is **mainly horizontally polarised**.

Brewster's law

At a special angle of incidence known as Brewster's angle the reflected ray is completely horizontally polarised and the reflected and refracted rays make a right angle between them. (This assumes that the surface is not metallic.)

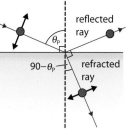

reflected ray

electric field along plane of paper

refracted ray

electric field into or out of plane of paper

In this case the angle of refraction is $90° - \theta_P$ and so Snell's law gives $1 \times \sin\theta_P = n \times \sin(90° - \theta_P) = n \times \cos\theta_P$ and so $n = \tan\theta_P$, a result known as Brewster's law.

You must know how to reproduce this proof in an exam.

Test yourself **9**

Unpolarised light is incident on three polarisers that are arranged one behind the other. The transmission axes of the first and third polariser are vertical and that of the middle polariser is at 45° to the other two. What fraction of intensity is transmitted?

Test yourself **10**

Light is moving from water (refractive index 1.33) into air. Calculate the angle of incidence such that the light that is reflected back into the water is completely polarised.

Optical activity and stress analysis

Certain materials (crystals and various solutions including sugar solutions) **rotate** the plane of polarisation of polarised light that is transmitted through the material. This is called **optical activity**. The angle of rotation depends on the thickness of the material and, in the case of solutions, on the concentration of the solution.

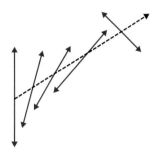

The electric field is rotating (here clockwise) as we move along the direction of propagation of the wave. To investigate optical activity, send a vertically polarised beam of light through the solution and then observe the beam through a second polariser whose axis is also vertical. Now rotate the second polariser by an angle θ until no light is transmitted. The angle by which the solution rotated the electric field is then $90° - \theta$. Repeat for a different thickness of the solution to see the dependence of angle of rotation with thickness. The explanation of this phenomenon is very complex and has to do with the way molecules of the material showing optical activity are put together.

Stress analysis

A piece of plastic placed in between two polarisers with their transmission axes at right angles to each other and illuminated with white light will show a complicated pattern of coloured and dark regions **if it is subjected to stress**. The phase difference, and hence colour, depends on the amount of stress and so the pattern seen is a stress 'map' of the plastic.

This phenomenon is complex. To learn more you should look up 'birefringence'.

> Keep your explanations simple and break them down step by step when you analyse these complicated processes.

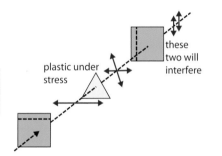

Plastic is placed in between two crossed polarisers.
Light through first polariser is horizontally polarised.
Light through stressed plastic has two components at right angles.
The two components, after transmission through the second polariser, are vertically polarised and so interfere.

> Two waves must have the same polarisation in order to interfere.

Liquid crystal displays (LCDs)

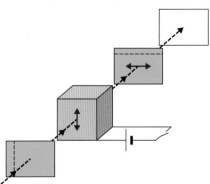

An LCD consists of a surface covered with pixels, and each pixel contains liquid crystal molecules that are long and thin.

Light enters the first polariser. The transmitted light is vertically polarised.

The liquid crystals rotate the plane of polarisation so that the transmitted light is now horizontally polarised.

The light thus can be transmitted through the second polariser, hit a reflecting screen and return along the same path. The screen looks bright.

If, however, a potential difference is applied to some pixels, the liquid crystal molecules will align and will not rotate the plane of polarisation. The light will therefore be blocked and those pixels will appear dark.

Magnetic flux

A loop of wire of area A is placed in a region of **uniform** magnetic field B. If the angle between the direction of the magnetic field and the **normal** to the area is θ, then we define the magnetic flux through the loop to be $\Phi = BA\cos\theta$.

If the wire of the loop is wrapped around the loop N times the **magnetic flux linkage** through the loop is $\Phi = NBA\cos\theta$.

Think of magnetic fields as real 'arrows'. The flux has to do with how many 'arrows pierce the loop's area'.

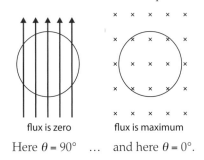

area A

The heavy arrow is the normal to the area of the loop.

In the first diagram the field is parallel to the surface. There is zero flux. In the second diagram the field is normal to the loop (it is directed into the page) and so the flux is a maximum.

flux is zero   flux is maximum

Here $\theta = 90°$ ...   and here $\theta = 0°$.

Faraday's law

The induced emf in a loop is equal to minus the rate of change of magnetic flux linkage with time:

$$\text{emf} = -\frac{\Delta\Phi}{\Delta t}$$

If the loop is made of conducting wire then the emf will produce a current. Thus Faraday's law creates a current out of a changing magnetic flux.

Examples of Faraday's law
Example 1

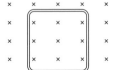

The magnetic field strength is **increasing** at a rate of $5.0\times10^{-3}\,\text{T s}^{-1}$. The area of the loop is $6.0\times10^{-2}\,\text{m}^2$. The rate of change of flux is $\dfrac{\Delta\Phi}{\Delta t} = \dfrac{\Delta B}{\Delta t}A = 3.0\times10^{-4}\,\text{V}$.

Example 2

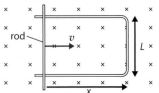

The rod is pushed to the right with speed v and so the area of the loop is decreasing, decreasing the flux in the loop. The rate of change of flux is $\dfrac{\Delta\Phi}{\Delta t} = \dfrac{\Delta(BLx)}{\Delta t} = BL\dfrac{\Delta x}{\Delta t} = BLv$

Example 3

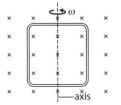

The loop rotates about the axis shown with constant angular frequency $\dfrac{d\theta}{dt} = \omega$. The flux changes because the angle changes. Using calculus, $\dfrac{d\Phi}{dt} = \dfrac{d(BA\cos\theta)}{dt} = -BA\sin\theta\dfrac{d\theta}{dt} = -BA\,\omega\sin\theta$. So the induced emf is $V = -\dfrac{d\Phi}{dt} = BA\,\omega\sin\theta$.

Lenz's law

The direction of the induced emf is such so as to oppose the change in flux that created it. This is a restatement of the law of conservation of energy.

This means that

- if the flux is increasing the induced current must produce a magnetic field opposite to the external field
- if the flux is decreasing the induced current must produce a magnetic field parallel to the external field.

Let's apply this law to the three previous examples on page 68.

Example 1
The flux is **increasing**. The magnetic field is directed into the page. We must oppose the change, i.e. we must decrease the flux. We do so by having a current in the loop whose own magnetic field will be out of the page, i.e. opposite the external field. The current is then counterclockwise.

Example 2
The flux is **decreasing**. The magnetic field at the loop is into the page. We must oppose the change, i.e. we must increase the flux. We do so by having a current in the loop whose own magnetic field will be into the page, i.e. parallel to the external field. The current is then clockwise.

Example 3
The flux is **decreasing** initially, but after half a revolution the current will change direction. The current is initially clockwise then changes to counterclockwise.

Another example of induced emf

Consider a conducting rod of length L that moves at right angles to a uniform magnetic field B with speed v. The field is out of the plane of the page.

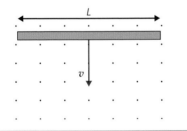

An electron in the rod moves with speed v and so experiences a magnetic force $F_m = evB$ directed to the right. Electrons will therefore move towards the right end of the rod, making it negatively charged and the left end positively charged. An electric field E will therefore be established in the rod (from right to left) opposing any further motion of electrons to the right: $evB = eE \Rightarrow E = vB$. This means there will be an emf induced at the ends of the rod of magnitude V such that $E = \frac{V}{L}$, i.e. $V = BLv$.

Test yourself **1**
In example 2 above the rod is given an initial velocity to the right and is then left alone. Explain why the velocity of the rod decreases. A lamp placed in the loop will light up. State and explain where the energy comes from.

➡ **Before you answer**
Looking for where the energy comes from means looking for something doing work.

Test yourself **2**
A battery is connected in series to a device D. The switch is closed at $t = 0$.

The current in the device varies with time as shown. Suggest what device D is and calculate its resistance.

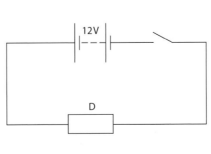

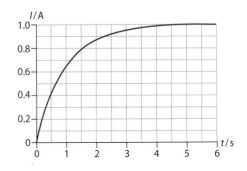

Alternating current

Electricity for commercial and home use comes mainly from **generators** that involve a coil rotating in a magnetic field. If the coil is rotating at a constant rate, the flux varies with time according to the graph. In this example the coil rotates with a period of 20 ms.

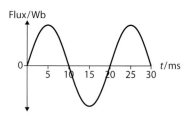

The corresponding induced emf and current in a domestic supply are shown below.

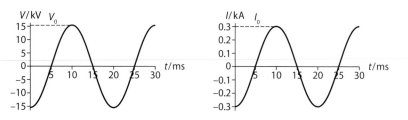

The current has the same dependence on time as the voltage (they are 'in phase')

Notice that when the flux is zero the emf (and the current) have large values and vice versa.

Rms values

The rms current is that current which in a dc circuit would give the same power dissipation as the average power in the ac circuit.

The voltage and current in an ac circuit have peak values called V_0 and I_0. We define the rms values of the voltage and current through

$$V_{rms} = \frac{V_0}{\sqrt{2}} \qquad I_{rms} = \frac{I_0}{\sqrt{2}}.$$

Do **not** use these formulae if you are asked to define rms values. Use the definition in words above.

In the graphs above, $V_0 \approx 15.5\,\text{kV}$ and $I_0 \approx 0.30\,\text{kA}$ so that $V_{rms} \approx \frac{15.5}{\sqrt{2}}$ $\approx 11\,\text{kV}$ and $I_{rms} \approx \frac{0.30}{\sqrt{2}} \approx 0.21\,\text{kA}$. (The resistance of the circuit is thus $R = \frac{15.5}{0.3} \approx 52\,\Omega$).

Power

Because the voltage and the current constantly vary in an ac circuit, the power dissipated in a resistor also varies. The **average** power dissipated (which is half of the peak power) is given by the usual formulae of dc circuits, provided we use rms quantities.

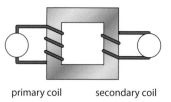

$$P_{ave} = V_{rms}I_{rms} = \frac{V^2_{rms}}{R} = RI^2_{rms}$$

Transformers

Consider two coils: a primary and a secondary with N_p and N_s turns of wire, respectively. An alternating voltage V_p is applied to the primary coil. Because the magnetic field it produces is varying, the flux linkage in the secondary coil is also changing and so an emf V_s is induced such that

$$\frac{V_p}{V_s} = \frac{N_p}{N_s}.$$

Assuming a perfectly efficient transformer, we have that the power in the secondary coil equals that in the primary coil and so $V_p I_p = V_s I_s$.

Therefore $\frac{I_p}{I_s} = \frac{N_s}{N_p}$.

Transformers can only be used with alternating current.

Transformers do not change the frequency of the ac current.

Power loss in transmission

Power loss in cables is reduced by transmitting the power at high voltage. This requires transformers.

A power station must produce a large amount of power. Assume that power produced is $P = 500\,\text{MW}$ at a voltage V. A current I will then flow into the external circuit. Then $P = VI$.

Let R be the total resistance of the cables. The power lost in the cables is $P_{\text{lost}} = RI^2$.

To minimise this loss the current must be as small as possible. This means that V must be large. A transformer must therefore be used to step up the voltage to a high enough value.

Suppose that the voltage at which the power is produced is a low 50 kV. The current is

$$I = \frac{500\,\text{MW}}{50\,\text{kV}} = 10^4\,\text{A}$$

and so the power lost is $P_{\text{lost}} = RI^2 = R \times 10^8$.

With a higher voltage, say 200 kV, the current is less,

$$I = \frac{500\,\text{MW}}{200\,\text{kV}} = 2.5 \times 10^3\,\text{A}$$

and the power lost is $P_{\text{lost}} = RI^2 = R \times (2.5 \times 10^3)^2 = R \times 6.25 \times 10^6$, i.e. 16 times **less**.

A step-down transformer must then again be used to reduce the voltage to a suitable value for supplying to consumers.

Test yourself **3**

The graph shows how the emf in the primary coil of an ideal transformer varies with time. There are 900 turns of wire in the primary coil.

a Draw a sketch graph to show how the magnetic flux in one loop of the primary coil varies with time.
b The emf in the secondary coil has a peak value of 16 V. Calculate **i** the rms value of the voltage in the secondary coil and **ii** the number of turns in the secondary coil.
c The current in the secondary coil has an rms value of 2.4 A.
i Calculate the resistance of the secondary coil.
Calculate **ii** the average and **iii** the peak power in the secondary coil.
d Draw a sketch graph to show how the power in the secondary coil varies with time.

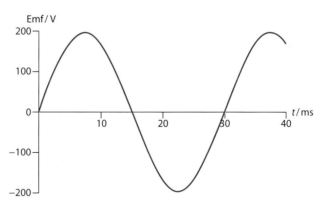

The quantum nature of radiation

Definitions
Photoelectric effect   The emission of electrons from a metal surface when electromagnetic radiation is incident on the surface. This is evidence for the behaviour of light as **photons**, i.e. as particles or **quanta** of energy.

Work function (ϕ)   The minimum energy required to eject an electron from a metal.

The key experimental facts are:

1   The kinetic energy of the emitted electrons depends on the light **frequency** and not the light intensity.

2   The light **intensity** only affects the number of electrons emitted (i.e. the photocurrent).

3   There is a frequency (the **threshold frequency**) below which no electrons are emitted (no matter how large the intensity).

4   Electrons are emitted within one nanosecond from the incidence of light on the surface, i.e. with essentially **no time delay**.

> You must be prepared to explain how the photon theory explains these observations.

These facts are in contradiction with the classical **wave theory of radiation**.

Einstein's explanation based on photons
Light is made up of particles called **photons** – bundles or quanta of energy. The mechanism for emitting electrons is that **one** electron absorbs **one** photon, each of energy $E = hf$. If the minimum energy to escape from the metal is ϕ (the **work function**) then the electron is emitted with kinetic energy $E_K = hf - \phi$.

The **stopping potential** is that potential for which the photocurrent in a photoelectric experiment becomes zero. This means that the kinetic energy of the electrons just becomes zero when they reach the collecting plate. Then, since the electric potential at the photosurface is V_s and the potential at the collecting plate is zero, by energy conservation: $E_{max} + (-e)V_s = 0 + 0$, i.e. $E_{max} = eV_s$.

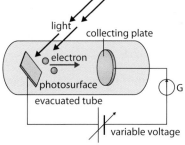

Test yourself **1**
The work function of a metal surface is 1.8 eV. Monochromatic light of wavelength 4.8×10^{-7} m is incident on the metal. Calculate **a** the threshold frequency and **b** the speed of the emitted electrons.

> **Before you answer**
> You want to find speed so you can first find the kinetic energy of the electrons. What is the equation relating kinetic energy and frequency? How do you find the frequency when you know the wavelength?

Test yourself **2**
The graph shows the variation with frequency of the stopping voltage in a photoelectric experiment. The line of best fit has been extrapolated to zero frequency.

Calculate the work function of the metal and a value for the Planck constant.

> **Before you answer**
> What is the equation relating stopping voltage and frequency?

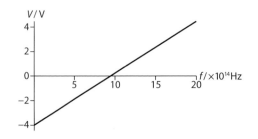

Wave nature of matter

De Broglie's hypothesis states that all moving particles (electrically charged or neutral) show wave behaviour with a wavelength given by $\lambda = \dfrac{h}{p}$, where h is the Planck constant and p the momentum of the particle.

> This does **not** mean that particles move along sine wave paths!
> It means that particles may show interference and diffraction effects.

The diagram shows the apparatus used for verifying de Broglie's hypothesis.

The wave nature of electrons can be seen in **electron diffraction** experiments in which a beam of fast electrons is directed at a crystal. The electrons diffract off the **regularly spaced** crystal atoms and create a diffraction pattern, similar to that created by light.

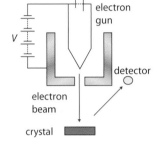

At the minima of the diffraction pattern the electron waves interfere destructively and cancel each other out. No mass or momentum would be measured there. This situation would be absurd if we insisted on an interpretation of the experiment in terms of electrons as particles.

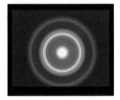

There are many electrons in the regions of this image that are white. There are no electrons in regions that are dark.

The image is very similar to that of diffraction of ordinary light by a circular aperture.

Calculations of the wavelength from the observed diffraction pattern agree with the de Broglie formula.

Test yourself **3**

Calculate the de Broglie wavelength of an electron that has been accelerated from rest through a potential difference of 250 V.

> ➡ **Before you answer**
> What is the work done when a charge is accelerated through a pd
> – and what becomes of this work? Think of a convenient formula for
> kinetic energy in terms of momentum.

Test yourself **4**

Explain why an electron microscope can resolve objects that cannot be resolved using visible light.

The Bohr and Schrödinger models

Niels Bohr showed that the energy of the electron in the hydrogen atom is given by $E_n = -\dfrac{13.6}{n^2}$ eV, i.e. it is discrete or **quantised**.

> Compare the energy levels of hydrogen with those for the electron in the box.
>
> Every time an electron makes a transition from a high energy state to a lower one it emits **one** photon. The photon energy is equal to the difference in energy between the levels of the transition. See Topic 7, page 37.

The Schrödinger theory

This is the current theory of atoms and molecules. Unlike Bohr's theory, it can be applied to **any** atom.

Electrons are described by **wavefunctions**. The wavefunction squared is a mathematical probability density function (a pdf) that can be used to calculate the probability for finding an electron in a small volume δV in the neighbourhood of a point:

probability $= |\Psi|^2 \delta V$

Since there is only a probability for finding the electron somewhere this implies that we cannot think of the electron as localised in space. There is only an **electron cloud** around the nucleus. This is consistent with the **Heisenberg principle** (see later).

Imposing **boundary conditions** on the wavefunction determines the energy.

The theory predicts **energy levels** with **discrete energies** for the electrons in atoms and also predicts the intensities of the **spectral lines** (something the Bohr model does not do).

The graph on the right is a wavefunction where the electron has a well-defined wavelength. Since the wavelength is related to momentum through the de Broglie formula $\lambda = \dfrac{h}{p}$ a small uncertainty in wavelength means a small uncertainty in momentum. In turn this implies a large uncertainty in position. We don't really know where this electron is.

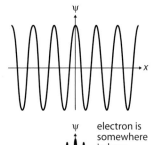

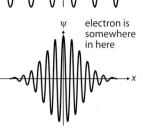

For this electron, the wavefunction allows the determination of the position of the electron with a low uncertainty. In turn this implies a large uncertainty in momentum.

Test yourself 5

The graph shows the variation with position of the wavefunction of an electron confined within a region of linear size 1.0×10^{-10} m.

a State what is meant by a wavefunction.
b Use the graph to estimate **i** the momentum of the electron and **ii** the kinetic energy of the electron.
c State one position where it is highly unlikely for this electron to be found.

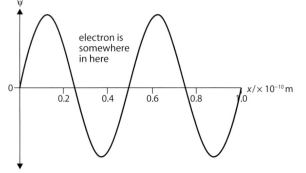

The Heisenberg uncertainty principle and the particle in the box model

The Heisenberg uncertainty principle

The Heisenberg uncertainty principle states that it is not possible, in principle, to determine both the position **and** the momentum of an electron with infinite precision at the same time. The more accurately the position is known the more inaccurately the momentum is known, and vice versa.

$$\Delta x \, \Delta p \geq \frac{h}{4\pi}$$

Δx, Δp are the uncertainties in the measurement of position and momentum and h is the Planck constant.

The principle also applies to measurements of energy and time: in measuring the energy of a state, a measurement that is completed within time Δt results in an uncertainty ΔE in the measured value of the energy.

$$\Delta E \, \Delta t \geq \frac{h}{4\pi}$$

The particle in the box model

Imagine an electron that is free to move along a line of length L. Imposing the condition that the wave associated with the electron is zero at the ends of the line means that the wave of the electron must be a standing wave with nodes at the ends of the line. This implies that the wavelength of the electron is $\frac{2L}{n}$ where n is an integer.

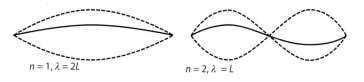

$n = 1, \lambda = 2L$ $n = 2, \lambda = L$

> Notice that imposing **boundary conditions** (e.g. nodes at the ends) **determines** the wavelength and in turn the **energy**.

The momentum is therefore $p = \frac{h}{\lambda} = \frac{h}{\frac{2L}{n}} = \frac{nh}{2L}$ and so the kinetic energy is

$$E_K = \frac{p^2}{2m} = \frac{n^2 h^2}{8mL^2}.$$

These are **discrete** energies. The energy can only take the values $\left\{ \frac{h^2}{8mL^2}, \frac{4h^2}{8mL^2}, \frac{9h^2}{8mL^2}, \dots \right\}$.

> The energy levels arise because the wave of the electron must be zero at the ends.

Notice that the lowest possible energy of this electron is (for $n = 1$),

$E_K = \frac{h^2}{8mL^2}$, i.e. E_K is non-zero. This electron cannot be at rest! This is consistent with the uncertainty principle.

> This model is too unrealistic. For one thing it does not take into account forces on the electron (e.g. electrical). As n increases the difference in energy between levels increases. In real atoms the opposite is true.

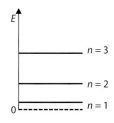

Test yourself **6**

An electron is confined within a hydrogen atom of linear size 10^{-10} m. Using the uncertainty principle, estimate that the kinetic energy of the electron is at least a few eV, explaining your working.

> **Before you answer**
> The uncertainty in the position of the electron is of the order 10^{-10} m.

Test yourself **7**

The energy of an excited level is to be measured. The electron will only stay in that excited level for less than 0.1 ns. **a** What is the uncertainty in the measured value of the energy level? **b** State and explain what your answer in **a** implies about the wavelengths of spectral lines.

> **Before you answer**
> How is the wavelength of a photon in a transition calculated?

Distance of closest approach

An alpha particle of electric charge $2e$ and kinetic energy E_K is directed head on at a nucleus of atomic number Z. The alpha particle will come to rest (for an instant, and will then be repelled) a distance d from the centre of the nucleus where

$$E_K = k\frac{(2e)(Ze)}{d} \Rightarrow d = k\frac{(2e)(Ze)}{E_K}.$$

We see that the kinetic energy of the electron gets transformed to just electric potential energy at the point of closest approach.

Experiments of this kind show that the radius of a nucleus with nucleon number A is approximately given by $R \approx 1.2 \times 10^{-15} \times A^{1/3}$ m and this implies that all nuclei have approximately the same density, about 2×10^{17} kg m^{-3}. This is because, density $= \dfrac{\text{mass}}{\text{volume}} \propto \dfrac{A}{(A^{1/3})^3}$ independent of A.

The mass spectrometer

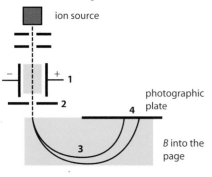

The mass spectrometer is an instrument that may be used to measure atomic masses. It consists of (1) a velocity selector, (2) collimators, (3) a magnetic field to bend ions into circular paths and (4) a detector (photographic film). In (1) ions of positive charge q enter a region of crossed electric and magnetic fields. The ions that continue undeflected satisfy $qvB = qE \Rightarrow v = \dfrac{E}{B}$.

Thus the beam that passes through the collimators (2) consists of ions of the same speed v. The ions enter the region of the second magnetic field (3) and are bent into circular paths of various radii depending on the mass of the ions: $qvB' = m\dfrac{v^2}{R} = R_i = \dfrac{m_i v}{qB'}$. Thus different radii R_i imply isotopes of **different mass to charge ratios**.

Test yourself **8**

A proton (to be treated as a point particle) is accelerated from rest by a potential difference V. The accelerated proton is directed at a nucleus of molybdenum ($^{96}_{42}$Mo). Given that the radius of a nucleus of mass number A is $R \approx 1.2 \times 10^{-15} \times A^{1/3}$ m, calculate the value of the accelerating potential if this proton just reaches the surface of a nucleus of molybdenum.

➡ **Before you answer**
What is the kinetic energy of the proton after acceleration? What becomes of this kinetic energy when the proton just stops on the surface of the nucleus?

Test yourself **9**

The ratio of mass to charge was measured for a sample of a pure element in a mass spectrometer. The values obtained were

$17.5\dfrac{m}{q}$ $18.5\dfrac{m}{q}$ $35.0\dfrac{m}{q}$ $37.0\dfrac{m}{q}$

where $\dfrac{m}{q}$ is the mass to charge ratio for hydrogen ($^{1}_{1}$H) nuclei. The data suggest that two isotopes are present with masses of

A 17.5 u and 18.5 u   **B** 17.5 u and 37.0 u   **C** 18.5 u and 35.0 u   **D** 35.0 u and 37.0 u

© IB Organization 2008

➡ **Before you answer**
Try to understand the meaning of the number in front of $\dfrac{m}{q}$. Hydrogen ($^{1}_{1}$H) nuclei have $q = e$ and $m = 1$ u. Our sample has $m = A$ u and the charge can be a multiple of e – the atoms may not be just singly ionised.

Nuclear energy levels

It is an important fact that the alpha and gamma particles produced in radioactive decay have **discrete** energies.

This can be explained in terms of **nuclear energy levels**. The protons and neutrons in a nucleus exist in discrete energy levels just as the electrons in atoms do. In a transition from one energy level to a lower one the emitted alpha or gamma particles have the discrete energy that is the difference in energy between the levels involved.

For the two alpha decays shown in the diagram below ($^{242}_{94}Pu \rightarrow {}^{4}_{2}\alpha + {}^{238}_{92}U$) the energies released are $4.983 - 0.307 = 4.676$ MeV and $4.983 - 0.148 = 4.815$ MeV.

The diagram below shows a gamma ray photon emitted in the decay of a nucleus of $^{24}_{12}Mg$ ($^{24}_{12}Mg \rightarrow {}^{0}_{0}\gamma + {}^{24}_{12}Mg$), with energy $5.24 - 1.37 = 3.87$ MeV.

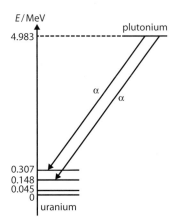

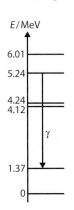

By contrast to alpha and gamma energies, beta particle (i.e. electron) energies are continuous!

Shown in the diagram to the right are the decays:

$$^{211}_{83}Bi \rightarrow {}^{0}_{-1}e + {}^{211}_{84}Po + {}^{0}_{0}\bar{\nu}$$

$$^{211}_{84}Po \rightarrow {}^{4}_{2}\alpha + {}^{207}_{82}Pb$$

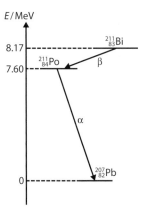

In beta minus decay a third particle is produced: the **antineutrino**. The three particles then **share** the available energy in many different ways depending on their direction of motion. The electron in the beta minus decay above would always have an energy of (approximately) $8.17 - 7.60 = 0.57$ MeV if there was no antineutrino produced, but this is **not** the case. The electrons in these decays have an energy that ranges **continuously** from 0 to a maximum of 0.57 MeV.

This is similar in beta plus decay such as $^{40}_{19}K \rightarrow {}^{40}_{18}Ar + {}^{0}_{+1}e + \nu$ where a positron and a neutrino are produced.

Test yourself **10**
a State the experimental evidence in support of nuclear energy levels. **b** Use the energy level diagram for plutonium to explain why in the alpha decay $^{242}_{94}Pu \rightarrow {}^{4}_{2}\alpha + {}^{238}_{92}U$ photons are also expected to be emitted.

Test yourself **11**
In nuclei, nucleons exist in nuclear energy levels, and in atoms, electrons exist in atomic energy levels. The order of magnitude of nuclear energy levels is 1 MeV whereas the energy of atomic energy levels is of the order 1 eV. Use this information and the particle in the box model to make an order-of-magnitude estimate of the ratio $\dfrac{\text{size of atom}}{\text{size of nucleus}}$.

Radioactivity

Definitions

Radioactive decay law   The rate of decay is proportional to the number N of nuclei present that have not yet decayed: $\dfrac{dN}{dt} = -\lambda N$.

The decay constant   The constant λ is called the **decay constant** and is the **probability of decay per unit time**.

Activity, A The number of decays per second. Initial activity $A_0 = \lambda N_0$.

Half-life, $T_{1/2}$ The time taken for the activity of a sample to halve.

The radioactive decay law implies that $N = N_0 e^{-\lambda t}$ and $A = \lambda N_0 e^{-\lambda t}$, i.e. the number of nuclei that have **not yet** decayed after time t and the activity after time t are both given by exponential decay laws.

If we know the molar mass of a pure radioactive sample, we can determine the number of nuclei present, N_0, by measuring the mass of the sample. Measuring the initial activity, A_0, then allows determination of the decay constant (through $\lambda N_0 = A_0$) and hence the half-life.

> The method described here is useful for determining very long half-lives.

Recall that, after a half-life, the initial activity of a sample is reduced by a factor of 2. The decay constant and half-life are related by $\lambda T_{1/2} = \ln 2$, which can be derived as shown below.

$$A = A_0 e^{-\lambda t}$$
$$\frac{A_0}{2} = A_0 e^{-\lambda T_{1/2}}$$
$$e^{-\lambda T_{1/2}} = \frac{1}{2}$$
$$\lambda T_{1/2} = \ln 2$$

> You may be asked to derive this relation in an exam.

Test yourself **12**
The activity of a 50 g freshly prepared sample of strontium ($^{90}_{38}$Sr) is 2.5×10^{14} Bq. Estimate the half-life of strontium.

Test yourself **13**
The half-life of an isotope is 2.45 minutes. Calculate the fraction of the original activity of the isotope 1.00 minute after it has been prepared.

Test yourself **14**
An isotope X has a half-life of 2.0 minutes. It decays into isotope Y that is stable. Initially no quantity of isotope Y is present. After how much time will the ratio of the number of Y nuclei to X nuclei be equal to 4?

Test yourself **15**
An isotope X decays into an isotope Y that is itself unstable. Isotope Y decays to a stable isotope Z. The graph shows the variation with time of the numbers of the nuclei of isotopes X and Y that have not yet decayed. Initially, the number of nuclei of isotope Y is zero.

Estimate the half-lives of isotopes X and Y, explaining your method.

> ➡ **Before you answer**
> Why must you look beyond 2.5 minutes to calculate the half-life of Y?

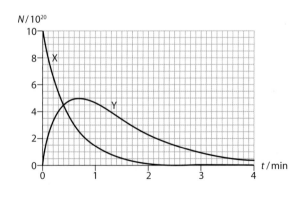

Binary numbers

A binary number is a number expressed in base 2 and consists of 0s and 1s. A sequence of 0s and 1s is called a **word**.

A number that is expressed in base 10 is called a decimal number. For example the number 5037 can be written as

$$5037 = \underline{5} \times 10^3 + \underline{0} \times 10^2 + \underline{3} \times 10^1 + \underline{7} \times 10^0$$

In other words, the digits we use to express the number are the coefficients of powers of 10 as shown above. In the same way we can express binary numbers where now we will use powers of 2 rather than 10. Thus, since $5 = \underline{1} \times 2^2 + \underline{0} \times 2^1 + \underline{1} \times 2^0$ we express the decimal number 5 in binary form as $5_2 = 101$. The coefficients we use are 0 or 1. Similarly the number 12 is

$$12 = \underline{1} \times 2^3 + \underline{1} \times 2^2 + \underline{0} \times 2^1 + \underline{0} \times 2^0$$
$$12_2 = 1100$$

Given a number in binary form, we call the leftmost digit (starting from the left) the most significant bit (MSB) and the digit the number ends with the least significant bit (LSB). For example, $\underset{\text{MSB}}{0} \ 111 \ \underset{\text{LSB}}{0}$.

Analogue and digital signals

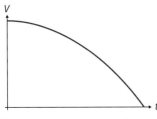

Analogue signals are **continuous** signals, varying between two extreme values in a way that is proportional to the physical mechanism that created the signal.

A digital signal is a coded form of a signal that takes the discrete values 0 or 1 only.

Compact disc (CD)

A CD is a device on which information can be stored in digital form. The analogue signal (e.g. music) is first converted into a digital signal (a series of 0s and 1s). This sequence is now **imprinted** on the CD by making marks (called pits) on the CD. The **edge** of a pit corresponds to binary 1. A series of pits is then made along a path that spirals from the centre of the disc outwards. The distance between adjacent paths is very small, about 1600 nm.

The diagram shows two rays in the laser beam. One reflects from a pit and the other from a land. The reflected rays will interfere. The path difference is $2d$ and so if $2d = \frac{\lambda}{2}$ the two reflected rays will interfere destructively. This is how the edge of a pit is detected and assigned binary 1. In other words the pit depth must be $d = \frac{\lambda}{4}$. So with a wavelength of 600 nm we need a pit depth of 150 nm.

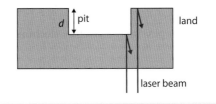

You must be able to explain the relation $d = \frac{\lambda}{4}$.

Test yourself **1**
Express the 5-bit binary number 10101 as a decimal.

Test yourself **2**
How many numbers can be represented with 5-bit words?

Test yourself **3**
Information is being imprinted on a CD at a rate of 44 100 words per second. The information consists of 32-bit words. A CD lasts for 74 minutes. Calculate the storage capacity of a CD.

Analogue and digital storage devices

LPs (analogue)	LPs have a very limited storage capacity and are subject to damage (by scratches and dust).
Cassettes (analogue)	These devices use **magnetic recording** to store data in analogue form. The cassette is a sequential device, i.e. to access information stored you must first go through all the information stored before the point you want to access. **Advantages** • low price • can be easily erased and reused **Disadvantages** • easily damaged by exposure to high temperatures and careless handling • sequential storage of data
Floppy disks (digital)	Data are stored magnetically (in much the same way as on the cassette) but the information imprinted is coded into 0s and 1s. **Advantages** • easily erased and reused • direct access device **Disadvantages** • limited quantity of data • damaged by exposure to high temperatures and careless handling • corrupted by magnetic fields
DVDs (digital)	Similar to the CD (see page 79) but here the pit length is shorter than on a CD allowing more data to be stored along the spiral. In addition, data can be stored on both sides of the disc or in a double layer on the same side. Since the pit length is shorter the wavelength used must be smaller as well.
Hard disks (digital)	Once used only in computers, hard disks can now be found in digital cameras and digital video recorders, mobile phones and other such devices. The disk may be thought to be divided into a very large number of tiny regions (the size is of order 10^{-6} m) and each such region is the seat of a 0 or a 1 of digitised data. The data can be accessed almost instantly irrespective of its position on the disk.

Advantages of digital storage

These advantages include:

• huge capacity for data storage in digital devices
• fast access to and retrieval of stored data
• storage is reliable and can be encrypted
• stored data can be copied or erased easily
• data can be processed and manipulated by a computer
• data can be transported easily physically as well as electronically.

On the negative side, whereas an analogue storage system such as ordinary photographic film degrades slowly with time, a serious error with a digital storage device is usually catastrophic in the sense that the data may never be recoverable. Digital storage thus requires back-up storage.

The CCD

Capacitance, C

Capacitance is the amount of electric charge that can be stored on a body per unit voltage. The unit of capacitance is the farad (1 F = 1 coulomb per volt.).

For a body of capacitance C and voltage V the charge that can be stored is $Q = CV$.

The charged-coupled device (CCD)

CCDs are used to create images in a wide range of the electromagnetic spectrum.

The CCD is a silicon chip that is covered with light sensitive elements called pixels (picture elements). Typical chip sizes vary from 20 mm × 20 mm to 60 mm × 60 mm.

Each pixel releases electrons when light is incident on the pixel (through a process similar to the photoelectric effect). A pixel acts as a small capacitor. The electrons released in the pixel correspond to a certain amount of electric charge Q and therefore a certain potential difference V develops at the ends of the pixel equal to $V = \dfrac{Q}{C}$, where C is the capacitance of the pixel. The value of V can be measured with electrodes attached to the pixel.

Pixels vary in size from 5×10^{-6} m to 25×10^{-6} m.

Image formation

The amount of charge (and hence the voltage V) is proportional to the **intensity** of light incident on the pixel. This means that if we can measure the voltage in **each** pixel we will know the intensity of light in each pixel, i.e. we will have an image.

Measuring the voltage

The idea is to measure the voltage in a particular pixel as well as the position of that pixel.

Charge is created in each pixel when the shutter of the camera (for example) opens. Charge accumulates in the pixel. By appropriately changing the potential, the charge in each pixel in the same row is made to move downwards.

Eventually, the charge in each pixel **in the same row** gets to a register where the voltage is amplified, measured and converted into digital form (in the analogue-to-digital converter, ADC) until the charge in the entire row is read. The computer processing all this now has stored two pieces of information. The first is the value of the voltage in each pixel and the second is the position of each pixel. The process is now repeated with the next row until the voltage in each pixel in each row is measured, converted and stored.

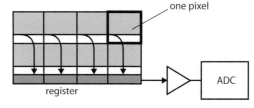

Each row is coupled to the next, hence the term 'charged coupled device'.

Test yourself **4**

The capacitance of a pixel is 25 pF. Calculate the voltage on the device when electrons accumulate in the pixel at a rate of $2.0 \times 10^8 \, s^{-1}$ for 30 ms.

CCD characteristics

Definitions

Quantum efficiency (QE)   The ratio of the number of electrons emitted to the number of incident photons. A high QE means you can acquire the image in less time.

One of the great advantages of the CCD is their very high quantum efficiency. It ranges between 70% and 80% (depending on the wavelength of light used). This is to be compared to 4% for the best quality photographic film and 1% for the human eye.

Magnification   The ratio of the length of the image as it is formed on the CCD to the actual length of the object.

Resolution   A CCD just resolves (i.e. 'sees' as distinct) two closely spaced points on the object if the images of these points are separated by at least a distance equal to 2 pixel lengths. (This means there is at least one empty pixel in between the images.)

High resolution implies that more detail can be seen in the image.

Notice that there is an additional constraint on resolution from diffraction. To 'see' two pixels as distinct their separation must be larger than the wavelength of light used. With a pixel size of 5×10^{-6} m and visible light ($\lambda \approx 10^{-7}$ m) this condition is easily satisfied. Diffraction would cause problems for pixels of much smaller size.

Uses of CCDs

Apart from their use in digital cameras and video recorders, CCDs have revolutionised endoscopy in medicine and they are also used as X-ray detectors in both medicine and astronomy. Their use in astronomy has made possible the formation of images of greatly different brightness in the same photograph. With photographic film the brighter object tends to wipe out the fainter object.

Advantages of CCD images over those on film
- Image is digital and so can be manipulated/stored/transmitted with a computer.
- The quantum efficiency is high so fainter images can be recorded in less time.
- The response is uniform over a wide range of wavelengths.
- Faint as well as bright objects can both be seen clearly in the same image.

Test yourself **5**

Light of intensity 6.8×10^{-4} W m^{-2} and wavelength 5.0×10^{-7} m is incident on the collecting area of the CCD of size 30 mm × 30 mm with 2.0×10^{6} pixels (i.e. 2.0 Mpixels).

a Calculate the number of photons incident on each pixel in a period of 25 ms.
b The capacitance of a pixel is 22 pF. Calculate the potential difference across the pixel assuming a quantum efficiency of 80%.
c Determine if this camera can resolve two points a distance 0.025 mm apart, assuming a magnification of 1.4.

(For this option you will need to study the material in this chapter as well as all of Topic 11.)

The eye

The eye is almost spherical in shape with a diameter of about 2.5 cm.
Its main parts are shown in the diagram.

Definitions

Cornea   A transparent membrane through which light enters the eye.
Most of the refraction takes place here.

Aqueous humour   A liquid-filled chamber in between the cornea
and the eye lens.

Iris   A coloured membrane covering the eye lens.

Pupil   An aperture in the iris through which the light enters the **eye
lens**. The pupil can increase or decrease its diameter in order to adjust
to varying intensities of light.

Eye lens   Provides some of the refraction of light rays through the eye.

Ciliary muscle   Muscle attached to the eye lens by ligaments.
It controls the curvature of the lens.

Retina   Membrane covering the back of the eye with light sensitive
cells.

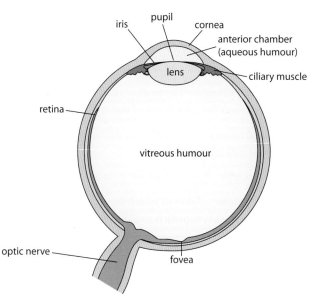

Cone and rod cells   There are two types of cells on the retina, **rods**
and **cones**. Close to the beginning of the optic nerve and essentially on
the principal axis of the eye, is an area called the **fovea**, a spot of diameter of about 0.25 mm, where vision is
exceptionally acute. This is filled with cones each connected to a different nerve fibre (unlike elsewhere on
the retina, where many different cones are connected to the same fibre).

Distribution of cones and rods on the retina   At the fovea there are many cones but no rods. The density
of cones at the centre of the fovea reaches 150 000 per mm². The rods are mainly found at the edges of the
retina (i.e. away from the principal axis of the eye) whereas the concentration of the cones increases as we
approach the fovea.

Test yourself **1**
Explain why in low intensity light it is easier to obtain a clearer image of an object by peripheral vision, i.e. by
looking at the object a bit sideways rather than directly at it.

Sight

Definitions

Depth of vision   The range of distances from the eye within which an object can be moved and still be seen acceptably clearly. The depth of vision depends on the distance to the object. The further the object is from the eye, the larger the depth of vision. If the object is put close to the eye, the depth of vision is greatly reduced. However, if brighter light is used the depth of vision will increase. This is because in brighter light the pupil diameter will decrease.

Accommodation   The ability of the eye lens to change its focal length. This is done by contractions of the ciliary muscle. When the muscle is relaxed, the lens is thin and the eye can focus on distant objects without fatigue. By contrast, when the muscle is tensed, the lens is fat and the eye can focus on objects nearby. This is an active process leading to fatigue.

Near point distance   The nearest distance at which an object can be seen clearly, without undue strain on the eye, is called the near point of the eye. For a normal healthy eye this distance is 25 cm.

Far point distance   The furthest distance the eye can focus on clearly; for all practical purposes this may be taken to be infinity.

Scotopic vision   Vision in which rods are the main detectors of the incident light in the eye.

Photopic vision   Vision in which the cones are the main detectors of the incident light. There are three types of cones, each sensitive to a different colour.

Scotopic vision	Photopic vision
used at night and when there is very little light available (because many different rods are connected to the same nerve fibre)	used during the day and when there is a lot of light available
distinguishes shapes but not colours	distinguishes shapes and colours
distinguishes little detail	distinguishes a lot of detail

Spectral response of rods and cones

The graph on the left shows that rods are more responsive to light of low wavelength. The graph on the right shows the response of the cones to different wavelengths. The dotted curve in the graph on the right is the response of the rods.

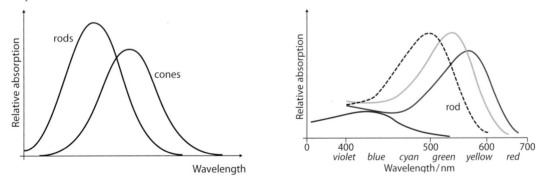

Use these spectral response graphs to answer Test yourself questions 2 and 3.

Test yourself **2**
Red and blue papers are viewed in low-intensity light. State and explain which one will be most clearly seen.

Test yourself **3**
In bright sunlight, red roses appear brightly red but in twilight, their red colour 'fades'. Explain this observation.

Colour and colour perception

The perception of colour is made possible by the fact that there are three types of cone cells, sensitive to blue, green and red light, respectively.

Definitions

Colour blindness   A general term referring to people with deficiency in the perception of colour. Colour blindness is associated with non-functioning cone cells or insufficient numbers of one or more types of cone cells. Red–green blindness is the most common.

Primary colours   Three colours whose combinations give (almost) all other colours. These are red, green and blue (R, G, B).

Colour addition   Obtaining a colour by overlapping different amounts of three primary colours.

Secondary colours   The colours obtained when two primary colours are mixed. B + G = C, cyan (bluish green, i.e. turquoise), B + R = M, magenta (reddish purple), R + G = Y, yellow.

Complementary colours   The combination of a primary and a secondary colour that gives white light.

Colour subtraction   Refers to white light being transmitted through a coloured filter. The three primary filters used are cyan, magenta and yellow filters. In other words the three filters each remove their respective complementary colour.

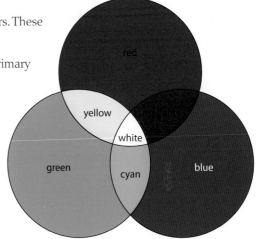

Light and perception

Architects, designers, interior decorators, advertisers and others create effects based on the perception of colour. For example:

- A room painted in bright red or yellowish colours gives a sense of a busy, hurried place. Another painted in soft, pastel colours gives the impression of a relaxed, calm place.
- Soft reddish or orange colours create a 'warm' atmosphere whereas bluish and violet colours give the impression of a cold, cool place.
- Small rooms can be made to 'look' bigger by painting them in light soft colours.
- A low ceiling can be 'raised' by painting it with a colour that is lighter than that used for the walls.
- A floor will look smaller if painted in dark colours rather than light colours.

Another effect is the inclusion of shadows. Deep shadows give the impression of a solid, massive object whereas light shadows, or the absence of them, give the impression of a light and 'airy' structure.

Test yourself **4**
Determine the colour obtained when yellow is mixed with blue.

→ **Before you answer**
Yellow is a secondary colour.

Test yourself **5**
White light transmitted through a yellow filter. Use colour subtraction to explain why the transmitted light is in fact yellow.

→ **Before you answer**
Filters subtract their complementary colour.

Test yourself **6**
White light is transmitted through a magenta filter. The transmitted light is then passed through a yellow filter. Determine the transmitted colour.

Option B: Quantum physics and nuclear physics – SL

The content of this option is identical to Topic **13**, page 72, to which the reader is referred.

Option C: Digital technology – SL

The content of this option is identical to Topic **14**, page 79, and HL sections of Option **F**, pages 99–110, to which the reader is referred.

Option D: Relativity and particle physics – SL

The content of this option is identical to sections in Options **H** and **J**, pages 123–135 and 145–156, to which the reader is referred.

Objects in the universe and stellar quantities – Core

Definitions

The solar system Our solar system consists of eight **planets** that revolve around a **star** called the Sun. The order of the planets is (starting from the one closest to the Sun) Mercury, Venus, Earth, Mars, Jupiter, Saturn, Uranus and Neptune (remembered as My Very Elegant Mother Just Served Us Noodles). All of these, except the first two, have moons orbiting them. In between the orbits of Mars and Jupiter we find the **asteroid belt**, a region of small rocky objects in orbit around the Sun. Pluto has recently been demoted from the status of a planet and is now called a **dwarf planet**.

Planets vary in size in the order: Mercury (smallest), Mars, Venus, Earth, Neptune, Uranus, Saturn and Jupiter (largest). A sometimes spectacular phenomenon in the solar system is the appearance of **comets**, small objects no more than about 10 km across, in very large and very elliptical orbits. (Some comets do not orbit the Sun and just appear through the solar system once.)

Distances in astronomy The average distance between the Earth and the Sun is called an astronomical unit (AU) and $1\,\text{AU} = 1.50 \times 10^{11}\,\text{m}$. The diameter of the solar system is about 80 AU. The distance travelled by light in one year is called the light year; $1\,\text{ly} = 9.46 \times 10^{15}\,\text{m}$. Another convenient unit is the parsec; $1\,\text{pc} \approx 3.09 \times 10^{16}\,\text{m}$.

Stars A star is in equilibrium under the action of the opposing pressures of gravity and radiation. A normal star is a large mass of mostly hydrogen with a temperature in the core that is high enough for nuclear fusion reactions to take place. The energy released produces an outward pressure on the outer layers of the star, thus preventing gravity from collapsing the star.

Stellar clusters and constellations A stellar cluster is a large number of stars relatively close to each other that affect each other through their gravitational forces. A constellation is a group of stars in a recognisable pattern that are not necessarily close to each other in space. Stars and constellations appear to rotate around the Earth in the course of the night because the Earth rotates around its axis. In the course of a year, as the Earth rotates around the Sun, different parts of the night sky are visible from Earth and so different stars and constellations are visible.

Galaxies Galaxies consist of **very many** stars (of the order 10^9) that attract each other gravitationally. Galaxies can be spherical, elliptical or spiral in shape but also irregular. The average separation of stars in a galaxy is of order a few pc and the average separation of galaxies is of order a few hundred kpc.

Radiation from stars – Core

Definitions

Luminosity The total power radiated by a star. It equals $L = \sigma A T^4$ where A is the star's surface area and T its surface temperature in kelvin. The constant σ is the Stefan–Boltzmann constant, $\sigma = 5.67 \times 10^{-8}\,\text{W}\,\text{m}^{-2}\,\text{K}^{-4}$. Luminosity is measured in watts.

A star with low luminosity may appear brighter than another star of higher luminosity because it is closer.

Apparent brightness The power received per unit area (of the receiver). It is measured in watts per square metre. Comparison of apparent brightness shows which star **appears** brighter from Earth. It equals $b = \dfrac{L}{4\pi d^2}$ where d is the distance to the star from Earth.

Apparent magnitude, m A measure of the apparent brightness of a star on a logarithmic scale.

The higher the magnitude, the dimmer the star appears.

In fact $m = -19 - \dfrac{5}{2}\log b$ where b is in $\text{W}\,\text{m}^{-2}$. The naked eye can see stars up to $m = +6$.

This formula is not on the syllabus but it is worth knowing since it makes the connection between b and m clear.

Absolute magnitude, M This is the apparent magnitude a star **would** have if observed from a distance of 10 pc.

Calculations with *m* and *M*: Cepheid stars – Core

> This is very important for exam questions.

If two stars **differ** by Δm units in apparent magnitude, they have a **ratio** of apparent brightness of $(2.512)^{\Delta m}$. So if they differ by 5 units they have a **ratio** of apparent brightness equal to $(2.512)^5 = 100$.

Thus, the star Achernar with apparent magnitude 0.50 (appears bright) and the star Ceti with apparent magnitude 3.50 (appears dimmer) have a ratio of apparent brightness $\dfrac{b_A}{b_C} = (2.512)^3 \approx 16$. In other words, Achernar appears 16 times brighter.

Definitions

The magnitude distance relation   Absolute magnitude, apparent magnitude and distance are related through the equation $m - M = 5\log\dfrac{d}{10}$ or $d = 10 \times 10^{\frac{m-M}{5}}$ where d is **necessarily in pc**.

Cepheid stars   An important class of stars, which have **variable** luminosity with a **definite period**.

Cepheids as 'standard candles'

The distance to a Cepheid up to 15 Mpc can be determined by the following methods.

The surface of the star **expands** (luminosity increases) and **contracts** (luminosity decreases). The period of variation of luminosity T (in days) is related to the average **absolute magnitude** of the star M through $M = -2.81 \times \log T - 1.43$.

Thus δ-Cephei with a period of 5.4 days has average absolute magnitude $M = -2.81 \times \log 5.4 - 1.4 = -3.49$. From the graph, the average apparent magnitude is about $m = 4.0$ and so using the magnitude distance relation we find the distance to the star to be

$$m - M = 5\log\frac{d}{10} \Rightarrow 4.0 - (-3.49) = 5\log\frac{d}{10}$$
$$\log\frac{d}{10} = \frac{7.49}{5} = 1.50 \Rightarrow d = 10 \times 10^{1.5} \approx 320\,\text{pc}$$

Brightness variation of δ-Cephei magnitude 3.6 to 4.3

It is easy to measure a star's apparent brightness (with the CCD of a digital camera) **but not** its luminosity. A Cepheid is a star of known luminosity (i.e. a 'standard candle'). If we can be sure that a particular Cepheid star belongs to a particular galaxy then another star **in the same galaxy** has essentially the same distance. If we then compare its **apparent brightness** to that of the Cepheid we will get information on the star's **luminosity**:

$$L_{star} = \frac{b_{star}}{b_{Cepheid}} L_{Cepheid}$$

Test yourself 1
The Sun has an apparent magnitude of approximately –27. Estimate, in AU, the distance from which the Sun becomes invisible to the naked eye.

➡ **Before you answer**
How does apparent brightness depend on distance?

Test yourself 2
The star Achernar has absolute magnitude $M_A = -2.77$ and Barnard's star absolute magnitude $M_B = 13.22$. What is the ratio of the luminosity of Achernar to that of Barnard's star?

➡ **Before you answer**
What is the ratio of apparent brightnesses when the distance is the same?

Test yourself 3
A star has apparent magnitude 3.2 and absolute magnitude 4.8. Explain without a calculation whether the star is closer or further than 10 pc.

➡ **Before you answer**
Does a higher number on the magnitude scale imply a brighter or a dimmer star?

Test yourself 4
Vega has apparent magnitude 0.03 and absolute magnitude 0.58. Calculate its distance from Earth.

Types of stars and stellar spectra – Core

Binary stars are two stars that orbit a common centre. The heavier star is in the inner orbit. The stars have a common period of revolution which means they are always diametrically opposite each other. The common period is determined by the separation of the stars and the total mass of the stars.

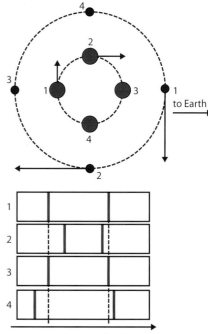

The period of revolution is T.

At $t = 0$ (and at $t = \frac{T}{2}$) the stars are moving at right angles to the line of sight to Earth and so there is no Doppler shift (positions 1 and 3).

At $t = \frac{T}{4}$ (and at $t = \frac{3T}{4}$) the stars are either approaching or moving away from Earth so there is a Doppler shift (positions 2 and 4).

Definitions

Spectroscopic binaries   If the light received from the binary stars is analysed through a diffraction grating so we can see the individual wavelengths in the light, the binary star is called a spectroscopic binary. Because the stars sometimes move towards the Earth and sometimes away, the light received shows a Doppler shift.

Eclipsing binaries   If the Earth happens to be on the same plane as the plane of the orbits of the two stars, one star will, periodically, be hiding behind the other star, i.e. there will be **eclipses**. This means that the light of the hidden star will be blocked and so Earth will receive less light than usual.

Increasing wavelength

The **light curve** of eclipsing binaries is a graph of apparent brightness (or apparent magnitude) versus time.

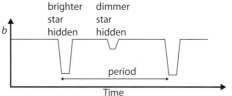

Stellar spectra   Can be used to tell the surface temperature and chemical composition of a star.

Wien's law   The wavelength at which most of the energy is emitted is related to the surface temperature through $\lambda_0 T = 2.9 \times 10^{-3}\,\mathrm{m\,K}$.

Chemical composition

This absorption spectrum shows the missing lines corresponding to hydrogen. If this was from a star it may be deduced that the star contains hydrogen. A real absorption spectrum of a star contains many more dark lines, i.e. **missing lines**, which are wavelengths corresponding to photons that have been absorbed by other elements in the outer layers of the star. **Specific elements absorb specific wavelengths** and so the missing lines give us information about what **elements exist in the star**.

The spectrum of the Sun

The peak wavelength corresponds to a yellowish-orange colour.

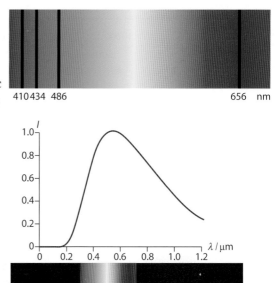

Test yourself **5**

A star has a surface temperature of 3000 K. Calculate the wavelength at which most of its energy is emitted and state the colour of the star.

The Hertzsprung–Russell diagram – Core

Hertzsprung and Russell independently pioneered a plot of stars according to luminosity (vertical axis) and surface temperature (horizontal axis). Notice that temperature increases as we move to the left.

In such a plot stars appear to be grouped in three major areas: the **main sequence**, the **white dwarfs** and the **red giants and super red giants**.

> You can answer (almost) everything in the Astrophysics Option if you learn the HR diagram well!

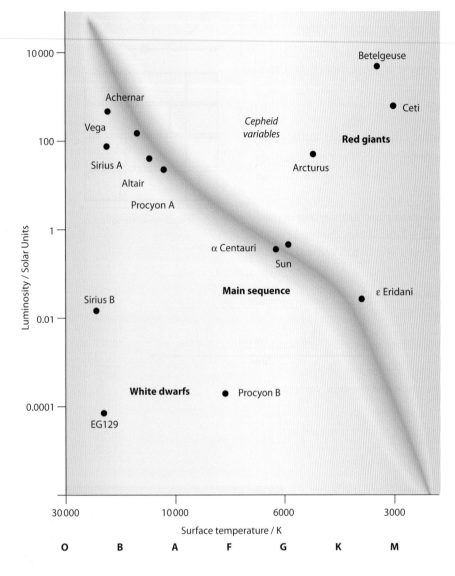

Spectral class

The letters O, B, etc. on the horizontal axis of the HR diagram refer to the spectral class of the star. This is simply another way of telling the surface temperature of the star. M denotes red stars, O white and B bluish. Our Sun is a class G star and is yellow.

Test yourself **6**

Using the HR diagram, calculate the ratio of **a** the radius of Achernar to that of EG 129 and **b** the radius of Ceti to that of Achernar. Comment on the results.

Distances in astronomy – Core

It is a major problem to determine distances in astronomy. We have available the Cepheid method (see page 88) and the parallax and spectroscopic parallax methods.

The parallax method

For nearby stars (at a distance less than 300 pc), the parallax method can be used. For larger distances, the parallax angle is too small to be measured.

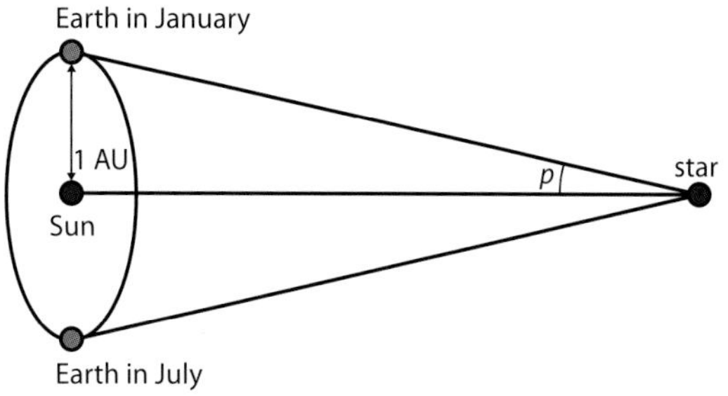

The method consists of observing a star at two times, six months apart. In the six months, the Earth has moved in its orbit around the Sun and so the star will be observed to have **shifted relative to the background of the very distant stars**. If the parallax angle (shown in the diagram) is measured to be p arc seconds, the distance to the star in parsec (pc) is $d = \dfrac{1\,\text{AU}}{\tan p} \approx \dfrac{1\,\text{AU}}{p}$ since the angle is very small. We define a new unit of distance, the parsec (pc) to be the distance at which the parallax angle is $1''$. Then if the parallax angle, expressed in arc seconds is p, the distance in pc is given by $d = \dfrac{1}{p}$.

Earth in January

1 AU

Sun

p star

Earth in July

One **parsec** is the distance at which the parallax of a star is one arc second/star subtends a distance of 1 AU.

To find the pc in metres,

$$1\,\text{pc} = \frac{1\,\text{AU}}{\tan 1''} = \frac{1.49 \times 10^{11}}{\tan \dfrac{1}{3600}} = 3.1 \times 10^{16}\,\text{m}$$

The spectroscopic parallax method

Despite the name, no parallax is involved in this method. It can be used for larger distances than the parallax method, up to a few kpc.

Summary of method:

- Measure apparent brightness
- Measure temperature from spectrum
- Determine star type from absorption spectrum
- Find luminosity from HR diagram
- Use $d = \sqrt{\dfrac{L}{4\pi b}}$

In this method, the distance to a star is calculated by measuring the apparent brightness b and luminosity L and then using: $b = \dfrac{L}{4\pi d^2} \Rightarrow d = \sqrt{\dfrac{L}{4\pi b}}$. The difficulty is in measuring the luminosity. To do that we must examine the spectrum of the star, get the wavelength at which most of the energy is emitted and then use Wien's law to get the star's surface temperature. We then refer to an HR diagram. Knowing the temperature is not enough to determine luminosity from the HR diagram. However, if we know the star's type we may then use the HR diagram to estimate luminosity. The star's type is determined by studying its absorption spectrum. Stars in the same area of the HR diagram have similar absorption spectra.

Test yourself **7**

A main sequence star has temperature $10\,000\,\text{K}$ and apparent brightness $4.4 \times 10^{-10}\,\text{W m}^{-2}$. Determine its distance from Earth. (Solar luminosity $L_s = 3.9 \times 10^{26}\,\text{W}$.)

➡ **Before you answer**
Use the HR diagram.

Worked examples of calculations in astrophysics: hints and common mistakes – Core

1. The distance to the star Wolf-359 is 4.93×10^5 AU and its apparent brightness is 1.97×10^{-12} W m^{-2}. Calculate the luminosity of this star.

© IB Organization 2008

This requires direct substitution in the formula $b = \dfrac{L}{4\pi d^2}$ and solving for luminosity we get $L = 4\pi d^2 b$.

This means that we must express all quantities in this formula in SI units.

We get $L = 4\pi \times (1.97 \times 10^{-12}) \times (4.93 \times 10^5 \times 1.50 \times 10^{11})^2 = 1.35 \times 10^{23}$ W.

2. Star A is at a distance of 100 pc from Earth. Its luminosity is 4 times greater than that of star B and its apparent brightness is 100 times greater than that of star B. Deduce that the distance of star B from Earth is 500 pc.

© IB Organization 2007

We apply $b = \dfrac{L}{4\pi d^2}$ to star A and star B to get $b_A = \dfrac{L_A}{4\pi d_A^2}$,

$b_B = \dfrac{L_B}{4\pi d_B^2}$ and now divide the equations side by side to get

This is a comparison problem. Units do not have to be changed.

$\dfrac{b_A}{b_B} = \dfrac{\frac{L_A}{4\pi d_A^2}}{\frac{L_B}{4\pi d_B^2}} = \dfrac{L_A}{L_B}\dfrac{d_B^2}{d_A^2}$ i.e. $100 = 4\dfrac{d_B^2}{d_A^2} \Rightarrow \dfrac{d_B^2}{d_A^2} = 25 \Rightarrow \dfrac{d_B}{d_A} = 5 \Rightarrow d_B = 5 \times 100 = 500$ pc

The original distance was in pc so the new distance will be in pc as well.

3. The table gives information on the Sun and the star Sirius A.

Star	Apparent brightness	Luminosity (relative units)
Sun	1.4×10^3 W m^{-2}	1.0
Sirius A	1.1×10^{-7} W m^{-2}	23

Deduce that the distance of Sirius from Earth is 5.4×10^5 AU.

© IB Organization 2007

The problem is again a comparison problem and completely identical to the previous one – supply the details. (Remember that the distance between the Earth and the Sun is 1 AU.)

It would be wrong to find the distance through $b = \dfrac{L}{4\pi d^2} \Rightarrow d = \sqrt{\dfrac{L}{4\pi b}}$ and substituting $L = 23$. This gives $d = \sqrt{\dfrac{23}{4\pi \times 1.1 \times 10^{-7}}} = 4.1 \times 10^3$ and is wrong for the simple reason that the luminosity is not just 23 but 23 times that of the Sun; but the luminosity of the Sun is not given. The distance obtained has unspecified units and hence is meaningless.

4. A binary star system consists of two stars Antares A and Antares B. The temperature of A is 3000 K and that of B is 15000 K. The luminosity of A is 40 times that of B. Calculate the ratio of the radius of A to that of B.

© IB Organization 2002

This is again a ratio problem. Write $L_A = \sigma A_A (3000)^4$ and $L_B = \sigma A_B (15000)^4$. Take ratios side by side to get $\dfrac{L_A}{L_B} = \dfrac{\sigma A_A (3000)^4}{\sigma A_B (15000)^4} \Rightarrow 40 = \dfrac{A_A}{A_B}\left(\dfrac{1}{5}\right)^4 \Rightarrow \dfrac{A_A}{A_B} = 25000$. Since area is related to radius through $A = 4\pi R^2$ it follows that $\dfrac{R_A}{R_B} = \sqrt{25000} \approx 160$.

You must learn this method involving dividing equations side by side.

Cosmology – Core

In the 19th century it was believed that the universe was **infinite** in extent, without a beginning, **static** and containing an infinite number of stars more or less uniformly distributed in space. This was the Newtonian model of the universe.

Olbers' paradox

This picture was challenged by a simple observation made by Olbers (and many others before him) who asked why the night sky was dark.

The idea is that stars far away appear very dim individually but there are also very many of them. The result is that the distant stars contribute as much light as the near stars.

The outer shell is **further away** so the apparent brightness of **each** of the stars it contains is **lower** than that of a star in the inner shell.

But the outer shell has **more** stars than the inner shell.

The two effects compensate each other exactly so that both shells contribute the **same** apparent brightness on Earth.

Details

Olbers provided a simple argument leading to the conclusion that the night sky should not be dark.

Olbers considered a thin shell of radius d and thickness δr around the Earth. The number of stars in the shell is therefore the average number of stars per unit volume, n (the star number density), multiplied by the volume of the shell, $4\pi d^2 \delta r$ (area of shell × thickness).

number of stars in shell $= n \times 4\pi d^2 \delta r$

> The volume of the shell
> $$V = \frac{4\pi}{3}r^3$$
> $$\frac{dV}{dr} = 4\pi r^2$$
> $$dV = 4\pi r^2 dr$$

If the average luminosity of the stars is L, then the total luminosity of the stars in the shell is

$$L_{total} = L \times \text{number of stars in shell}$$
$$= L \times n \times 4\pi d^2 \delta r$$

So the apparent brightness received on Earth from all the stars in the shell is

$$b = \frac{L_{total}}{4\pi d^2} = \frac{L \times n \times 4\pi d^2 \delta r}{4\pi d^2} = n\delta r L$$

In other words, **even if the shell is very far away**, it contains so many stars that each shell contributes a **constant amount** of apparent brightness on Earth. If the universe is infinite, it contains an infinite number of such shells and so the apparent brightness on Earth should theoretically be infinite. (Of course, some stars block others and this reduces the amount from infinite to very large.)

The sky at night should be ablaze with light and should not be dark!

Resolution

- The universe does not contain an infinite number of stars.
- The stars do not live forever.
- The universe has a finite age and so some stars are so far away their light has not yet reached us.

Expanding universe

There is a lot of hydrogen in the universe so we expect that a lot of the light we receive has been emitted by hydrogen. We know the wavelengths at which hydrogen emits from experiments in the lab.

Light from distant galaxies is received on Earth at a wavelength that is longer than that emitted, i.e. it is **red-shifted**. This is evidence that the galaxies are moving **away** from us.

The Big Bang – Core

The expansion of the universe suggests that in the past the universe was smaller and had a beginning. The Big Bang marks the beginning of time. It took place at a point, which was all that the universe was then. So the Big Bang happened everywhere in the universe.

Does the universe expand into anything?

The universe is all that there is and so there is nothing the universe can expand into.

General relativity says that space is created in between galaxies (the space expands) giving the illusion of galaxies moving away. It is impossible to visualise expanding space in three dimensions, so we usually make a two-dimensional analogy with the two-dimensional surface of an expanding balloon.

> It is a **common mistake** to think of the universe as a cloud of smoke that expands in a room, taking up more and more of the space of the room.

> The expansion of the universe does not imply that the Earth is at the centre of the universe. An observer anywhere in the universe would reach the same (erroneous) conclusion about his or her position.

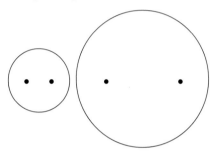

When the balloon in the diagram expands, the distance between the two dots increases. An observer on one dot would say that the other has moved away.

CMB (cosmic microwave background) radiation

CMB radiation is **black body** radiation in the **microwave** region coming from **all directions**. It is the remnant of the radiation that filled the universe in its early stages when the temperature was very high. As the universe expanded, the temperature fell and so the peak wavelength of this radiation shifted to microwave wavelengths.

The present peak wavelength is about 1.07 mm, indicating a temperature of the universe of just below 3 K.

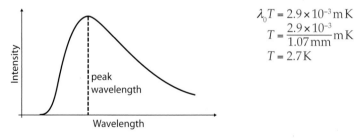

$$\lambda_0 T = 2.9 \times 10^{-3}\,\text{m K}$$
$$T = \frac{2.9 \times 10^{-3}}{1.07\,\text{mm}}\,\text{m K}$$
$$T = 2.7\,\text{K}$$

The CMB was discovered in 1964 by A. Penzias and R. Wilson but had been predicted in 1948, on theoretical grounds, by R. Alpher and R. Herman (in work that went, mainly, unappreciated and unacknowledged).

Test yourself **8**

State and explain two pieces of experimental evidence in support of the Big Bang model of the universe.

The fate of the universe – Core

Standard theory predicts that there are only three possible outcomes in the evolution of the universe. It may:

- expand forever (an open universe)
- expand forever at a rate that becomes zero after an infinite time (a flat universe)
- expand and then collapse back to a point (a closed universe).

(But this is an outdated answer!)

Notice that the age of the universe depends on which model one assumes.

These three possibilities are shown in the graph, coincident at the present time.

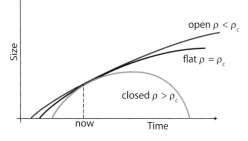

Which model fits our universe?

The path the universe will actually follow depends on the comparison of the density ρ of the universe to a **critical density**, ρ_c. If $\rho < \rho_c$ the universe will expand forever, if $\rho = \rho_c$ it will expand forever at a slowing rate, stopping at infinity and if $\rho > \rho_c$ the universe will collapse. The critical density is determined from theory: $\rho_c \approx 10^{-26}\,\text{kg}\,\text{m}^{-3}$.

$\rho = \rho_c$

Recent measurements show that $\rho = \rho_c$. But, despite $\rho = \rho_c$ the universe is actually accelerating in its expansion rate. **Dark energy** (a kind of vacuum energy making up as much as 70% of the energy of the universe) has been invoked to explain this.

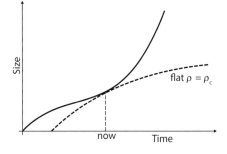

Dark matter

Determining the density of the universe is difficult because there appears to be mass that is too cold to radiate light and so cannot be seen. Its existence is determined from the gravitational effects this mass has on other masses. Candidates for dark matter include neutrinos, black and brown dwarfs, possible exotic particles predicted by theories of particle physics (WIMPS), matter around galactic halos (MACHOS) and others. With 70% of the mass-energy of the universe composed of dark energy, the remaining 30% is formed by dark matter and ordinary matter. Of this 30%, only 5% is accounted for by ordinary matter. In other words, ordinary matter is only about 17% of the **total matter** in the universe.

> Do not confuse dark matter with dark energy.

Test yourself **9**
State the significance of the critical density of the universe.

Stellar evolution – HL

Stars will spend most of their lifetime on the main sequence. There, they fuse hydrogen into helium.

Once about 12% of the hydrogen is used up, the star will develop instabilities and will start to expand.

As it expands, the surface temperature of the star decreases. The decrease in temperature would normally result in a reduction in luminosity but the increase in surface area more than compensates and so the luminosity actually increases. The star will become a red giant or red supergiant star.

What happens next depends on the mass of the star. In a low-mass star, no further nuclear reactions take place and the core remains composed of helium. In higher-mass stars, nuclear reactions continue in the core but now involving heavier elements. The more massive the star, the heavier the elements produced in nuclear reactions. The process stops at the production of iron/nickel. No heavier elements can be produced by nuclear fusion. (Recall the binding energy curve, page 40.)

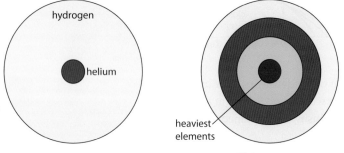

Low-mass star　　　　　**High-mass star**

The star will then undergo a catastrophic explosion. The explosion will be a **planetary nebula** if the mass of the star is low and a **supernova** if it is high.

Both explosions leave behind the **core** of the star.

What happens to the core is discussed next.

The Chandrasekhar limit (the largest mass a white dwarf can have)

If the **core** left after the planetary nebula stage has a mass such that $M < 1.4 M_s$ it will become a stable **white dwarf star**. It does not collapse further because of a pressure created by electrons.

The largest mass a white dwarf can have is about 1.4 solar masses and this is known as the Chandrasekhar limit.

The Oppenheimer–Volkoff limit (the largest mass a neutron star can have)

This is close to three solar masses.

A star with a **core** mass after the supernova stage of $1.4 M_s < M < 3 M_s$ does not collapse further because of a pressure created by neutrons. It becomes a stable **neutron star**. These are very small and dense stars composed of neutrons.

> A very massive star can still end up as a white dwarf if the mass of the core is less than the Chandrasekhar limit.

Pulsars

If the neutron star rotates around its axis it is called a pulsar. Because of its very strong magnetic field, it emits radio waves along the direction of the magnetic field. This radiation may be detected with radio telescopes. The radiation arrives at the observer **once** in every star revolution if the direction of the magnetic field is different from that of the rotation axis.

Black holes

If the mass of the core is larger than the Oppenheimer limit then no known mechanism exists to stop the further collapse of the star – it becomes a black hole – a star from which nothing can escape.

Evolutionary paths and the mass–luminosity relation – HL

The diagrams show the paths followed by stars as they leave the main sequence to become **a** red giants or **b** supergiants.

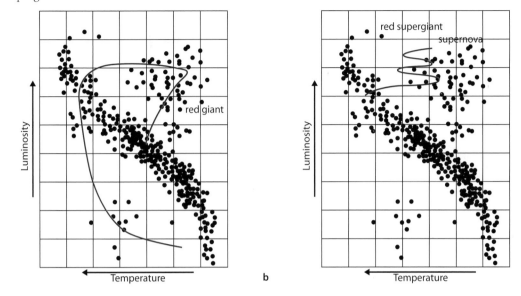

a   Temperature   b   Temperature

The mass–luminosity relation

Main sequence stars show a relationship between their luminosity and their mass: $L = kM^n$ where the exponent n is between 3 and 4. We will take $n = 3.5$ (k is a constant).

> It is important to recognise that it is **only** main sequence stars that obey this relation.

The total time that will be spent by the Sun on the main sequence (its lifetime) will be about 9×10^9 y.

Stars leave the main sequence after using about 12% of their hydrogen. We can use this to estimate the time they spend on the main sequence.

$$L = kM^{3.5} = \frac{E}{T}$$

where E is the energy produced and T is the lifetime on the main sequence. But $E = 0.12Mc^2$

and so $kM^{3.5} = \dfrac{0.12Mc^2}{T} \Rightarrow T = \dfrac{0.12c^2}{k}M^{-2.5}$.

Thus, a star with a mass 100 times greater than the mass of the Sun will spend much less time on the main sequence:

$$\frac{T_{star}}{T_S} = \frac{\frac{0.12c^2}{k}M_{star}^{-2.5}}{\frac{0.12c^2}{k}M_S^{-2.5}} = \frac{M_S^{2.5}}{M_{star}^{2.5}} = \left(\frac{1}{100}\right)^{2.5} = \frac{1}{100\,000}$$

and so $T_{star} = \dfrac{1}{100\,000} \times 9 \times 10^9 = 9 \times 10^4$ y.

Test yourself **10**

A star has a mass that is 50 times larger than the mass of the Sun and a luminosity that is 80 000 times the luminosity of the Sun. Could this star be a main sequence star?

Hubble's law – HL

Distant galaxies move **away** from each other with a speed that is proportional to their separation: $v = Hd$.

The presently accepted value of the Hubble constant is $H = 72\,\text{km}\,\text{s}^{-1}\,\text{Mpc}^{-1}$. (The value is uncertain because of the difficulty in measuring speeds and, especially, distances.)

The speed of the receding galaxies is measured using the Doppler formula $\dfrac{\Delta\lambda}{\lambda_0} = \dfrac{v}{c}$.

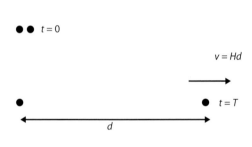

> Hubble's law only applies to **distant** galaxies. Andromeda, for example, is actually approaching our Milky Way because of the mutual gravitational attraction between the two galaxies.

> The slope of this graph is the Hubble constant. The graph passes through the origin.

Estimating the age of the universe – Hubble time

The diagram shows points that were very close to each other at the time of the Big Bang. Now, they are separated by a distance d and one moves with speed $v = Hd$ relative to the other.

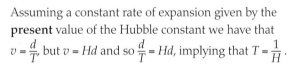

Assuming a constant rate of expansion given by the **present** value of the Hubble constant we have that $v = \dfrac{d}{T}$, but $v = Hd$ and so $\dfrac{d}{T} = Hd$, implying that $T = \dfrac{1}{H}$.

(Not assuming a constant rate of expansion does not significantly change the result. Note that since the age of the universe increases, the Hubble 'constant' is not really a constant.)

Formation of structures in the universe

The very early universe existed at an enormous temperature, $10^{32}\,\text{K}$ at $10^{-43}\,\text{s}$ after the Big Bang. This meant that the kinetic energy of individual particles (e.g. quarks, electrons) was so high that these particles could not bind into nucleons, nuclei and atoms.

Only after the temperature dropped sufficiently (due to the universe expanding) was the formation of these structures possible.

- Nuclei formed 3 min after the Big Bang.
- Atoms formed 10^5 years after the Big Bang.
- Stars and galaxies formed 10^6 years after the Big Bang.

Test yourself **11**

A line in the spectrum of hydrogen is measured to have a wavelength of 656.3 nm in the lab. The same line observed in the spectrum of a distant galaxy has a wavelength of 689.1 nm. Calculate the distance to the galaxy using $H = 72\,\text{km}\,\text{s}^{-1}\,\text{Mpc}^{-1}$.

Test yourself **12**

a Estimate the age of the universe using a Hubble constant $H = 72\,\text{km}\,\text{s}^{-1}\,\text{Mpc}^{-1}$. **b** Explain why this is actually an **overestimate** of the age of the universe.

Signals, carriers and modulation – Core

Definitions

Modulation   The modifying of a signal so that it can be used to transmit information.

Information signal wave   Can be either audio, i.e. sounds or a voice, or video, i.e. a picture or a movie or data.

Carrier wave   The means by which the information is to be transmitted – this is usually an electromagnetic wave, e.g. a radio wave or visible light, or alternating current.

Bandwidth   The range of frequencies a communication channel can transmit.

AM (amplitude modulation) – Core

In AM modulation the **amplitude** of the carrier wave gets modulated (i.e. modified) by the addition of the information signal wave to the carrier's amplitude. This is shown in the three graphs below right.

For a carrier of frequency f_C and an information signal of frequency f_S the modulated wave's spectrum contains three frequencies as shown in the AM power spectrum below.

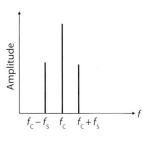

The frequencies $f_C - f_S$ and $f_C + f_S$ are known as the lower and upper sideband frequencies.

The difference between the upper and lower sideband frequencies is the **bandwidth**:

$$\Delta f = (f_C + f_S) - (f_C - f_S)$$
$$= 2f_S$$

Test yourself **1**

The AM wave graph below shows a carrier wave modulated by a single audio frequency. Using the graph, determine **a** the frequency of the carrier, **b** the frequency of the information signal, **c** the bandwidth and **d** the amplitude of the information signal.

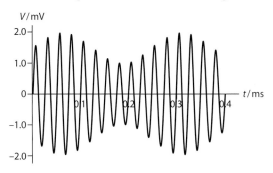

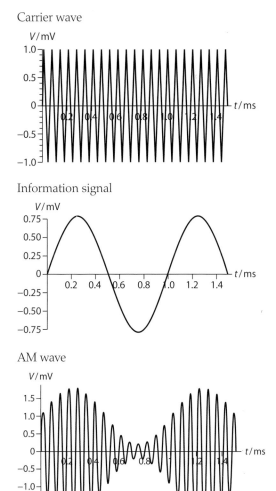

Carrier wave

Information signal

AM wave

FM (frequency modulation) – Core

In frequency modulation (FM) the carrier wave's **frequency** is changed (modulated) according to the instantaneous displacement of the information signal. The graphs below show the variation with time of an information signal wave, carrier wave and the resulting FM wave.

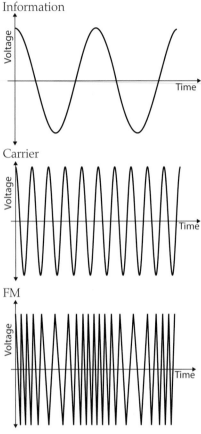

The frequency of the modulated signal is greatest when the information signal has its greatest positive value and the frequency is least when the information signal has its most negative value.

In FM modulation we have a parameter k, called the **frequency deviation constant**, that determines by how much the modulated wave's frequency deviates from the carrier's frequency. The unit of k is $Hz\,V^{-1}$. The frequency of the modulated wave varies from a minimum of $f_C - kA_S$ to a maximum of $f_C + kA_S$. A_S is the information signal wave amplitude.

A related quantity in FM modulation is the modulation index defined by $\beta = \frac{\Delta f}{f}$. Here, Δf is the maximum deviation of the modulated carrier's frequency relative to the unmodulated carrier frequency and f is the (highest) frequency in the information signal.

The importance of this index is that it is related to bandwidth. The FM bandwidth is given (approximately) by the equation:
FM bandwidth $\approx 2(\Delta f + f)$

In radio FM broadcasts, $\Delta f = 75\,kHz$ and the modulation index β used is typically 5.

> Notice that in the FM modulated signal the frequency changes but the amplitude stays constant.

Comparing AM and FM modulation

- FM has a better signal-to-noise ratio. This is because noise adds to the amplitude of the carrier wave and so is included in the received signal. Notice that when amplifying an AM signal the noise gets amplified as well.
- The same information can be transmitted with less power with FM compared to AM.
- The bandwidth for FM is greater than that for AM.
- In FM, the amplitude of the carrier is small compared to the amplitude of the sidebands. This means that most of the power in transmission goes to the sidebands, which is where the information is.
- The modulators and demodulators for FM are more complex compared with those for AM and so more expensive.
- AM transmissions travel further because the signal is reflected off the ionosphere whereas FM transmissions travel along straight lines.

Test yourself 2

A carrier of amplitude 12 V and frequency 600 kHz is FM modulated by an information signal wave of amplitude 2.0 V and frequency 8.0 kHz. The frequency deviation constant is $k = 20\,kHz\,V^{-1}$. Determine **a** the amplitude of the FM modulated signal, **b** the highest and lowest frequencies in the FM modulated wave and **c** the modulation index β.

> ➡ **Before you answer**
> Read the main features of FM modulation again.

Test yourself 3

A high quality FM radio station has a frequency deviation of 75 kHz and contains audio signals varying from 50 Hz to 15 kHz. What is the modulation index and the bandwidth of the FM transmissions?

AM radio receiver – Core

The components of the AM radio receiver are represented in the block diagram on the right and described in the table.

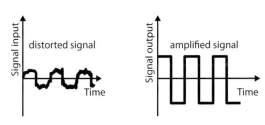

Aerial	The antenna is needed in order to pick up the carrier signal that has been emitted by the transmitter.
Tuning circuit	It isolates the frequency of the particular carrier wave one wants to tune to.
Radio Frequency amplifier	The voltages sent by the tuning circuit to the demodulator are generally extremely small. They have to be increased so that the demodulator can work.
Demodulator	It extracts the information carried by the carrier and the carrier is then rejected.
Audio Frequency amplifier	The signal sent by the demodulator is weak and needs to be amplified before sending it to the loudspeaker, otherwise the loudspeaker cannot be driven.
Loudspeaker	The audio frequency signal is still electrical in nature. This signal will then drive the diaphragm of the loudspeaker so that the sound content of the information signal can be recovered.

Binary numbers – Core

Binary numbers are numbers expressed in base 2 and consist of 0s and 1s.

Since $5 = \underline{1} \times 2^2 + \underline{0} \times 2^1 + \underline{1} \times 2^0$ we express the decimal number 5 in binary form as $5_2 = 101$. The coefficients we use are 0 or 1. Similarly the number 12 is $12 = \underline{1} \times 2^3 + \underline{1} \times 2^2 + \underline{0} \times 2^1 + \underline{0} \times 2^0 \Rightarrow 12_2 = 1100$.

Given a number in binary form, we call the first digit (starting from the left) the most significant bit (MSB) (because it has the biggest effect on the value of the number) and the digit the number ends with the least significant bit (LSB). For example, 1 111 0 .

MSB   LSB

Definitions

Analogue signal   A signal that varies continuously between two extreme values.

Digital signal   A signal that can only take the value 0 or 1.

A digital signal will be distorted during transmission due to noise and attenuation (see page 105). The signal can easily be reshaped using circuits involving Schmitt triggers.

A Schmitt trigger device is needed as an amplifier will also amplify the noise carried along with the signal.

The advantages of digital communication
- Digital signals can be regenerated perfectly, i.e. noise and distortion can be eliminated.
- Digital circuits are relatively inexpensive, reliable and readily available.
- Error correcting codes ensure that errors in the transmission of the signals are eliminated.
- The signals can be encrypted, by scrambling the bits in the signal, so that they can only be read at the desired destinations, providing privacy and security.
- The signals can be stored, processed, compressed and controlled by computers.
- Digital signals can be stored on devices such as CDs and DVDs that are readily available.
- Time division multiplexing (see later) can be used with digital signals.

Test yourself **4**
Express the 5-bit binary number 10101 as a decimal and the decimal number 25 as a 5-bit binary number.

Test yourself **5**
How many numbers can be represented with 5-bit words?

Digital transmission – Core

ADC (analogue to digital conversion)

An analogue signal is **sampled**, i.e. the voltage is measured every 0.50 ms, and the values are recorded in the graph to the right. The sampling frequency is

$$\frac{1}{0.50\,\text{ms}} = 2.0\,\text{kHz}.$$

We will convert the measured voltages into 3-bit binary words.

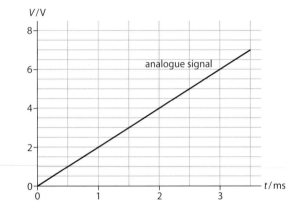

With three bits we can have at most $2^3 = 8$ **quantisation levels**. So we divide the range of the voltages (0 to 8 V) into eight intervals.

A measured value within a given interval is assigned the value of the **lower** boundary of the interval. For example at 2 ms the measured voltage is 4 V. This belongs to the interval [4, 5) and so is assigned the value 4 V. The decimal number 4 is now converted to the 3-bit binary number 100. This gives the values in the table.

Range	Sampling time / ms	Signal / V	PAM signal / V	Binary code
$[0,1) \to 0$	0	0	0	000
$[1,2) \to 1$	0.5	1	1	001
$[2,3) \to 2$	1.0	2	2	010
$[3,4) \to 3$	1.5	3	3	011
$[4,5) \to 4$	2.0	4	4	100
$[5,6) \to 5$	2.5	5	5	101
$[6,7) \to 6$	3.0	6	6	110
$[7,8) \to 7$	3.5	7	7	111

Reconstructing the signal

A low sampling frequency (compared to the information signal frequency) results in aliasing, i.e. unfaithful reconstructions of the signal.

The sampling frequency must be at least twice as large as the largest frequency in the information signal. This is known as the **Nyquist** frequency.

Block diagram for digital transmissions

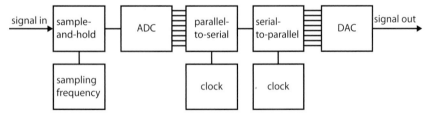

Definitions

Sample-and-hold   The signal is sampled according to the sampling frequency used and stored.

ADC   Every sample of the signal is converted into an n-bit binary code in the ADC (as an example take n to be 8). The output of the ADC is a set of 8 bits making up one sampled signal.

Parallel-to-serial   The 8 bits are sent **simultaneously** in the device called the parallel-to-serial converter. Each bit is then transmitted **one by one** from this device along a single conducting line.

Serial-to-parallel   At the other end, the bits, arriving one by one, are registered in the device called the serial-to-parallel converter. Once all the bits have arrived, they are put together to make one 8-bit word. The 8 bits are then **simultaneously** fed into the DAC.

DAC   In the digital-to-analogue converter, the (digital) signal is now turned into an analogue signal.

Clocks   The purpose of the devices labelled 'clocks' is to control the process of transmitting the bits in the parallel-to-serial and the serial-to-parallel converters. The bits must be sent before the next batch of bits arrives.

Bit rate

The **bit rate** is the number of bits that can be transmitted per second. If each bit has a duration of τ seconds then the bit rate is given by $B = \dfrac{1}{\tau}$. Equivalently, if the number of bits per sample is n and the signal is sampled f times a second we also have $B = f \times n$.

The bandwidth for the transmission of a digital signal is equal to the bit rate.

A small bandwidth will distort the pulses to such an extent that reconstructing the analogue signal from its digital form may be impossible.

Test yourself 6

The first graph shows the variation with time of the voltage of an analogue signal.

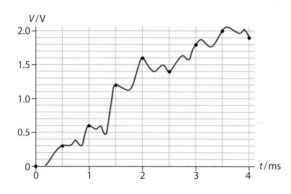

The signal is converted into a digital signal and, after transmission, it is converted into an analogue signal again. The second graph shows the variation with time of the voltage of the transmitted signal.

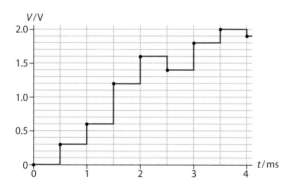

Use the graphs to determine **a** the sampling frequency, **b** the minimum number of bits in a sample and **c** the minimum bit rate for this transmission. **d** State and explain values of an appropriate sampling frequency and number of bits in each sample that would allow a better reconstruction of the original signal.

Test yourself 7

A telephone call is sampled 8000 times a second and each sample contains 8 bits. Calculate the duration of a bit and the total number of bits generated in a 12-minute phone call.

Test yourself 8

A transmission line carries signals of frequency ranging from 50 Hz to 3.0 kHz. What is the highest bit rate in this transmission line?

Time division multiplexing (TDM) – Core

Time division multiplexing is a way to transmit many digital signals along the same channel at the same time.

Consider a signal (solid line) in which the sample has a duration of $8\,\mu s$ (typical in telephone communications). The sampling frequency is $8\,kHz$ and so the time in between samples is $\dfrac{1}{80 \times 10^3} = 125\,\mu s$. There is, therefore, a wasted time of $125 - 8 = 117\,\mu s$. This could be used (theoretically) to send an additional $\dfrac{117}{8} \approx 14$ samples in between (here only one is shown in dotted line).

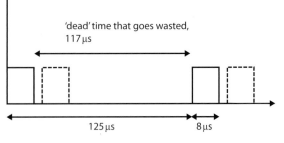

'dead' time that goes wasted, $117\,\mu s$

$125\,\mu s$ $8\,\mu s$

Total internal reflection – Core

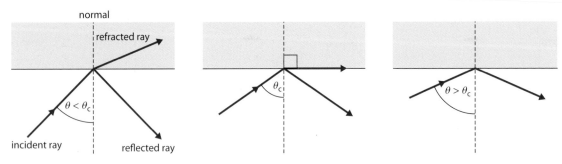

normal

refracted ray

$\theta < \theta_c$

incident ray

reflected ray

θ_c

$\theta > \theta_c$

When a ray of light enters a medium of low refractive index from a medium of high refractive index, the refracted ray bends away from the normal.

As the angle of incidence is increased, the angle of refraction will eventually become $90°$. The angle of incidence in this case is called the **critical angle** θ_c.

For an angle of incidence greater than the critical angle, no refraction takes place. The ray simply reflects back into the medium from which it came. This is called **total internal reflection**.

The critical angle can be found from Snell's law: $n_1 \sin \theta_c = n_2 \sin 90°$, $\sin \theta_c = \dfrac{n_2}{n_1}$, $\theta_c = \arcsin \dfrac{n_2}{n_1}$

Optical fibres – Core

Optical fibres consist of a thin glass core surrounded by a material of slightly lower refractive index called the cladding.

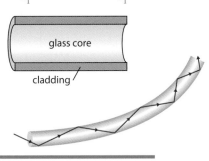

glass core

cladding

Such a thin fibre can easily be bent and a ray of light can be sent down the length of the fibre core. For most angles of incidence, total internal reflection occurs so that the light ray stays within the core and never enters the cladding.

Test yourself **9**

A ray of light in water (refractive index 1.33) is incident on a water–air boundary. Calculate the critical angle of the water–air boundary.

Dispersion, attenuation and noise – Core

Definitions

Dispersion   Different rays will, in general, arrive at the end of the fibre at different times. This may cause bits of information to arrive at the end in the wrong order.

Dispersion limits the bit rate and the maximum frequency that can be transmitted.

Attenuation   The loss of power when a signal travels through a medium.

Noise   Power due to unwanted signals that travel along a given medium along with the signal of interest. There is noise in a communications channel even when there is no signal.

Dispersion

There are two kinds of dispersion:

1 **Material dispersion**   Different wavelengths will travel through the glass core of an optical fibre at different speeds because the speed of the wave depends on wavelength. Therefore, a set of light rays of different wavelengths will reach the end of a fibre at different times even if they follow the same path.

> ! Material dispersion may be limited by using single-frequency light.

2 **Modal dispersion**   Rays of light entering an optical fibre will in general follow different paths. Rays that undergo very many internal reflections over a given distance are said to follow **high-order mode** paths while those suffering fewer reflections follow **low-order mode** paths.

> ! Modal dispersion may be limited by using very thin fibres, called monomode fibres.

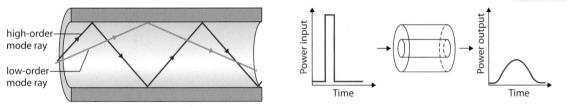

In the diagram on the right the area under the pulse is the energy carried by the pulse. In the output pulse the area is somewhat less because some energy has been lost along the transmission. Since the width increases as a result of dispersion, the associated carrier wave period increases as well and this implies that the maximum frequency that can be transmitted decreases.

Definitions

Attenuation in optical fibres   Mainly due to impurities in the glass core.

Power loss   Power loss in decibels (dB) $= 10 \log \frac{P_{final}}{P_{initial}}$.

Specific attenuation   Power loss in decibels per unit length travelled,

i.e. $\dfrac{10 \log \frac{P_{final}}{P_{initial}}}{L}$. It is measured in decibels per kilometre.

> ! In optical fibres, the specific attenuation depends on the wavelength of the wave. It is minimum for infrared wavelengths and this is why these are used in optical fibre transmissions.

Signal-to-noise ratio (SNR) $SNR = 10 \log \frac{P_{signal}}{P_{noise}}$, where P_{signal} and P_{noise} are, respectively, the power of the signal and the noise.

> ! Amplifiers amplify the signal as well as the noise and so the SNR remains unchanged.

Noise in optical fibres

The **main** source of noise in an optical fibre is the **dark current** in the photodiode – the small current that exists even when the photodiode is dark. This current is due to radiation other than the light it is intended to record falling on the photodiode and the workings of the semiconductor junctions in the photodiode.

Test yourself **10**

A signal of initial power 8.0 mW suffers a **power loss** of 16 dB. What is the output signal power?

Test yourself **11**

A signal of power 180 mW is input to a cable of specific attenuation 3.0 dB km⁻¹. Calculate the power of the signal after it has travelled 12 km in the cable.

Test yourself **12**

An amplifier has a gain of 6.8 dB. The signal that is input to the amplifier has power 0.25 mW. Calculate the power of the output signal.

Test yourself **13**

A signal travels along a monomode fibre of attenuation per unit length 4.0 dB km⁻¹. The signal enters a number of equally spaced amplifiers, each providing a gain of 20 dB. How many amplifiers must be used so that after travelling a total distance of 400 km the signal emerges from the last amplifier with no power loss?

Channels of communication – Core

These are all media that can be used to transmit information.

Copper wires and wire pairs		Used only for simple links nowadays, for example connections for a loudspeaker.
		Advantages: cheap, easy to handle and install wire pairs have reduced cross talk.
		Disadvantages: susceptible to interference from other nearby wires (cross talk), low bandwidth, needs frequent amplification, signal distortion due to dispersion.
Coaxial cables		Carry cable TV signals and telephone communications.
		Advantages: high bandwidth, reduced attenuation and crosstalk effects.
		Disadvantages: the average distance between amplification varies a lot with frequency. There is still noise.
Optical fibres		Used for high-quality telephone communication, secure transfer of digital data.
		Advantages: very high bandwidth, low attenuation, very secure.
		Disadvantage: complex electronics.
Satellites		Used for transmitting telephone communications, TV signals, navigation signals, espionage, surveillance and weather prediction.
		Advantages: very high volumes of data can be transmitted.
		Disadvantages: costs are enormous.
Radio waves		Electromagnetic waves covering a vast range of wavelengths. Used in a variety of communications depending on the frequency. Three types of radio waves are given below in the table.
Frequency below about 3 MHz	Surface waves	Mainly used for AM radio transmissions. Can travel large distances, well beyond the horizon of the transmitter, due to diffraction.
		Advantage: very large range.
		Disadvantage: attenuation and distortion significant.
Frequency range 3 MHz to 30 MHz	Sky waves	Mainly used for amateur radio operators, international radio broadcasts and ship communications. The waves are directed upwards towards the atmosphere where they suffer (a complicated) total internal reflection from a layer of the atmosphere called the **ionosphere**.
		Advantage: large range.
		Disadvantages: substantial attenuation in the ionosphere. Unreliable due to unpredictable ionosphere conditions and interference.
Frequency above 30 MHz	Space waves	This is the method used for radio FM transmissions as well as Earth-bound and satellite TV transmissions.
		The waves travel along straight lines. The range is then dictated by the height of the transmitting station and is typically a few tens of km for ground-based stations.
		Advantages: the ionosphere has no effect on these transmissions so they are more reliable. Can be used by satellites.
		Disadvantage: small range (for ground-based stations).

Test yourself 14

The specific attenuation of a coaxial cable is $14\,\text{dB km}^{-1}$. A signal is input to such a cable of initial power $200\,\text{mW}$. **a** Calculate the power of the signal after it has travelled a distance of $3.0\,\text{km}$ along the cable. **b** State whether a signal of similar power to that in **a** but of much higher frequency would suffer a larger or smaller attenuation.

Test yourself 15

A microwave link station emits microwaves of power $28\,\text{MW}$ uniformly in all directions. **a** Calculate the power received by an antenna dish of area $A = 1.2\,\text{m}^2$ at a distance of $100\,\text{km}$. **b** Determine the attenuation of the signal in dB.

Satellite communications – Core

Uplink frequency   The frequency used to transmit to the satellite.

Downlink frequency   The frequency used by the satellite to transmit down to Earth.

The uplink and downlink frequencies are always different, with the uplink frequency being the higher of the two (by convention).

The reason for the difference in frequencies is that the receiver on the satellite is designed to be able to pick up very small signals and so is very sensitive. It operates at the uplink frequency. The transmitter, operating at the downlink frequency, is powerful. If the frequencies were the same, a kind of resonance would occur in which the arrival of a tiny signal creates a large, unwanted output signal.

Polar orbit satellites	Geosynchronous satellites
low height (a few hundred km), north–south orbits	large orbits – about 42 000 km from the centre of the Earth above the equator
low height means they use less power for transmissions	needs substantial power for transmissions
used for communications, geological surveying and cartography, meteorology, oceanography, military espionage, etc.	used mainly for communications
cheaper to put in orbit	very expensive to put in orbit
serve polar regions	just three satellites can cover the entire Earth's surface area (except the poles)
need tracking systems	no tracking required
are above a particular point on the Earth's surface for only about 10 minutes	are above the same point on the equator all the time

The operational amplifier (op-amp) – HL

The op-amp is a versatile device with two inputs and one output. The output depends on the potential difference between the two inputs, $V_{OUT} = G(V_+ - V_-)$ where G is known as the (open loop) gain of the op-amp.

The maximum output is $\pm V$ where V is voltage of the power supply. (In practice it is a bit less.)

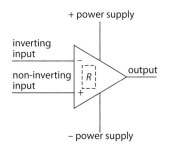

An **ideal** op-amp has the properties:

1   The resistance R between the two inputs is infinite (in practice it is very large). This means that the op-amp does not take in any current.

2   The gain G is infinite (in practice it is very large.)

The inverting amplifier

In this **inverting** amplifier, the output voltage has an opposite sign to that of the input voltage.

The non-inverting input is connected to the 0 V line.

As long as the op-amp does not saturate, the difference in potential between the inverting and the non-inverting inputs is very small and so the potential at the inverting input is also approximately zero.

The diagram assumes a positive potential at the inverting input. This implies that current flows as shown, which means that the output potential V_0 is negative, i.e. opposite to the input.

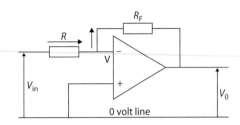

The **virtual Earth approximation** assumes that point V has zero potential. This is because the op-amp has a very high input resistance and a very high open loop gain.

Voltage across R is $V_{in} - 0$ so current in R is $\dfrac{V_{in}}{R}$.

Voltage across R_F is $0 - V_0$ so current in R_F is $\dfrac{-V_0}{R_F}$ (recall, V_0 is negative).

These currents are equal since no current is taken in by the op-amp, and so

$$\frac{V_{in}}{R} = -\frac{V_0}{R_F}.$$

The ratio $G = \dfrac{V_0}{V_{in}}$ is known as the closed loop gain of the inverting amplifier and so

$$G = -\frac{R_F}{R} \text{ (closed loop inverting amplifier gain).}$$

Test yourself 16

An inverting op-amp (see diagram) has a saturated output of ±9.0 V and $R_F = 80\,k\Omega$ and $R = 16\,k\Omega$.

a Determine the closed loop gain of the op-amp.
b Calculate the output voltage when $V_{in} = -0.60\,V$.
c Calculate the input voltage for which positive saturation is achieved and hence state the output when $V_{in} = -2.0\,V$.
d What is the current in the R_F resistor when $V_{in} = +1.2\,V$?
e The signal shown is input to the op-amp. Copy this and draw the output signal on the same axes.

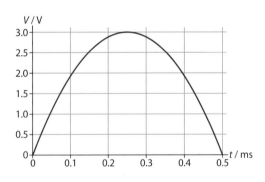

The non-inverting amplifier

In the non-inverting amplifier shown, notice the following points:

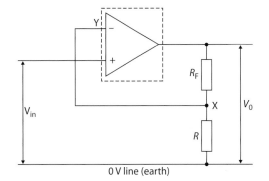

As long as the op-amp does not saturate, the difference in potential between the inverting and the non-inverting inputs is very small and so the potential at the non-inverting input is approximately V_{in}.

Since no current is drawn by the op-amp, the current in R is the same as the current in R_F.

Current in R_F: $\dfrac{V_0}{R_F + R}$

Current in R: $\dfrac{V_{in}}{R}$

Therefore, $\dfrac{V_0}{R_F + R} = \dfrac{V_{in}}{R}$

Hence the closed loop gain is $G = \dfrac{V_0}{V_{in}} = \dfrac{R_F + R}{R} = \dfrac{R_F}{R} + 1$

Test yourself **17**

A non-inverting op-amp (see diagram) has a saturated output of $\pm 6.0\,V$ and $R_F = 100\,k\Omega$ and $R = 25\,k\Omega$.
a Determine the closed loop gain of the op-amp. **b** Calculate the output voltage when $V_{in} = -0.50\,V$.
c Calculate the input voltage for which positive saturation is achieved and hence state the output when $V_{in} = 3.0\,V$.

Reshaping digital pulses – the Schmitt trigger

In the transmission of a digital signal, dispersion, noise, attenuation and other factors may contribute to a distortion of the digital signal.

The Schmitt trigger works as a standard comparator (it compares the input voltage to a reference value). However, there are two separate reference values, one when the input is increasing (V_2) and another when it is decreasing (V_1). To understand how the trigger works, consider the Schmitt trigger circuit (in which the op-amp is used in the non-inverting mode).

Here the output is at $-9.0\,V$ because the potential at X is below $2.0\,V$. (This means that the input voltage is sufficiently low.)

As the input voltage increases, so does the potential V_X at X.

Eventually, V_X will become $2.0\,V$ **while the output is still** $-9.0\,V$.

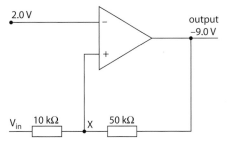

In this case the potential difference across the $50\,k\Omega$ resistor is $2 - (-9) = 11\,V$. Hence the current is $\dfrac{11}{50 \times 10^3} = 0.22\,mA$. The op-amp takes negligible current and so this is also the current in the other resistor. The potential difference across the $10\,k\Omega$ resistor is $V_{in} - 2 = IR \Rightarrow V_{in} = 2 + 0.22 \times 10^{-3} \times 10 \times 10^3 = 4.2\,V$.

In other words, as V_{in} increases, the output will suddenly switch to $+9.0\,V$ when $V_{in} = 4.2\,V$. This is the upper switching voltage of the trigger.

The lower switching voltage

We now have the output at +9.0V. Then $V_X > 2.0$V. As V_{in} now begins to decrease, V_X will decrease too and eventually will become equal to 2.0V **while the output is still at +9.0V**. In this case, the potential difference across the 50 kΩ resistor is $9.0 - 2.0 = 7.0$V. Hence the current is $\frac{7.0}{50 \times 10^3} = 0.14$ mA. The op-amp takes negligible current and so this is also the current in the other resistor. The potential difference across the 10 kΩ resistor is $2 - V_{in} = IR \Rightarrow V_{in} = 2 - 0.14 \times 10^{-3} \times 10 \times 10^3 = 0.60$V.

Output of the Schmitt trigger circuit

The red line on the graph shows the signal that is fed into the Schmitt trigger circuit. What will be the output?

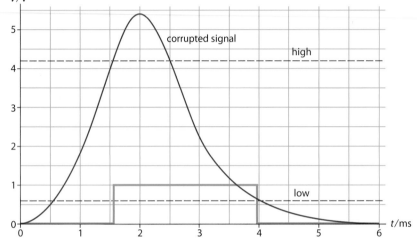

- The high and low switching voltages are shown in dashed lines.
- Starting at $t = 0$, we see V increasing. The first switchover will be when we reach the high switching voltage. V becomes binary 1.
- As V decreases we wait until we reach the lower switching voltage. V becomes binary 0.
- The regenerated signal is shown by the green line (binary 0 corresponds to output voltage −9.0V and binary 1 to +9.0 V).

The mobile phone system – HL

The main components of the mobile phone system are the **mobile phones** themselves, the **base stations** and the **cellular exchange**.

A geographic area is divided into different cells with a base station in each cell. When a mobile phone is turned on, it sends a radio signal that registers its presence to the nearest base station.

Base stations

Their main function is to assign a frequency for a particular call to a phone within the cell. The same frequency can be used for other calls at the same time using time division multiplexing. The base station is connected via cables to the cellular exchange computers that control the operation of very many base stations.

The cellular exchange

Its main function is to allocate a range of frequencies to each cell, with neighbouring cells being allocated different frequency ranges in order to avoid overlap and interference.

The cellular exchange also offers entry into the fixed telephone system network. If the mobile phone moves during the call, from one cell to another, the cellular exchange will automatically reroute the phone call to the base station at the centre of the new cell.

The nature of electromagnetic waves – Core

Electromagnetic waves (and so also visible light) consist of oscillating electric and magnetic fields at right angles to each other. Both are at right angles to the direction of energy transfer of the wave.

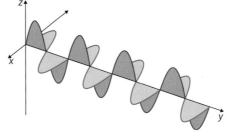

The diagram below shows the approximate orders of magnitude for the wavelength and frequency of various parts of the electromagnetic spectrum.

accelerated charges	molecular transitions	molecular transitions	atomic transitions	atomic transitions	atomic transitions	nuclear transitions
radio	microwave	infrared	optical	ultraviolet	X-rays	gamma rays

1   10^{-1} 10^{-2} 10^{-3} 10^{-4} 10^{-5} 10^{-6} 10^{-7} 10^{-8} 10^{-9} 10^{-10} 10^{-11} 10^{-12} 10^{-13} m

10^{8} 10^{9} 10^{10} 10^{11} 10^{12} 10^{13} 10^{14} 10^{15} 10^{16} 10^{17} 10^{18} 10^{19} 10^{20} Hz

> You must know the approximate orders of magnitude for the wavelength of various parts of the spectrum.

Definition
Dispersion   The phenomenon in which the refractive index depends on wavelength.

Due to dispersion, white light is split into the colours of the rainbow when it enters a glass prism. This is because glass has a different refractive index for different wavelengths. For example, the refractive index for red light is lower than for blue light. Red light will deviate less than blue light as it refracts in a prism. (Smaller refractive index means larger angle of refraction θ_r and hence smaller deviation.)

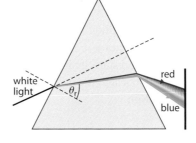

Rayleigh scattering – Core

When electromagnetic radiation is incident on a medium, part will be absorbed, part will be transmitted through the medium (in the same direction as that of the incident beam) and part will be scattered, i.e. radiation will be emitted in all directions.

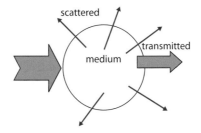

The incident radiation forces electrons in the medium to oscillate and these now emit radiation; this is the scattered radiation.

The **scattered intensity** is proportional to the inverse fourth power of the wavelength, $I \propto \dfrac{1}{\lambda^4}$ (Rayleigh scattering). This means that blue light, with its smaller wavelength, scatters much more than red light.

The colour of the sky

During the day	Light from the Sun entering the Earth's atmosphere scatters when it travels through air molecules and dust particles. The degree of scattering is largest for shorter wavelengths (i.e. blue and violet) and least for red. This means that during the day, if one is not looking directly at the Sun, the colour of the atmosphere is dominated by the colour that scatters the most, i.e. blue.
During a sunset	During a sunset (or sunrise) the Sun is low in the atmosphere and the light travels a longer distance in the atmosphere to get to the observer looking at the Sun. The blue and violet components of the light have been scattered away, leaving red and orange as the dominant colours reaching the observer.
The sky from the Moon	The Moon has no atmosphere and so there is no scattering of light in the lunar sky. The sky looks black (when one looks away from the Sun).

You must be prepared to explain the colour of the sky during the day and during a sunset.

Lasers (Light Amplification by Stimulated Emission of Radiation) – Core

Laser light is highly coherent and monochromatic radiation. To understand how laser light is produced we must first understand the difference between **spontaneous** emission and **stimulated** emission of radiation.

Definitions

Spontaneous emission   The electron in the excited state makes a transition to the ground state, emitting one photon of energy equal to the difference in energy between the ground and the excited state.

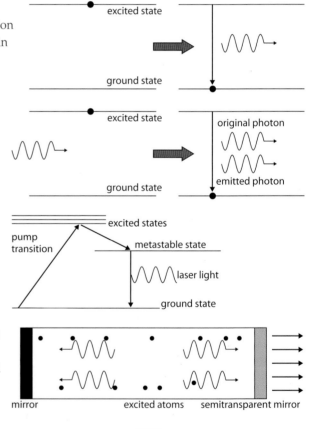

Stimulated emission   Einstein suggested that a photon incident on an atom with an electron **in an excited state** can force or **stimulate** the electron to make a transition down to the ground state, emitting a photon in the process. The emitted photon will be identical to the first, i.e. it will have the same **frequency, phase and direction**.

Optical pumping   The idea is to force electrons to make transitions to excited states. The electrons will then very quickly (within 10^{-8} s) return to a metastable state (a state where electrons spend a relatively long time).

Population inversion   The situation when the number of electrons in the metastable state is far greater than the number in the ground state.

Laser action   The electrons in the metastable state make transitions to the ground state, emitting the laser light photons. These photons, going back and forth in between mirrors, are used to stimulate the emission of identical photons. For every photon causing stimulated emission we get a second identical photon and so very quickly the intense, coherent laser beam is built up. Part of the laser beam emerges from the semitransparent mirror.

In any exam question you must be prepared to describe the role of optical pumping, population inversion and stimulated emission of radiation.

Uses of lasers include: modulating light to be used for communications in optical fibres, measuring distances in surveying, reading information on CDs, DVDs and bar codes, applications to medicine such as the endoscope and surgery, drilling holes in metals, etc.

Lenses – Core

Definition
Focal point The point on the principal axis through which rays **parallel to the principal axis** pass, after refraction through the lens.

Converging lenses
A ray of light will, upon entering a lens, refract at **both faces** of the lens.

In practice, we draw rays halfway into the lens and show the bending taking place only once, inside the lens.

The line through the middle of the lens and at right angles to its face is called the **principal axis** of the lens. There are two important points of the principal axis at equal distances from the lens, the **foci** or **focal points.**

If the rays enter the lens from the 'other' side they will pass through the second focus f' of the lens. The **two foci** are at equal distances from the lens. This distance is called the focal length f. Rays that are parallel to each other but not parallel to the principal axis refract as shown.

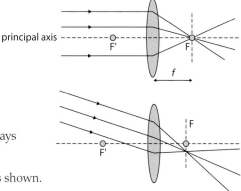

To construct an image we must know how at least two rays will refract through the lens.

Three standard rays refract through a converging lens as shown.

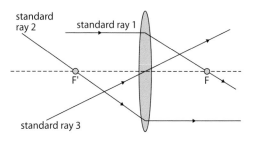

Determining the image using equations

Definitions
Real image An image formed by actual light rays.

Virtual image An image formed by mathematical extensions of light rays. It cannot be displayed on a screen.

In the two examples on the following pages, an object is placed in front of a converging lens. The position and size of the image may be determined either by a graphical method or by using the lens equation

$$\frac{1}{f} = \frac{1}{v} + \frac{1}{u} \text{ and } M = -\frac{v}{u}$$

where:

u = object distance from lens
v = image distance from lens
f = focal length

The first equation is used to find the image distance v. The second equation is for magnification, which is defined as $M = \frac{h'}{h}$ where h' is the image height and h the object height. These formulae use the convention: **real images are positive and virtual images are negative.**

Examples of image formation (1)

An object is placed a distance of 12 cm in front of a converging lens of focal length 4.0 cm. Determine the characteristics of the image.

➡ **Before you answer**
Use both the formula for image distance as well as that for magnification.

The equation gives: $u = 12\,\text{cm}$, $f = 4.0\,\text{cm}$ so that $\dfrac{1}{v} = \dfrac{1}{f} - \dfrac{1}{u} = \dfrac{1}{4.0} - \dfrac{1}{12} = \dfrac{1}{6} \Rightarrow v = 6.0\,\text{cm}$. Since $v > 0$ the image is real. The magnification is $M = -\dfrac{6.0}{12} = -0.50$ implying that the image is inverted ($M < 0$) and smaller ($|M| < 1$). If the object size is 4.0 cm the image size is $Mh = -0.50 \times 4.0 = -2.0\,\text{cm}$. The diagram shows a graphical solution to this problem.

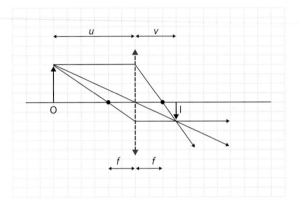

This construction of an image in a converging lens uses the three standard rays. The scale is 2 cm = 1 horizontal square. Notice that the image can be constructed with just two rays, but the third serves as a check that the diagram is drawn correctly. Here, the image is **real** (there are actual rays of light going through the position of the image), it is **inverted** and it is **smaller** in size than the object.

Test yourself **1**
Determine the characteristics of the image of an object 3.0 cm tall that is placed 8.0 cm from a converging lens of focal length 6.0 cm.

Test yourself **2**
Copy and complete the ray diagram below to form the image of the object.

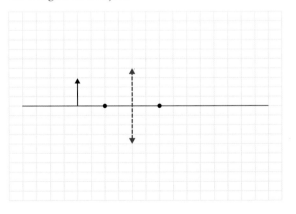

Test yourself **3**
Copy and complete the ray diagram below to form the image of the object.

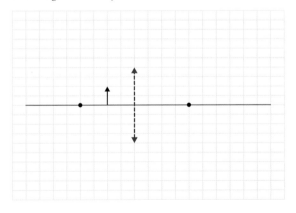

Examples of image formation (2)

An object is placed a distance of 4.0 cm from a converging lens of focal length 12 cm. Determine the characteristics of the image.

➡ **Before you answer**
Use both the formula for image distance as well as that for magnification.

The equation gives: $u = 4.0$ cm, $f = 12$ cm so that $\frac{1}{v} = \frac{1}{f} - \frac{1}{u} = \frac{1}{12} - \frac{1}{4.0} = -\frac{1}{6} \Rightarrow v = -6.0$ cm. Since $v < 0$ the image is virtual. The magnification is $M = -\frac{-6.0}{4.0} = +1.50$ implying that the image is upright ($M > 0$) and larger ($|M| > 1$). The diagram shows a graphical solution to this problem.

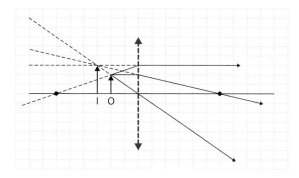

This construction of an image in a converging lens uses the three standard rays. The scale is 2 cm = 1 horizontal square. Notice that the image can be constructed with just two rays, but the third serves as a check that the diagram is drawn correctly. The image is **virtual** (there are no actual rays of light going through the position of the image, just their mathematical extensions), it is **upright** and it is **larger** in size than the object.

Test yourself 4

An object is placed in front of a converging lens and an image is formed. The top half of the lens is now covered with opaque paper. Discuss the changes, if any, in the appearance of the image.

➡ **Before you answer**
Does **any** light from the object go through the lens?

The simple magnifier – Core

Definitions

Near point   The closest point to the eye where the eye can focus without strain. The distance to the near point is denoted by D and is about 25 cm for a healthy eye.

Far point   The furthest point from the eye where the eye can focus without strain. The distance to the far point is taken to be infinite for a healthy eye.

A converging lens can be used as a simple magnifier. A small object is placed closer to the lens than the focal length. The lens produces a larger, virtual image and thus acts as a magnifier.

Unaided eye

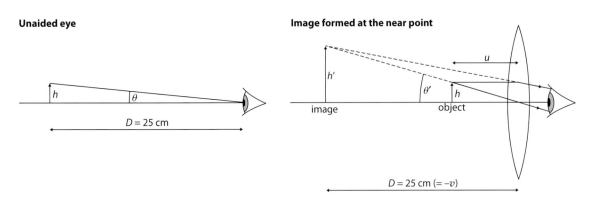

Image formed at the near point

The enlarged, virtual image is formed at the near point. The **angle the image subtends at the eye** (θ') is larger than when the lens is not in place (θ) and so the image appears larger.

The **angular magnification** is $M = \dfrac{\theta'}{\theta}$. Now, $\theta = \dfrac{h}{D}$ and $\theta' = \dfrac{h'}{D}$ so that $M = \dfrac{h'}{h}$.

This is the same as the **linear magnification** given by $\dfrac{-v}{u}$.

From the lens formula, $\dfrac{1}{u} = \dfrac{1}{f} - \dfrac{1}{v}$, so $\dfrac{-v}{u} = 1 - \dfrac{v}{f}$. But in this case the image is virtual and formed at the near point, so the image distance v is equal to $-D$ and $M = 1 + \dfrac{D}{f}$

> Use this formula for the image at the near point. D is the near point distance.

A simple magnifier with the image formed at infinity

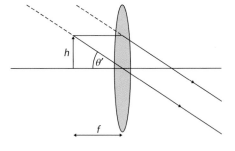

In this case, $v = \infty$ and so $u = f$. Thus, $M = \dfrac{\theta'}{\theta} = \dfrac{h/f}{h/D} = \dfrac{D}{f}$.

> Use this formula for the image at infinity.

Test yourself 5

An object is placed in front of a combination of two converging lenses as shown in the diagram. The objective lens forms an image of this object as shown. The final image in the eyepiece is formed on the screen. Draw a ray diagram to locate the position of the focus of the eyepiece. Use the diagram to determine the **linear** magnification of the **a** objective, **b** eyepiece and **c** combination of the two lenses.

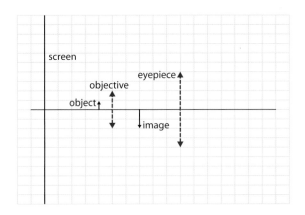

The compound microscope – Core

This is used to obtain an enlarged image of a small object very close to the microscope. It consists of two converging lenses: the objective (near the object) and the eyepiece (near the eye).

The objective lens forms a real enlarged image of the object. This image acts as the object for the eyepiece. The eyepiece now acts as a magnifier for this object.

In the diagram below, we draw the standard two rays (**1** and **2**) leaving the top of the object and extend these to meet the eyepiece lens. We now have a problem because we do not know how these refract in the eyepiece lens – these are not standard rays. To proceed we use **construction rays**. First we draw the red dotted line from the top of the image to the centre of the eyepiece lens. This will continue straight through the lens. We now extend this red line backwards. Next we draw the green dotted line that leaves the top of the image and is parallel to the principal axis. This will refract through the focal point of the eyepiece. We also extend this backwards. Where the green and red lines meet is the top of the final image. The original standard rays leaving the top of the object may now be completed by joining the top of the final image to where these rays join the eyepiece. Extending these gives their path after refraction in the eyepiece.

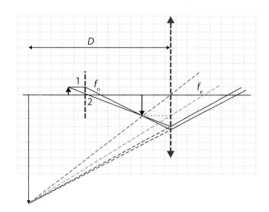

In this example, the final image is formed a distance D from the eyepiece equal to the near point distance, usually 25 cm. (In the diagram, each square horizontally corresponds to 2.0 cm.)

The magnification of the compound microscope

The magnification of the microscope is the product of the linear magnification produced by the objective times the angular magnification of the eyepiece. The objective produces a linear magnification of $M_o = -\dfrac{v}{u}$. The eyepiece produces an angular magnification of $1 + \dfrac{D}{f_e}$ where D is shown in the diagram and is the near point distance. Hence the overall magnification of the microscope is $M_o \times \left(1 + \dfrac{D}{f_e}\right)$. In the example shown in the diagram, $M_o = -3.3$ and $1 + \dfrac{D}{f_e} = 1 + \dfrac{25}{6} = 5.2$ for an overall magnification of approximately -17.

The telescope – Core

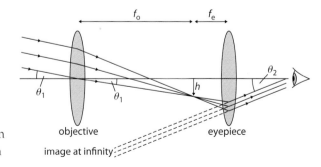

A distant object subtends a very small angle at the eye (θ_1). The telescope magnifies that angle to a larger angle θ_2. Since the object is far away, the image in the objective is formed a distance of f_o from the objective. Here the final image is formed at infinity. This means that the image in the objective is formed a distance equal to f_e from the eyepiece. The separation of the lenses is then $f_o + f_e$. The angular magnification of the telescope is given by $M = \dfrac{\theta_2}{\theta_1} = \dfrac{f_o}{f_e}$.

Test yourself **6**
Considering the diagram of the telescope, explain the formation of the final image by the eyepiece lens.

Lens aberrations – Core

Chromatic aberration

Because glass has a **slightly different refractive index** for different wavelengths of light, light of different wavelengths will come to focus at slightly different points. This results in a coloured, blurred image.

The situation may be partially corrected by using the lens in combination with a diverging lens. The chromatic aberration caused by the second lens is opposite to that caused by the first. (Strictly this corrects the problem for just two different wavelengths – the problem persists for the rest but is reduced.)

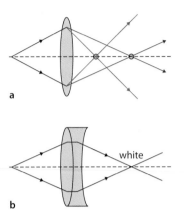

Spherical aberration

This is due to the fact that rays far from the principal axis come to a focus closer to the lens than where paraxial rays (rays close to the axis) focus. This results in an image with less detail, as well as blurring and curving at the edges. Because the rays far from the axis also have a different magnification, an image of a straight edge object may appear curved.

The problem is reduced by blocking those rays that are far from the principal axis of the lens, in a procedure known as **stopping down**.

This reduces the amount of light through the lens and so reduces the brightness of the image.

Two-source interference – Core

Conditions for two-source interference

- The two sources must be coherent sources of radiation of roughly the same amplitude. Coherence means that the phase difference between the sources is constant in time.
- In addition the two sources must produce radiation with the same polarisation.

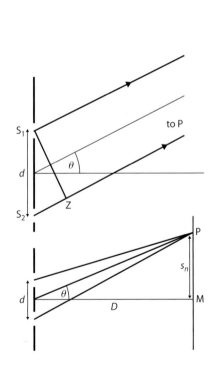

Young's two-slit experiment

Light that is incident normally on the two slits will diffract at each slit. This means light can be observed at an angle θ to the original direction of light.

The path difference is the distance S_2Z which equals $d \sin \theta$.

We have constructive interference when $d \sin \theta = n\lambda$ and n is an integer.

From the second diagram we see that $\tan \theta = \dfrac{s_n}{D}$.

Because the angle is small, $\sin \theta \approx \tan \theta$ and so $d\dfrac{s_n}{D} = n\lambda$. Thus the distance on the screen from the centre to the nth maximum is given by $s_n = \dfrac{n\lambda D}{d}$.

The intensity pattern from two sources

The diagrams show the intensity observed far from the two sources as a function of the distance s along the screen. The pattern shows equally spaced maxima whose intensity is the same.

The first graph shows the pattern with large slit separation. Fringes are close together.

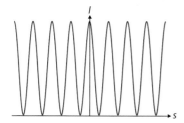

The second graph shows the pattern with smaller slit separation. Fringes are further apart.

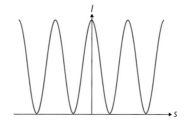

The separation Δs of two consecutive maxima (or minima) is given by $\Delta s = \dfrac{\lambda D}{d}$.

D = distance to screen
d = separation of slits

Test yourself 7
In a Young two-slit experiment, light of wavelength 656 nm is incident on two very narrow slits a distance of 0.125 mm apart. Calculate the angular width of the central maximum.

Test yourself 8
Light carries energy. What happens to the energy of two waves that interfere destructively?

> ➡ **Before you answer**
> Energy must be conserved.

Test yourself 9
Two coherent sources of light of equal amplitude produce an interference pattern. Describe the changes to the fringes if the amplitude of one of the sources is reduced.

> ➡ **Before you answer**
> Examine carefully what happens at **a** the maxima and **b** the minima.

The diffraction grating – Core

The discussion from the two-slit case shows that with a smaller slit separation we get fringes that are further apart.

This is exploited in the diffraction grating, a device that has a very large number of very narrow, parallel slits.

- With more than two slits we see that we have secondary maxima in between the primary maxima. (Shown here are six slits, diagram **a**.)
- The importance of the secondary maxima becomes negligible as the number of slits increases.
- The primary maxima become narrower and more intense.

Diagram **b** shows the fringe pattern for 2, 4 and 6 slits. Notice that the principal maxima are at the same location.

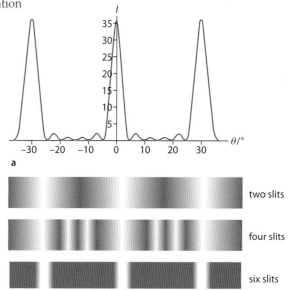

two slits

four slits

six slits

Test yourself 10
A diffraction grating has 600 lines per mm. Light consisting of two wavelengths 589.0 nm and 589.6 nm is incident normally on the grating. Determine the difference between the diffraction angles of the two wavelengths in **a** the first-order and **b** the second-order maxima.

X-rays – HL

In an X-ray tube, electrons are emitted from a
heated filament and are accelerated towards a
metal target. The electrons produce X-rays for **two
distinct reasons**. This can be seen in the spectrum
of the X-rays produced, which shows a curved
continuous spectrum and distinct peaks of intensity
at specific wavelengths.

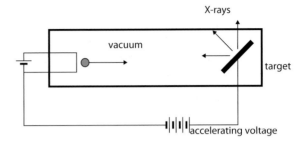

Continuous part of the spectrum: First, the electrons suffer enormous decelerations as they strike the
target and decelerated charges give out radiation. Because the magnitude of the acceleration varies, photons
of **many different wavelengths** are emitted.

Discrete part of the spectrum: Second, the electrons may collide with **electrons inside the target atoms**
and knock them out of the atoms. Atom electrons in higher energy states will then make a transition to the
vacated energy level thereby emitting photons of a **specific energy** (equal to the difference in energy of the
energy levels in the transition).

An electron accelerated from rest by a potential
difference V acquires a kinetic energy eV. When **all** of
this energy is converted to a **single** photon,
$\frac{hc}{\lambda} = eV$, and so $\lambda = \frac{hc}{eV}$.

This is the **smallest** possible wavelength that can be
emitted by an X-ray tube operating at a voltage V.

The graph shows the two X-ray spectra for the same
target element but different accelerating voltages.

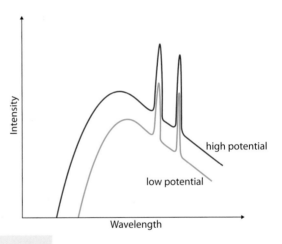

> Notice how the minimum wavelength shifts as V increases.

You must be prepared to describe and annotate an X-ray tube and explain the production of the
continuous and discrete part of the X-ray spectrum. You must also be able to explain why there is a
minimum wavelength produced.

Test yourself **11**
Calculate the minimum wavelength produced in a 25 kV X-ray tube.

X-ray diffraction

When X-rays are directed at a crystal, there are angles at which the reflected X-ray intensity is very large. This is explained by assuming that the maxima are due to constructive interference of X-rays diffracting off the regularly arranged atoms in various crystal planes.

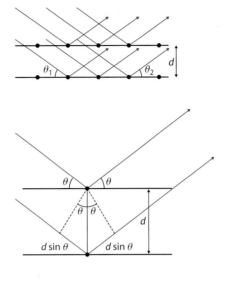

The diffracted beam is strong if two conditions are satisfied:

$$\theta_1 = \theta_2 \ (= \theta) \quad \text{and} \quad 2d \sin \theta = n\lambda \ \text{(the Bragg formula)}.$$

The first condition ensures that X-rays diffracting from the top layer constructively interfere with each other. The second condition ensures that X-rays diffracting from the top layer constructively interfere with those from the second layer.

From the diagram, the path difference is $2d \sin \theta$ and we will have constructive interference if this is an integral multiple of the wavelength.

Test yourself **12**

X-rays of wavelength 3.80×10^{-11} m are incident on a crystal. The smallest angle between the X-ray beam direction and the crystal surface where a maximum in scattered in intensity is observed is $25.3°$. Determine the spacing between the crystal planes.

Thin-film interference – HL

Parallel films

Phase change upon reflection: When a ray of light reflects off a surface that has a higher index of refraction than the medium from which the ray is incident, a phase change of π will take place. In the diagram, the ray in air reflects from the top surface of oil. Since the refractive index of oil is greater than that of air a phase change takes place. The second reflection at the bottom surface of oil does not result in a phase change.

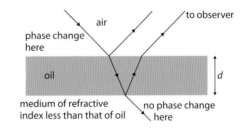

The two reflected rays will interfere. At **normal incidence**, the path difference is $2d$ where d is the thickness of the film. So we will have **destructive** interference if $2d = n\lambda$ ($n = 0, 1, 2, 3\ldots$) and **constructive** interference if $2d = (n + \frac{1}{2})\lambda$ ($n = 0, 1, 2, 3, \ldots$) where λ is the wavelength of light **in the oil**.

Thus, observing from above, a layer of oil floating in water will show a coloured oil film. The colour seen is determined by:

- white minus that colour whose wavelength that destructively interferes and
- the colour that constructively interferes.

Because the oil film has variable thickness, different colours are observed at different parts of the film.

Applications: The idea of thin-film interference is used mainly in high-quality lenses where a thin coating on the lens causes destructive interference for certain wavelengths of light, thus reducing the amount of reflected light.

Wedge films

In the diagram, a very thin object of thickness D is placed in between two glass plates a distance L from where the plates join. As a result, the angle θ between the plates is very small. The idea is to measure this small angle and hence the small thickness D.

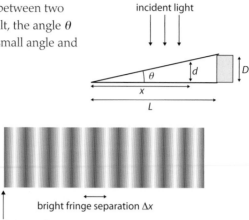

Let d be the separation of the plates at a distance x from where the plates join. Destructive interference takes place if

$2d = n\lambda$ ($n = 0, 1, 2, 3\ldots$)

Since $d = x\tan\theta$ we have that $\Delta d = \Delta x\tan\theta$.

Consecutive bright fringes correspond to air wedge heights that differ by $\frac{\lambda}{2}$. So if Δx is the separation of two consecutive bright fringes, $\tan\theta = \frac{\Delta d}{\Delta x}$. Then $D = L\tan\theta$.

bright fringe separation Δx

plates join here

Test yourself 13

White light is incident normally on a soap film of index of refraction 1.33. The thickness of the film is assumed to be uniform and equal to 0.26 μm. Explain why the soap film appears turquoise (cyan) in colour.

Test yourself 14

Referring to the standard diagram of wedge films shown, the wavelength of light used is 520 nm and the separation of two consecutive bright fringes is 0.15 mm. The length L is 5.0 cm. Calculate the thickness D.

Frames of reference – SL Option D and HL

Relativity deals with **events**, i.e. occurrences at specific times and specific places. To specify the times and positions of events we use **reference frames**.

Definitions

Reference frame   A coordinate system (three dimensions for space and one for time) used to record the time and position of an event. An event thus has four coordinates (x, y, z, t). In this course we mainly deal with just one space coordinate, x.

Inertial reference frame   A reference frame that is not accelerating.

Rest frame of an object   The frame of reference in which the object is at rest.

An event (lightning strike) is given the coordinates (x, t) by a stationary observer in reference frame S. An observer in reference frame S′, which is moving relative to frame S, assigns the coordinates (x', t') to the same event. An object is measured to have speed u by S and u' by S′.

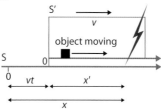

How are the two sets of measurements related? In **pre-relativity physics**, the answer is given by **Galilean transformation** equations:

Equation 1: $t' = t$
Equation 2: $x' = x - vt$
Equation 3: $u' = u - v$

The Galilean transformation equation, Equation 3, applied to light shows that light moves with different speeds relative to different observers. If S measured a speed $u = c$ for light then S′ would measure a speed $u' = u - v = c - v$. Conversely if S′ measured a speed c for light, S would measure $u = c + v$.

On the other hand, **Maxwell's laws of electromagnetism** showed that the speed of light in a vacuum is a **universal constant** independent of the speed of its source.

Einstein solved the problem by **trusting the laws of electromagnetism and changing the Galilean transformation equations**. And this implied great changes in physics!

The postulates of relativity

Postulate 1   The speed of light in a **vacuum** is the same for all **inertial** observers.

Postulate 2   The laws of physics are the same for all **inertial** observers.

Test yourself **1**
In a certain inertial reference frame S, lightning strikes at $x = 3 \times 10^8$ m. An observer is standing at the position $x = 6 \times 10^8$ m. Light from the strike arrives at the observer when his clock shows $t = 3$ s. What are the coordinates of the event 'lightning strikes' according to this observer?

The time of an event is recorded by the clock at the position of the event. This question illustrates a very common mistake.

Time dilation and length contraction – SL Option D and HL

Time dilation – the light clock
A ray of light leaves the base of a box and is directed parallel to the walls to a point directly above, where it is reflected and is received back at the source.

The first diagram represents the point of view of S′, the reference frame of an observer inside the box.

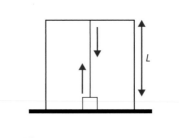

$$c = \frac{2L}{t'} \qquad \text{or} \qquad c^2(t')^2 = 4L^2 \qquad \text{I}$$

The next diagram represents the point of view of S, the reference frame attached to the ground.

> The speed of light is the same for both observers. This next derivation is frequently asked for in exams.

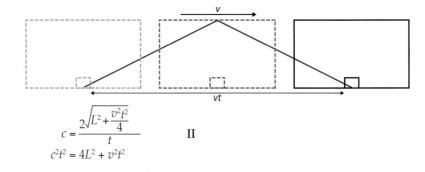

$$c = \frac{2\sqrt{L^2 + \frac{v^2 t^2}{4}}}{t} \qquad \text{II}$$

$$c^2 t^2 = 4L^2 + v^2 t^2$$

Substituting $4L^2$ from **I** into **II** gives

$$c^2 t^2 = c^2(t')^2 + v^2 t^2 \Rightarrow \underbrace{(c^2 - v^2)t^2 = c^2(t')^2}_{\substack{\text{bring this term} \\ \text{to the left}}} \Rightarrow \underbrace{t^2(1 - \frac{v^2}{c^2}) = (t')^2}_{\substack{\text{now divide} \\ \text{by } c^2}} \Rightarrow \underbrace{t = \frac{t'}{\sqrt{1 - \frac{v^2}{c^2}}}}_{\substack{\text{now take} \\ \text{square roots}}}.$$

Proper time interval
The time interval between two events that happen at the same point in space is called a **proper time interval**.

The time interval between any two events is equal to time interval = γ × proper time interval where v is the relative speed of the two observers.

> A very common mistake: do **not** think that the 'moving frame' always measures proper time intervals.

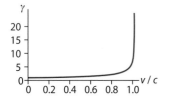

The 'Lorentz gamma factor' is: $\gamma = \dfrac{1}{\sqrt{1 - \dfrac{v^2}{c^2}}}$.

Notice that $\gamma \to \infty$ as $v \to c$.

Time dilation and length contraction – questions

Definition

Proper length (or rest length)   The length of an object as measured in the object's rest frame.

If the object moves with speed v with respect to an observer, that observer will measure a smaller length

given by $L = L_0 \sqrt{1 - \dfrac{v^2}{c^2}}$ or $L = \dfrac{L_0}{\gamma}$.

> Only those lengths in the direction of motion contract. The density of the object will increase since the volume will get smaller, according to the observer with respect to whom the object moves.

Test yourself 2

A container of radioactive material is in a rocket that moves past a lab at a speed of $0.80c$. The half-life of the radioactive material is 12 minutes according to an observer in the rocket. Consider the events:

Event 1 = rocket observer measures N_0 nuclei of the radioactive material in the container.

Event 2 = rocket observer measures $\dfrac{N_0}{2}$ nuclei of the radioactive material in the container.

What is the time interval between the two events according to **a** the rocket observer, **b** the lab observer? **c** At the time found in **b**, what is the number of radioactive nuclei in the container as measured by the lab observer?

Test yourself 3

A spacecraft moving at $0.80c$ relative to Earth, passes the Earth on its way past a planet a distance of 40 ly as measured by Earth. Calculate the time taken to arrive at the planet according to **a** Earth observers, **b** spacecraft observers.

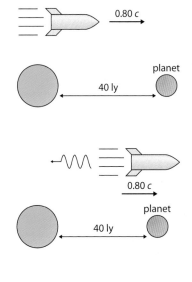

> ➡ **Before you answer**
> This is such a basic example that you must learn it well.

The spacecraft continues to move past the planet. As it passes the planet it sends a radio signal to Earth. Calculate the time taken for the signal to arrive at Earth according to **c** Earth observers, **d** spacecraft observers.

> ➡ **Before you answer**
> **c** Notice that the speed of the signal is c. **d** It is very tempting to use the answer in **a** in the time dilation formula. But we can only do that if we have a proper time interval and here we do not readily have one.

> It is important that you realise that 'spacecraft' clocks do not necessarily read proper time and that spacecraft clocks always read less time than 'stationary' clocks. The point of question 3 is to point this out. Motion is relative!

Simultaneity – SL Option D and HL

Two events are called **simultaneous** if they occur at the same time.

If the two events are simultaneous **and they take place at the same point in space according to one observer** then they will be simultaneous for all other observers as well.

However, if two events are simultaneous for one observer **and take place at different points in space**, then they will **not** be simultaneous for another observer in motion relative to the first.

A *gedanken* (thought) experiment

A box moves to the right with speed v relative to the ground. Two light signals are emitted towards the left and right ends of the box from a point midway in the box. The signals are emitted simultaneously according to an observer at the middle of the box. Do the signals arrive simultaneously at L and at R according to the observer inside the box and an observer on the ground?

The first diagram shows the view according to an observer inside the box.

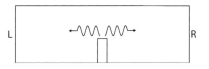

For the observer in the box:

- Light travels at the same speed, c, towards L and R.
- Distances to L and R are the same.
- Hence the light signals will arrive at the same time.

The second diagram shows the view according to observers on the ground.

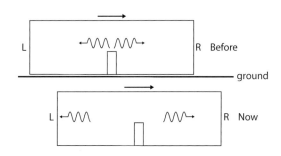

For the observer on the ground:

- Signals were **emitted** simultaneously according to the ground observer (because they were emitted simultaneously at the same point).
- Light signals move towards L and R with same speed, c.
- But end L is moving towards the light signal and R away from it.
- **The arrival of the signals will not be simultaneous. L will receive the signal first**.

Test yourself **4**

A ground observer G is halfway between two buildings. According to G, two lightning strikes hit the buildings at the same time, just as a rocket passes G. Which building is hit first according to the rocket observer R?

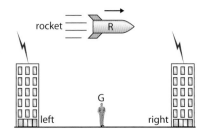

It would be meaningless to say that the rocket observer travels towards the right-hand building and so 'sees' the light from the right-hand building first.

Experimental evidence for special relativity – HL

Muon decay experiments

Muons are unstable particles that decay into electrons. Muons may be created in the atmosphere when cosmic rays from the Sun interact with air molecules.

Consider muons created at a height of 1 km from the Earth's surface (a height measured by Earth observers). Assume that the speed of the muons is $0.95c$ towards the Earth surface.

The proper lifetime of the muons is 2.2×10^{-6} s. The gamma factor for a speed of $0.95c$ is $\gamma = 3.2$.

Without relativity, the distance travelled by muons before they decay would be $0.95 \times 3 \times 10^8 \times 2.2 \times 10^{-6} = 630$ m. So most muons would have decayed before reaching the Earth's surface.

According to the Earth observer	According to the observer moving with muons
The muon lifetime is time dilated to $3.2 \times 2.2 \times 10^{-6} = 7.0 \times 10^{-6}$ s. In this time muons travel a distance of $0.95 \times 3 \times 10^8 \times 7.0 \times 10^{-6} \approx 2$ km. Hence most muons make it to the Earth's surface before decaying. This is evidence for time dilation.	The Earth surface is moving upward towards the muons at a speed of $0.95c$. The distance of 1 km is length contracted to $\dfrac{1000}{3.2} = 310$ m. In a time of 2.2×10^{-6} s the Earth's surface moves a distance of $0.95 \times 3 \times 10^8 \times 2.2 \times 10^{-6} = 630$ m. Hence by the time the Earth surface arrives at the position of the muons, most muons have not decayed. This is evidence for length contraction.

The Hafele–Keating experiment

In this experiment, two very accurate atomic clocks were compared after one of them had been put on a plane that travelled for a few hours. Upon comparison, the time that had elapsed according to the clock on the plane was slightly less than according to the clock that stayed on Earth, just as relativity predicts.

The Michelson–Morley experiment

The purpose of this experiment was to measure the speed of the Earth relative to the **ether** (an outdated hypothesis of a medium for light).

In a frame at rest relative to the ether, the speed of light was the constant c, but in frame that moved relative to the ether, the speed of light was expected to be different from c.

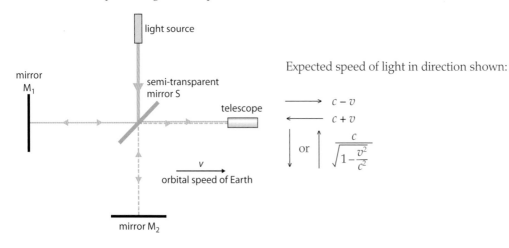

Light from a source followed the paths shown. The split beams of light were joined at the telescope where interference fringes were seen. The apparatus was then rotated by 90°. They expected a change in the phase difference between the split beams and so a **shift** of the interference fringes. But no such shift was detected! In relativity this 'null' result is explained by saying that no ether exists and the speed of light in vacuum is the same for all inertial observers.

Velocity addition – HL

Consider a frame of reference S' that moves with velocity v relative to another frame of reference S. The speed of an object is measured to be u by S and u' by S'. The two speeds are related by

$$u' = \frac{u-v}{1-\frac{uv}{c^2}} \quad \text{or} \quad u = \frac{u'+v}{1+\frac{u'v}{c^2}}$$

Velocity addition and light

If the 'object' above is a ray of light then both S and S' must measure the same speed, c. If for example $u = c$, then $u' = \dfrac{u-v}{1-\frac{uv}{c^2}} = \dfrac{c-v}{1-\frac{cv}{c^2}} = \dfrac{c-v}{1-\frac{v}{c}} = \dfrac{c-v}{\frac{c-v}{c}} = c.$

The twin 'paradox'

Arnold gets in a spacecraft that will take him on a long trip at relativistic speeds. He leaves behind his twin sister, Beatrice. Arnold returns after some time. Arnold expects that he has aged less than his sister. Beatrice, who studied relativity, claims that it is she who will be younger when she is reunited with Arnold because she claims that it is the Earth that moved away from the spacecraft.

Both cannot be right.

Resolution of the twin paradox

Arnold must have accelerated at some point in the trip. Either by stopping to turn around or by going in a circle. This means that he is in a **different** inertial frame of reference on the return trip. Beatrice was in the same inertial frame all the time. This lack of symmetry implies that Arnold aged less.

Test yourself **5**

Two spacecraft, A and B, are approaching each other head on. The speed of A as measured by an observer on the ground is $0.80c$. The speed of B relative to the ground is $0.40c$. Calculate the speed of B relative to A.

➡ **Before you answer**
What are v, u and u'?

Relativistic mechanics – HL

Definitions

Momentum   At low speeds, $\gamma \approx 1$, and the definition then agrees with Newtonian physics:

$$p = \frac{mv}{\sqrt{1-\frac{v^2}{c^2}}} \text{ or } p = \gamma mv$$

Total energy   This is the famous formula that can be interpreted as showing the **equivalence of mass and energy**.

$$E = \frac{mc^2}{\sqrt{1-\frac{v^2}{c^2}}} \text{ or } E = \gamma mc^2$$

Rest energy   This is the energy needed to create the particle from the vacuum. In the frame of reference where a particle is at rest (the particle's rest frame) there is still energy in the particle, $E_0 = mc^2$, since $\gamma = 1$ then.

Kinetic energy   In the particle's rest frame, $\gamma = 1$, and so $E_K = 0$. This is defined as the total energy minus the rest energy, i.e. $E_K = \gamma mc^2 - mc^2 = (\gamma - 1)mc^2$. (For low speeds, this formula approximates to $E_K \approx \frac{1}{2}mv^2$ but we never use this formula in relativity.)

Rest mass   This is the mass of a particle as measured in its rest frame.

Energy and momentum are related by $E^2 = (mc^2)^2 + p^2c^2$

Units

Given that the rest energy of a proton is $E_0 = 938\,\text{MeV}$ we use $E_0 = mc^2$ to find $m = \frac{E_0}{c^2} = 938\,\text{MeV}\,c^{-2}$.
Similarly, the momentum of a proton of total energy $E = 1250\,\text{MeV}$ is

$$E^2 = (mc^2)^2 + p^2c^2$$
$$1250^2\,\text{MeV}^2 = 938^2\,\text{MeV}^2 + p^2c^2$$
$$pc = \sqrt{1250^2 - 938^2}\,\text{MeV}$$
$$pc = 826\,\text{MeV}$$
$$p = 826\,\text{MeV}\,c^{-1}$$

A constant force is applied to a body initially at rest. In Newtonian mechanics (curve labelled N) the velocity increases without limit. In relativity (curve R) the body never reaches the speed of light (dashed line).

Notice that both curves are identical at low speeds. It is important to show this in an exam. You must be able to explain why a particle with non-zero rest mass cannot reach the speed of light by referring to the infinite amount of energy ($E \to \infty$ as $v \to c$) required, which makes it impossible.

Accelerating potentials

When a particle of charge q is accelerated by a potential difference V then $qV = \Delta E$, where ΔE is the change in the particle's **total** energy.

A few standard relativistic mechanics questions

Test yourself 6
Calculate the speed of a proton (mass $938\,\mathrm{MeV}\,c^{-2}$) whose momentum is $p = 2800\,\mathrm{MeV}\,c^{-1}$.

Test yourself 7
Calculate the accelerating voltage required to accelerate an electron (mass $0.511\,\mathrm{MeV}\,c^{-2}$) to a speed of $0.98\,c$.

Test yourself 8
Calculate the kinetic energy of a proton (mass $938\,\mathrm{MeV}\,c^{-2}$) of speed $0.950\,c$.

Test yourself 9
Calculate the momentum of a muon (μ^-, mass $106\,\mathrm{MeV}\,c^{-2}$) of total energy $540\,\mathrm{MeV}$.

Test yourself 10
Calculate the speed of a tau particle (τ^-, mass $1800\,\mathrm{MeV}\,c^{-2}$) whose total energy is $6500\,\mathrm{MeV}$.

Test yourself 11
The rest mass of the φ meson is about double that of the η meson. The speed of a φ meson is half that of an η meson. Which particle has the greater momentum?

> **Before you answer**
> Recall the definition of relativistic momentum – this is not a classical mechanics problem!

Test yourself 12
a Show that the speed of the particle of total energy E and momentum p is given by $v = \dfrac{pc^2}{E}$. Use this formula to deduce that a massless particle always moves at the speed of light. A particle has total energy $E = 654\,\mathrm{MeV}$ and momentum $p = 640\,\mathrm{MeV}\,c^{-1}$. Calculate **b** the speed of this particle, **c** the rest mass of the particle.

Test yourself 13
A proton is accelerated from rest by a potential difference $3.2 \times 10^9\,\mathrm{V}$. Calculate the speed and momentum of the accelerated proton.

> **Before you answer**
> Recall that $qV = \Delta E$.

> You will have to perform this calculation in most exam papers.

Test yourself 14
Calculate the speed of a proton whose momentum is $p = 2.40\,\mathrm{GeV}\,c^{-1}$.

> **Before you answer**
> Look at the available formulae and decide on the most convenient.

Test yourself 15
A Ψ meson has rest mass $3100\,\mathrm{MeV}\,c^{-2}$. It decays at rest in a lab into a muon–antimuon pair. The rest mass of the muon and that of the antimuon is $106\,\mathrm{MeV}\,c^{-2}$. Determine the momentum of the muon relative to the lab.

General relativity – HL

The equivalence principle and its consequences

'Acceleration mimics gravity': it is impossible to distinguish effects of acceleration and effects of gravitation.

However, you must also understand its other (more detailed) equivalent formulations.

It is important that you learn **both** versions of the principle.

Version 1   A frame of reference accelerating with acceleration a in outer space (i.e. far from all masses) is equivalent to a frame of reference that is at rest in a gravitational field of field strength $g = a$.

Version 2   An inertial frame of reference moving at constant velocity in outer space (i.e. far from all masses) is equivalent to a frame of reference that is falling freely in a gravitational field.

The diagram shows an example. If you drop an object in Frame 2 it will fall to the floor because of gravity.

If you drop the same object in Frame 1 it will also appear to fall to the floor because the floor is accelerating upwards.

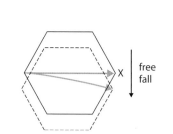

Two consequences of the equivalence principle

1 Bending of light

Consider a box that is **freely falling** in a gravitational field. A ray of light that is emitted from the left wall of the box will travel on a straight line and hit the right wall at a point (X) according to an observer inside the box (path of light shown by the yellow line).

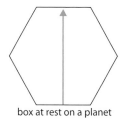

But the box is also seen to be falling by an observer outside. By the time the light ray goes across, the box has fallen and so the ray appears to be following the curved path shown in blue. Thus the outside observer claims that **in a gravitational field, light bends** towards the mass causing the field.

2 Gravitational redshift

The first diagram shows a box at rest on a planet. The second diagram shows a box accelerating in empty space. A ray of light is emitted from the base of the box. To observers outside, the top of the box is moving away from the light and so the frequency measured at the top will be less than that emitted, according to the Doppler effect. Hence a ray of light rising in a gravitational field will have its frequency reduced.

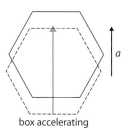

box at rest on a planet

box accelerating

Gravitational time dilation – HL

You must be prepared to use the equivalence principle in order to **deduce** the bending of light in a gravitational field, gravitational redshift and gravitational time dilation.

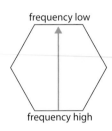

frequency low

frequency high

We have learned that a ray of light travelling higher in a gravitational field will have its frequency reduced: the gravitational redshift.

But frequency is the number of wavefronts received per second, so how can the frequency change? The answer has to be that when one second goes by, according to a clock at the base, more than a second goes by, according to a clock at the top, i.e. the equivalence principle predicts **gravitational time dilation**: the interval of time between two events is longer when measured by a clock far from the source of the gravitational field compared to a clock near the source.

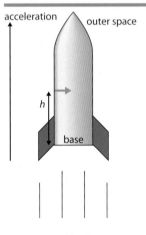

acceleration

outer space

h

base

Test yourself **16**
A rocket accelerates in outer space far from all masses. A ray of light is emitted in a direction that is initially parallel to the base of the rocket from a point a height h from the base. State and explain whether the ray will meet the opposite side of the rocket at a height that is less than, equal to or greater than h.

> **Before you answer**
> Use the equivalence principle to find an equivalent situation where you know the answer.

Test yourself **17**
A ray of light is emitted, initially horizontally, in a lab on Earth of length 300 m. Estimate the amount by which the ray will bend downwards after travelling the length of the lab.

> **Before you answer**
> Use the equivalence principle to find an equivalent situation where you know the answer.

Test yourself **18**
A rocket accelerates in outer space far from all masses.

A ray of light is emitted from the back to the front of the rocket. State and explain whether the observers at the front of the rocket will receive a smaller, equal or higher frequency of light than the emission frequency at the back.

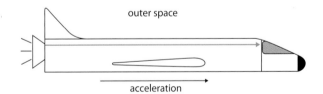

outer space

acceleration

> **Before you answer**
> Use the equivalence principle to find an equivalent situation where you know the answer.

Experimental evidence for general relativity – HL

The bending of light experiment

To test the amount of bending of light by the Sun, an observation was undertaken by A. S. Eddington in an expedition to West Africa in 1919.

A star was observed during a total solar eclipse (the eclipse was needed so that the star could be seen during the day). Rays from the star had to pass close to the Sun and so were slightly bent. This means that the position of the star in the sky appears slightly different than when the star is observed with the Sun out of the way. The measured angle of bending was in agreement with Einstein's theory.

The true position of the star was known from measurements at a time when light from the star reached the Earth without going past the Sun (i.e. 6 months before or after the situation shown in the diagram).

For a ray of light just grazing the surface of the Sun the angle of deviation is only about 4×10^{-4} degrees!

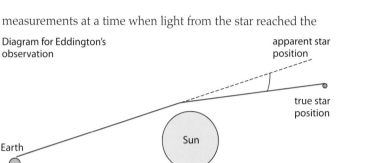

Diagram for Eddington's observation

Gravitational redshift

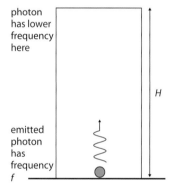

In the Pound–Rebka–Snider gravitational redshift experiment, photons of frequency f emitted on the surface of the Earth are observed a distance H higher, above the Earth's surface. The frequency is predicted to be **less** than the emitted frequency according to: $\frac{\Delta f}{f} = \frac{gH}{c^2}$.

Pound, Rebka and Snider performed experiments (in 1960 and 1964) to verify this relation. For a tower of height $30\,\text{m}$ we have that $\frac{\Delta f}{f} = \frac{10 \times 30}{9 \times 10^{16}} \approx 3 \times 10^{-15}$ so the experiment must be able to measure frequency to 15 decimal places!

The Shapiro time delay test

The two spacecraft are at equal distances from the Earth. Signals are sent to both spacecraft from Earth and their reflections are received back at Earth. The signal to the spacecraft at the right will return to Earth a short time **after** that from the left spacecraft, i.e. with a **time delay**.

The signal to and from the right spacecraft passes near the massive Sun and so suffers a time delay for **two reasons**:

- signal bends
- signal suffers gravitational time dilation.

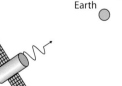

diagram not to scale

Curved spacetime – HL

Spacetime is the four-dimensional continuum (three space and one time) in which physical phenomena take place.

The theory states that four-dimensional spacetime gets curved by the mass and energy it contains.

When space contains no matter or energy it is flat …

… but it curves in the presence of matter or energy. Far from the source, the curvature is less.

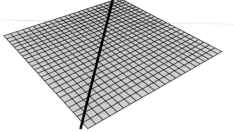

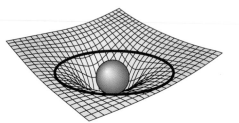

The straight line path shown above is a **geodesic** in flat spacetime, the path followed by an object on which no forces act. The curved line path shown on the right is a **geodesic** in curved spacetime, the path followed by an object on which no forces act. It is the path of least length.

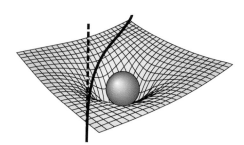

Light travels on geodesics.

Gravitational lensing refers to multiple images of the same object caused by the bending of light by a very massive object in the path of the light.

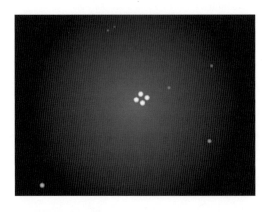

The picture shows four images of the same distant quasar. The images have been formed by light that has bent around the massive galaxy that is directly in front of the quasar and appears at the centre of this picture.

Test yourself **19**
Explain how Newton and Einstein would account for the motion of a planet around the Sun.

Black holes: the extreme prediction of general relativity – HL

A black hole is a 'singularity of spacetime', a point of infinite spacetime curvature.

Nothing taking place within the **event horizon** (a sphere around the black hole of radius equal to the **Schwarzschild radius**) can be communicated to the outside and nothing can move from inside the event horizon to the outside.

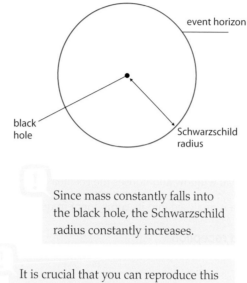

Definition

Schwarzschild radius This is the distance from the black hole where the escape speed is equal to the speed of light: $R_S = \dfrac{2GM}{c^2}$

For the Sun to become a black hole, its radius would have to be smaller than
$$R_S = \frac{2 \times 6.67 \times 10^{-11} \times 2.0 \times 10^{30}}{(3.0 \times 10^8)^2} \approx 3\,\text{km}.$$

Since mass constantly falls into the black hole, the Schwarzschild radius constantly increases.

It is crucial that you can reproduce this calculation for other masses.

Time dilation near a black hole.

This is an example showing that mass bends not just space but also time, i.e. spacetime.

The time interval between two events is measured by a clock near a black hole and by a clock very far from it: the clock near the black hole reads Δt_0 and that far away reads Δt. General relativity predicts that

$$\Delta t = \frac{\Delta t_0}{\sqrt{1 - \dfrac{R_S}{r}}}$$

where r is the distance of the near clock from the centre of the black hole and R_S the Schwarzschild radius of the black hole. As we get close to the event horizon, $r \rightarrow R_S$, $\Delta t \rightarrow \infty$, i.e. it appears to the far away observer that time near the event horizon is stopping. More precisely, according to the clock near the event horizon it takes $\Delta t_0 = 1\,\text{s}$ for the tick of the clock. According to the far away clock very many seconds are needed before the clock ticks again.

Test yourself **20**

A probe near a black hole of Schwarzschild radius $R_S = 5.0 \times 10^8$ m emits one pulse every second. The pulses are received every 5.0 seconds by a spacecraft far away. How far from the event horizon of the hole is the probe?

The parts of the ear and their functions

Definitions

Outer ear Consists of the pinna and the auditory canal ending at the eardrum (tympanic membrane).

Sound incident on the eardrum through the auditory canal forces the membrane to vibrate.

Middle ear With the eardrum at its entrance, the middle ear houses the ossicles. These are small bones that move as result of the vibrations and act as a lever system, amplifying the amplitude of the sound incident on the eardrum.

Inner ear Begins at the oval window and houses the cochlea.

Sound reaching the cochlea is analysed into its component frequencies.

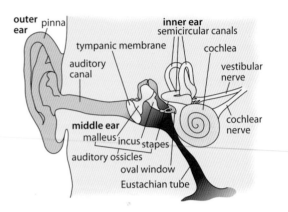

Sound amplification and reception

The action of the ossicles exerts a force on the oval window.

The same **force** acts on the eardrum and the oval window. But because the areas are different, the pressures are different:

$$F = p_1 A_1 \Rightarrow p_1 A_2 = \frac{p_2}{p_1} = \frac{A_1}{A_2}$$

The signal is now in the cochlea of the inner ear. The basilar membrane in the cochlea distinguishes the different frequencies present in the incoming sound and its many nerve endings feed the signal (now as electrical impulses) to the brain.

Mismatch of impedances

The acoustical impedance, Z, of a medium is defined as the product of the speed of sound in the medium multiplied by the medium's density, $Z = \rho c$.

> This material is also relevant for ultrasound imaging – see page 141.

When a wave moves from a medium of impedance Z_1 into a medium of impedance Z_2, the **fraction of the incident intensity that is reflected** is $\left(\frac{Z_1 - Z_2}{Z_1 + Z_2}\right)^2$. So for a wave to enter a new medium with as little reflection as possible, the two media must have very similar impedances.

But the region up to the oval window is filled with air of very low impedance and the region behind the oval window is filled with the cochlear fluid of very high impedance.

This mismatch of impedances means that it is necessary to **amplify** the sound wave arriving at the oval window so that some of it can be transmitted.

Sound intensity level

Intensity of sound The power of a wave (here sound) per unit area.

Sound intensity level, IL Defined in terms of the intensity of sound I and a reference intensity $I_0 = 10^{-12}\,\mathrm{W\,m^{-2}}$ as $IL = 10\log\dfrac{I}{I_0}$. This gives the IL in decibels (dB).

The healthy human ear is sensitive to sounds of a frequency ranging from 20 Hz to 20 kHz.

If the intensity of a sound is doubled, the ear does **not** perceive this change as a doubling in the hearing sensation of the sound, however. Rather, **the ear has a logarithmic response to intensity**: this means that if the intensity of sound increases from I_1 to I_2, the increase in the hearing sensation is $10\log\dfrac{I_2}{I_1}$.

Ordinary conversation IL The IL for ordinary conversation in a room is approximately 60 dB. This corresponds to a sound intensity of $60 = 10\log\dfrac{I}{I_0} \Rightarrow \log\dfrac{I}{I_0} = 6 \Rightarrow \dfrac{I}{I_0} = 10^6 \Rightarrow I = 10^6 \times 10^{-12} = 10^{-6}\,\mathrm{W\,m^{-2}}$.

Pain threshold This happens at a sound intensity of approximately $I = 1.0\,\mathrm{W\,m^{-2}}$ corresponding to an intensity level of $IL = 10\log\dfrac{1.0}{10^{-12}} = 10 \times 12 = 120\,\mathrm{dB}$.

Threshold of hearing The minimum intensity of sound that can be perceived by a person at a given frequency. It depends on frequency according to the graph on the right.

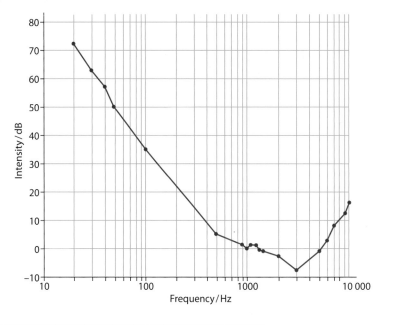

Test yourself 1
A sound is increased in intensity from $1 \times 10^{-6}\,\mathrm{W\,m^{-2}}$ to $2 \times 10^{-6}\,\mathrm{W\,m^{-2}}$. Another sound is increased from $2 \times 10^{-6}\,\mathrm{W\,m^{-2}}$ to $3 \times 10^{-6}\,\mathrm{W\,m^{-2}}$. Would a healthy normal ear perceive the change in loudness in the two cases to be the same or not? Explain your answer.

Test yourself 2
The intensity of a sound increases from $1.0 \times 10^{-10}\,\mathrm{W\,m^{-2}}$ to $1.0 \times 10^{-8}\,\mathrm{W\,m^{-2}}$. By how many decibels does the sound intensity level change?

Test yourself 3
The sound intensity level due to a machine is 95 dB. How many machines must be operating at the same time for the sound intensity level to become 102 dB?

Audiograms and hearing loss

Hearing can be monitored with an audiogram: the patient is supplied with very faint sounds of a specific frequency through earphones and their intensity is increased until they are just audible to the patient. A typical example is the audiogram at the bottom of the page (consider first the data points represented by circles). At a frequency of 1000 Hz, a sound must increase in intensity by 45 dB and by 70 dB at 4000 Hz, if these sounds are to be audible by the patient. This defines what is called a **hearing loss** in dB. At 1000 Hz, therefore, the intensity of sound must be increased (for example by a hearing aid) by a factor of

$$\Delta\beta = 45\,\text{dB} = 10\log\frac{I}{I_o} \Rightarrow I = I_o \times 10^{4.5}$$ where I_o is the intensity prior to amplification.

Definitions

Air conduction   Sound that reaches the inner ear via the outer and middle ears.

Bone conduction   Sound can reach the cochlea through the bones of the head and thus the audiogram is performed not only with earphones but also with an oscillator (placed at the bottom of the skull) that transmits the sound into the bones.

Types of hearing loss

Sensory nerve deafness	Damage to the hair cells in the cochlea and neural pathways to the brain (e.g. due to tumours of the acoustic nerve or meningitis). Audiograms in which the data points for air and bone conduction **almost coincide** are certainly due to **cochlea/nerve** problems in the inner ear.
Conduction deafness	Damage to the middle ear prevents the transmission of sound into the inner ear and the cochlea. This may be due to the plugging of the auditory canal by foreign bodies, such as wax, thickening of the ear drum due to repeated infections, destruction of the ossicles, and too rigid an attachment of the stapes to the oval window.

Exposure to noise and loud sounds

There are short- and long-term effects to exposure to loud sounds. Short-term effects are usually associated with a condition called tinnitus, a 'ringing' sound in the ear. Long-term effects include permanent damage to nerves.

The graph below shows an audiogram for air (circles) and bone (arrows) conduction.

There is a **gap** between the two sets of data points of about 25 dB (at 1000 Hz). This is most likely an indication of a **conduction** hearing problem, the origin of which is in the middle or outer ear.

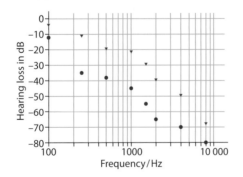

Medical imaging

Definitions

PET scanning (positron emission tomography)   A positron-emitting radioisotope is injected into the patient. The positron produces two photons when it collides with an electron in the patient. The two photons move in opposite directions and can be used to locate the point of emission. By using a radiopharmaceutical that can accumulate in a particular organ, the function of that organ may be monitored.

X-rays   Short wavelength (10^{-10} m) electromagnetic radiation.

Attenuation   The reduction in the intensity of the X-rays transmitted due to absorption and/or spreading of the X-ray beam.

Half-value thickness   The distance after which the intensity of the transmitted X-rays is reduced to half the original intensity. This denoted by $x_{1/2}$.

Attenuation coefficient   The probability per unit length that a particular X-ray photon will be absorbed. This denoted by μ.

Transmitted intensity   X-rays of intensity I_0 are incident on a medium. After travelling a distance x in the medium the intensity of the X-rays is given by $I = I_0 e^{-\mu x}$.

Relation between half-value thickness and attenuation coefficient

When $x = x_{1/2}$, $I = \dfrac{I_0}{2}$ and so substituting in $I = I_0 e^{-\mu x}$ we find $\dfrac{I_0}{2} = I_0 e^{-\mu x_{1/2}}$ and so $\dfrac{1}{2} = e^{-\mu x_{1/2}} \Rightarrow \ln 2 = \mu x_{1/2}$.

> You must be able to derive this relation.

Choice of energy for X-ray imaging

The attenuation coefficients, in general, depend on X-ray photon energy. The choice of energy is dictated by, for example, having the attenuation coefficients for soft tissue and bone to be as different as possible. In this way, a contrast in the images of the bone and the tissue is achieved.

Test yourself 4

The attenuation coefficient for tissue at a particular energy is $0.52\,\text{mm}^{-1}$. Calculate the fraction of X-ray intensity that is transmitted through $1.2\,\text{mm}$ of soft tissue.

Test yourself 5

Two sources of attenuation of X-rays are the photoelectric effect and Compton scattering. The attenuation coefficient for the photoelectric effect depends on the atomic number Z of a sample through $\mu \propto Z^3$ and for Compton scattering μ is independent of Z. Suggest whether the photoelectric effect or Compton scattering is more useful for medical imaging with X-rays.

X-ray imaging and Computed Tomography (CT)

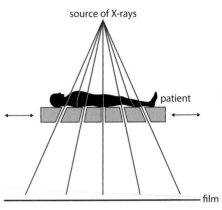

Sharpness of image

The image can be made sharper by having a source of X-rays that is as point-like as possible. The image is also made sharper by preventing stray X-rays scattering through tissue and bone from reaching the photographic film. This is achieved by having metal strips in between the patient and the film that are oriented along the direction of the incident X-ray beam. These block scattered X-rays.

Barium meal

In situations where there is no substantial difference between the attenuation coefficients of different parts of the body, a contrast may be achieved with a barium meal. The patient swallows a quantity of barium, which absorbs X-rays more strongly than the tissue surrounding the intestinal tract.

Intensifying screens

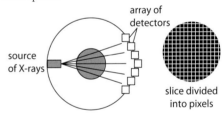

X-rays need considerably longer times to expose photographic film than visible light and this means that the exposure of the patient to X-rays can be long. To reduce this, intensifying screens are used: the X-rays incident on the screens cause visible light to be emitted and this light can then be used to expose photographic film.

Computed Tomography (CT)

In CT, X-rays are directed at the patient through a horizontal plane and the transmitted radiation is detected on the opposite side. Each horizontal 'slice' is divided up into a large number of pixels and a computer reconstructs the amount of radiation absorbed in each pixel. In this way an image of the slice is constructed. The procedure is repeated for other slices of the body so that a three-dimensional image is obtained. A computer can then rotate the image so it can be seen from various angles.

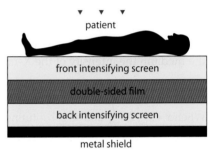

A CT image is thus superior to the plain two-dimensional images obtained with ordinary X-ray imaging techniques and also produces images much faster (which can be critical in the case of an accident).

Test yourself 6

The graph shows the variation of the linear absorption coefficient μ of soft tissue with X-ray photon energy E. **a** Define linear absorption coefficient μ. **b** To obtain an X-ray image in soft tissue, X-rays of energy 50 keV are being used. Use the graph to state and explain whether any significant change will occur to the quality of the image if low-energy X-rays are filtered out. **c** Calculate the fraction of the incident intensity that is transmitted through 2.2 mm of soft tissue for X-rays of energy 50 keV.

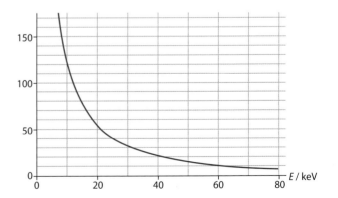

Ultrasound

Ultrasound is sound of frequency higher than the 20 kHz limit of the human ear.

Typically, ultrasound for medical uses has a frequency in the MHz region.

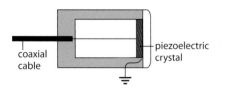

Ultrasound is produced by crystals that are subjected to an **alternating voltage** that forces the crystal to vibrate and emit ultrasound in a phenomenon known as **piezoelectricity**.

Resolution

Definitions

Impedance matching   In using ultrasound a gel-like substance is placed on the patient's skin between the skin and the probe. The gel has an impedance close to that of tissue and so most of the ultrasound gets transmitted into the body rather than being reflected. The ultrasound that enters the body gets reflected off organs and can also exit the body so it can be picked up by a detector.

> It is important to point out the need for gel for ultrasound both entering and exiting the body.

A-scan (Amplitude modulated)   An A-scan is a map of the intensity of the reflected ultrasound signal from the skin and various organs inside the body.

An ultrasound pulse is directed at the body by placing a transducer (a probe) on the skin. There are reflected pulses from various interfaces in the body. In the diagram, the first pulse is reflection from the skin. The next two are from the front and the back surface of an organ. The last is from bones in the skeleton. The diagram is actually a graph of the strength of the reflected signal versus time. The fact the signal strength decreases is a sign of attenuation (absorption of energy by the body). (The last signal is large because there is little attenuation by the bones.)

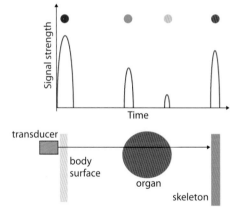

B-scan (Brightness modulated)   In the A-scan above, the signal strength may be converted to a dot whose brightness is proportional to the signal strength. We now imagine a series of transducers along an area of the body.

Putting together the images (as dots) of each transducer forms a **two-dimensional image** of the surfaces that cause reflection of the ultrasound pulses. This creates a B-scan.

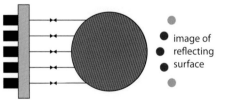

Test yourself **7**
Explain why in ultrasound imaging pulses rather than continuous waves of ultrasound are emitted by the transducer.

NMR and lasers

Nuclear magnetic resonance imaging or MRI

In this imaging technique, the patient is not exposed to any harmful radiation, which is a big advantage of nuclear magnetic resonance imaging (MRI) over CT scanning. Other advantages include obtaining high-quality images without contrast agents and the ability to image any cross-section of the body. A disadvantage is the high cost of installation.

The method is based on the fact that protons have a property called spin. The proton's spin will align parallel or anti-parallel to a magnetic field and the energy of the proton will depend on whether its spin is **up** (i.e. parallel to the magnetic field) or **down** (opposite to the field). The state with spin up has a lower energy than that of spin down. The **difference** in energy depends on the magnetic field strength.

Uniform magnetic field separates spin up from spin down states

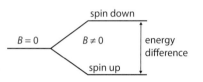

The patient is placed in an enclosure that creates a very **uniform** magnetic field throughout the body. A source of radio frequency forces protons with spin up to make a transition to a state with spin down. As soon as this happens the protons will make a transition back down to the spin up state, emitting a photon in the process.

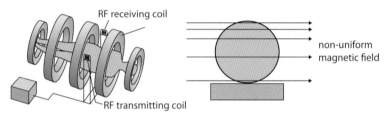

Non-uniform field required

The idea is to detect these photons and correlate them with the point from which they were emitted.

This is done by exposing the patient to an **additional non-uniform** magnetic field. Since the difference in energy for spin up and down states depends on the magnetic field strength, only those protons in regions where the magnetic field has the 'right' value will be absorbed and so it is possible to determine where these photons have been emitted from.

Lasers in medicine

Pulse oximetry

This technique measures the amount of oxygen that is absorbed in the haemoglobin of blood.

A source of laser light at two different wavelengths is placed at the finger or ear lobe of the patient (thin parts of the body so the light can be received on the other side). The transmitted light is detected. The amount of absorption at the two wavelengths chosen is different for blood with lots of oxygen so the ratio of absorption gives a measure of the oxygen in the blood.

The laser as a scalpel

A laser beam can be made very thin and so when it is focused on a tiny spot a large intensity of light is achieved. This can be used to vaporise tissue.

The advantages over an ordinary scalpel are that there is less bleeding and less damage to nerve cells. This results in less pain to the patient during the recovery period after an operation.

Endoscopy

The laser can be directed to the required spot via a thin tube that can be inserted into the patient through the mouth or an artery. The patient no longer has to be opened up for the operation. The surgeon monitors the procedure via an endoscope, an optical fibre through which the laser light is transmitted.

Radiation in medicine

Definitions

Physical half-life   The time for the activity of the radioisotope in the body to be reduced by half through the physical process of radioactive decay as discussed in Topic **7**. This is denoted by T_P.

Biological half-life   The time for the activity of the radioisotope in the body to be reduced by half through biological processes such as sweating, urinating, etc. This is denoted by T_B.

Effective half-life   The time for the activity of the radioisotope in the body to be reduced by half through both physical and biological processes. This is denoted by T_E and it is related to the physical and biological half-lives through the equation $\frac{1}{T_E} = \frac{1}{T_P} + \frac{1}{T_P}$. (This implies $\lambda_E = \lambda_P + \lambda_B$)

Absorbed dose   The energy absorbed per unit mass of material: $D = \frac{E}{m}$. It is measured in joules per kilogram and this unit is called the gray, Gy.

Quality factor (relative biological effectiveness)   A numerical factor that is a measure of the relative damage done by different radiations of the **same energy**.

Dose equivalent   The energy absorbed per unit mass of material multiplied by the quality factor for the radiation involved: $H = QD = \frac{QE}{m}$. It is measured in joule per kilogram and this unit is called the sievert, Sv.

> The sievert and the gray are both joules per kilogram, but are different!

Exposure   The amount of positive charge per unit mass, created as a result of ionisation: $E = \frac{q}{m}$. It is measured in coulombs per kilogram, $C\,kg^{-1}$.

> Exposure is a technical term – it does not mean the time that you are exposed to radiation!

Balanced risk   A patient who exposes himself to radiation for either diagnostic purposes (teeth X-rays, broken bone X-rays, CT scan, etc.) or therapeutic purposes (cancer radiation treatments) faces a risk. The patient must weigh this risk against the possibly much more dangerous consequences of what might happen if this risk is not taken.

Protection from radiation

The general rules are:
- keep the exposure time to radiation as short as possible
- keep the absorbed dose as little as possible
- stay away from radiation sources as far as possible
- use shielding as much as possible.

Test yourself **8**
A patient is injected with a gamma ray emitter. The radiation from the source creates an exposure in the body of $6.9 \times 10^{-3}\,C\,kg^{-1}$. The average energy required to singly ionise an atom in the human body is approximately $40\,eV$ and the quality factor for gamma radiation is 1. Calculate the dose equivalent received by the patient.

Test yourself **9**
A patient of mass 70 kg is injected with a quantity of technetium for diagnostic purposes. The average activity of technetium during the five hours it remains in the body of the patient is 380 MBq. Technetium decays by gamma photon emission. The energy of each of the photons emitted is 140 keV.

a Explain why, for diagnostic purposes, radioisotopes which are gamma emitters are preferable to alpha or beta emitters. **b** Calculate the dose equivalent received by the patient.

Test yourself **10**
An isotope has a physical half-life of 2 days and a biological half-life of 4 days. Calculate the activity 4 days later as a fraction of the initial activity.

Radiation therapy for cancer

Definition

Radiopharmaceutical targeting A chemical compound that can be used to carry a radioactive isotope to the precise location of the tumour.

Radiation can be used for **diagnostic** purposes but also to **cure** cancer. Cancerous cells are more vulnerable to radiation, especially when they are dividing. Also, the rate of repair of cancerous cells is lower than that of healthy cells.

The idea is to direct a beam of X-rays or gamma rays at a tumour and destroy it. The difficulty is that healthy cells are also exposed to radiation that may damage them. This is avoided with fine beams that enter the patient from different directions and overlap at the position of the tumour. In this way healthy cells receive less radiation than those in a tumour.

If possible, the tumour may be injected with alpha or beta emitters, destroying it from within.

A common isotope used for treatment is iodine-131 (a gamma ray emitter). It is used mainly for problems with the thyroid gland. The thyroid needs iodine to produce the hormone thyroxine. Little iodine is found naturally in the body so radioactive iodine injected in the body will collect at the thyroid gland. This isotope can destroy cancerous thyroid gland cells or, in lesser quantities, reduce the activity of the gland.

Comparing diagnostic to therapeutic uses

Diagnostic	Therapeutic
Generally, we require short half-life isotopes for diagnosis to minimise the damage done to the patient.	For therapeutic purposes X-rays and gamma rays are used.
We need gamma emitters so that the rays can be detected outside the body without being absorbed.	If isotopes are used to produce the gamma rays, we need longer half-life isotopes that can sustain a high activity within the body so that cancerous cells will be destroyed.
Commonly used isotopes include the gamma emitters technetium-99, cobalt-60, iodine-123 and iodine-131.	Alpha and beta emitters may also used (within the tumour) as well as gamma rays (from outside).

Test yourself **11**
A volume of 10 cm^3 of albumen containing a sample of technetium-99 is injected into the bloodstream of a patient. A 5.0 cm^3 sample taken from the blood of the patient some time later has an activity of 120 kBq. Another 10 cm^3 of albumen is mixed with 5.0×10^3 cm^3 of water. A volume of 5.0 cm^3 of this mixture has an activity of 125 kBq. Estimate the volume of blood in the patient.

The standard model

The currently accepted model of particle interactions is called the **standard model**. The model assumes that the **elementary particles**, i.e. the particles that are not made out of smaller constituents, belong to three different classes. They are the **quarks**, the **leptons** and the **exchange particles**. The exchange particles are associated with the four fundamental interactions (forces) of nature and they will be discussed separately later on. In addition, there is also the **Higgs particle**, which will be discussed separately later on in the AHL material.

Quarks – SL Option D and HL

Definitions

Quarks   Elementary particles which combine to form a class of particles called **hadrons**. Quarks combine in two ways.

Hadron   A particle made of quarks. There are two kinds of hadrons: baryons and mesons.

Baryon   A type of hadron consisting of three quarks. Protons and neutrons are typical baryons: proton = uud, neutron = ddu.

Meson   A type of hadron made of one quark and one antiquark.

Colour   Quarks have a fundamental property called colour. There are three colours for quarks: red, green and blue. (These have nothing to do with ordinary colour!) The colour of an antiquark may be described as antired, antiblue and antigreen.

In this book we will denote antiquarks with circles with a line through.

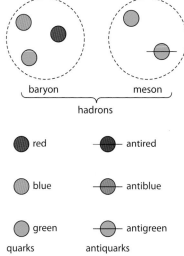

Confinement

Quarks cannot be observed as isolated free particles and so colour cannot be observed directly. The hadrons that quarks form always appear as **combinations with no colour**. For example, a proton consists of 2u quarks and 1d quark. The colour quantum numbers of the three quarks cannot be anything other than the colourless combination R(ed)G(reen)B(lue). We cannot have a proton whose quarks have colours, e.g. RRG or BBB. Similarly, the quarks in the meson $\pi^+ = u\bar{d}$ must have colours that are, e.g. R$\bar{R}$, but never R$\bar{G}$ or B$\bar{R}$.

Will energy liberate a quark?

If enough energy is supplied to a hadron, won't it be possible to remove a quark and so observe colour?

No, the supplied energy would increase the separation of the quarks but to increase it any further would require too much energy. Instead, a quark–antiquark pair is created out of the vacuum.

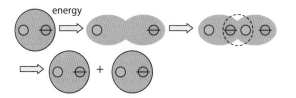

This is like breaking a bar magnet hoping to isolate a magnetic pole. Instead you will only succeed in creating two magnets!

Quantum numbers – SL Option D and HL

Quantum numbers are numbers (or properties) used to characterise particles. They include charge, baryon number, spin, strangeness, lepton number and colour.

Definitions

Charge, Q   We measure charge in units of e (the charge of the proton). Thus, a proton has quantum charge number $Q = +1$ and the neutron has $Q = 0$. The u quark has $Q = +\frac{2}{3}$ and the d quark $Q = -\frac{1}{3}$.

Baryon number, B   All **baryons** are assigned a baryon number B of +1. Thus the proton and the neutron both have $B = +1$. The **meson** $\pi^+ = u\bar{d}$ has $B = 0$ because it is not a baryon.

Spin   A property of particles that is similar, but not identical, to the notion of a ball spinning around its axis.

The spin of particles is measured in terms of $\frac{h}{2\pi}$. We call this combination $\hbar = \frac{h}{2\pi}$ (read 'h bar').

Particles have a spin that is one of these two options:

$$\begin{cases} n\hbar & \text{bosons, (exchange particles, mesons, Higgs)} \\ (n+\frac{1}{2})\hbar & \text{fermions (electrons, neutrinos, baryons)} \end{cases}$$

where n is an integer.

Baryons are made out of three quarks and so their spin can be $\frac{3}{2} \times \hbar$ (all three spin up) or $\frac{1}{2} \times \hbar$ (two spin up and one spin down).

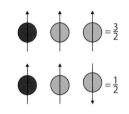

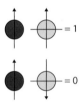

Mesons are made out of a quark and an antiquark and so their spin can be $1 \times \hbar$ (both spin up) or 0 (one spin up and one spin down).

Strangeness, S   A quantum number that applies only to hadrons. For every strange quark in a hadron we assign a strangeness quantum number of −1. For every antistrange quark we assign a strangeness of $S = +1$. Thus $\pi^+ = u\bar{d}$ has $S = 0$, $\Sigma^+ = uus$ has $S = -1$ and $\Xi^+ = \overline{dds}$ has $S = +1$.

Lepton number, L   A quantum number that applies to leptons only. Each lepton is assigned a lepton number of +1. Thus the electron and the neutrino both have $L = +1$.

Note: for Higher Level you will need to know more about lepton number. See HL material on page 153.

Antiparticles   To every particle there corresponds an antiparticle of the same mass as the particle but with **opposite electric charge** (and opposite any other quantum number). But some particles are their own antiparticle, e.g. the photon and the graviton.

> Particles that are their own antiparticles are therefore necessarily electrically neutral.

Conservation laws   In interactions between particles, various quantum numbers are conserved i.e. they have the same value before and after the interaction. The quantum numbers electric charge, baryon number, lepton number and colour are always conserved in all interactions in addition to energy and momentum. An important exception is strangeness that is conserved in the electromagnetic and strong interactions but not in the weak interaction.

> This is very important for examinations.

Test yourself **1**
State and explain whether the neutral K meson, $K^0 = d\bar{s}$, can be its own antiparticle.

The Pauli and Heisenberg principles – SL Option D and HL

Definitions

The Pauli principle   It is impossible for two **identical fermions** (particles with half integral spin) to occupy the same quantum state.

The quantum property **colour** was introduced because of the baryon with spin $\frac{3}{2}\hbar$ consisting of three identical u quarks in the same quantum state. This would violate the Pauli principle. To save the situation, colour was introduced to **distinguish** the three, otherwise identical, u quarks.

The Heisenberg uncertainty principle for time and energy

This principle is expressed in the equation $\Delta E \Delta t \geq \dfrac{h}{4\pi}$. In an interaction the total energy after the interaction may be larger than the energy before by an amount ΔE, i.e. energy conservation is violated(!), provided the process does not last longer than a time interval Δt given by $\Delta t \approx \dfrac{h}{4\pi\Delta E}$. In other words, energy conservation may be violated provided the time it takes for that to happen is not too long.

The vacuum in quantum physics

In classical physics the term **vacuum** applies to space in which there is no matter or radiation or energy. But in quantum theory the 'vacuum' is a completely different thing.

An electron that enters a region that is empty of other matter and energy (the classical vacuum) will be involved in energy-violating processes lasting for very short times. These processes involve emitting and reabsorbing photons.

Interactions – SL Option D and HL

There are three fundamental interactions in nature, in addition to gravitation:

Interaction	electromagnetic	weak	strong
Relative strength (at low energies) (HL only)	10^{-2}	10^{-6}	1
Exchange particle(s)	photon	Z^0, $W^\pm$	gluons
Basic Feynman diagram for interaction	The solid lines represent charged particles.	The solid lines represent leptons or quarks.	

The weak and strong interactions have many other interaction diagrams but in an exam these will be given if necessary.

Test yourself **2**

The reactions below do not take place because they violate one or more conservation laws. Which ones?

a $p \rightarrow e^- + \gamma$ **b** $p \rightarrow \pi^- + \pi^+$ **c** $n \rightarrow p + e^-$ **d** $e^- + e^+ \rightarrow \gamma$ **e** $e^+ \rightarrow \mu^+ + \nu_\mu$ **f** $p \rightarrow n + e^+ + \nu_e$

Test yourself **3**

The $\Sigma^+ =$ uus decays into a neutron and a positive pion ($\pi^+ = u\bar{d}$): $\Sigma^+ \rightarrow n + \pi^+$. **a** State and explain whether the interaction involved is strong, weak or electromagnetic. **b** Draw a Feynman diagram for this process. (See page 148 if you are still unsure about Feynman diagrams.)

Feynman diagrams – SL Option D and HL

Feynman introduced a pictorial way of viewing particle interactions. He noticed that every conceivable interaction in electromagnetism can be constructed out of **just one** basic **interaction vertex**, shown here.

The first diagram says that an electron (solid line) emits a photon (wavy line). The electron changes direction slightly as a result of this emission.

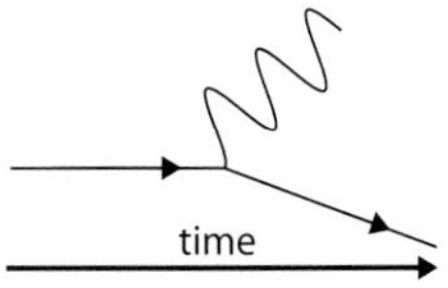

The second diagram shows what happens when two such interaction vertices are put together.

This is interpreted as two electrons exchanging a photon. Both electrons change momentum as a result of this exchange. But the change of momentum of the two electrons is classically explained by saying that there is force between them. Feynman interprets this 'force' to be just the exchange of the photon.

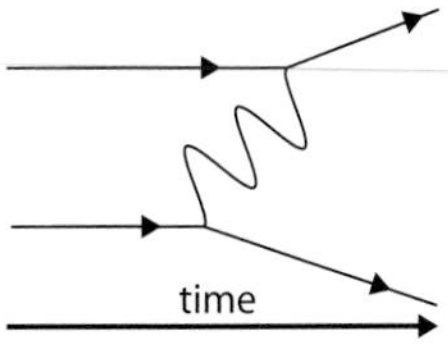

The third diagram shows another way of drawing the basic interaction vertex.

This is interpreted as an electron absorbing a photon.

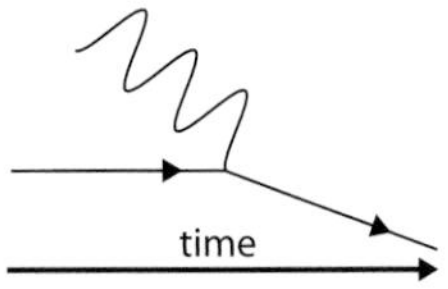

Feynman realised that he could represent antiparticles by lines with arrows pointing opposite to the direction of time.

This diagram shows a positron emitting a photon:

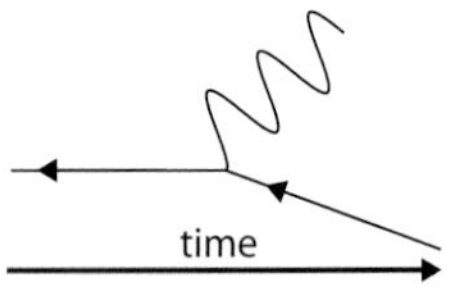

This diagram represents a positron absorbing a photon:

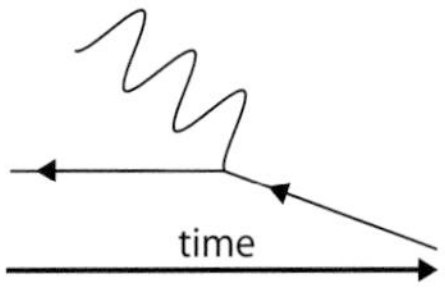

By drawing the vertex as in the last diagram we have the interpretation of a collision between an electron and a positron into a photon. This is called pair annihilation.

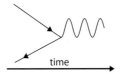

Finally, putting two copies of the last diagram together we get a fascinating possibility. It says that an electron can collide with a positron and produce another electron–positron pair.

But notice that we do not necessarily have to have an electron and a positron in the final state. Any quark or lepton pair with electric charge will do, for example a u quark and a u antiquark, or a c quark and an a antiquark, or a muon and an antimuon.

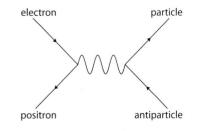

Test yourself **4**
A neutral meson consisting of a charmed and an anticharmed quark decays into two photons. Construct a Feynman diagram for the process.

Test yourself **5**
Construct a Feynman diagram for the process $e^- + e^+ \rightarrow e^- + e^+ + e^- + e^+$.

Test yourself **6**
Use one of the basic interaction vertices for the weak interaction to draw a Feynman diagram for the decay of a neutron into a proton by beta decay.

Virtual particles and gluons – SL Option D and HL

Definition

Virtual particles These appear in intermediate states in Feynman diagrams, are unobservable and temporarily violate energy conservation.

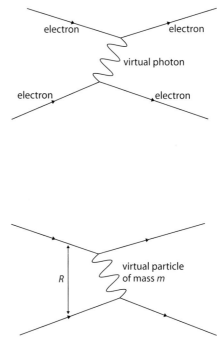

The Feynman diagram shows two electrons exchanging a photon. The photon is said to be **virtual**.

When the electron emits the photon, the law of conservation of energy is actually violated. It cannot take place unless the photon that is emitted is very quickly (i.e. within a time interval $\Delta t \approx \dfrac{h}{4\pi\Delta E}$) absorbed by the other electron so that the energy violation (and the photon itself) becomes undetectable.

The second diagram shows two particles exchanging a virtual particle of mass m. The range of the interaction is given by $R \approx \dfrac{h}{4\pi mc}$.

When the particles are further apart than R, the interaction between them is negligible.

Thus the electromagnetic interaction (which involves the exchange of the massless photon) has an infinite range.

The weak interaction that involves the exchange of (the very) massive W and Z bosons will have a short, finite range. Gluons are special.

Colour for gluons

There are eight gluons. Each carries one colour and one anticolour quantum number. There are six gluons with colour quantum numbers $B\overline{R}$, $R\overline{B}$, $B\overline{G}$, $G\overline{B}$, $R\overline{G}$ and $G\overline{R}$. The other two have colour quantum numbers that need not concern us further.

Colour is conserved: at any one interaction vertex colour is conserved, which means that the net colour entering a vertex equals the net colour leaving.

In the first diagram, red enters; antiblue and blue cancel leaving red as the net colour leaving the vertex.

In the second diagram, red and antigreen enter and the same leave.

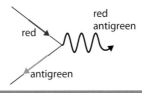

Test yourself **7**
The mass of the W boson is about $80\,\mathrm{GeV}\,c^{-2}$. Estimate the range of the weak interaction.

Test yourself **8**
The strong interaction also has a triple gluon vertex. If a red antiblue gluon joins a green antired gluon, what are the colour numbers of the resulting gluon?

Test yourself **9**
A green strange quark emits a gluon and becomes a red quark. State **a** the flavour (i.e. quark type) of the red quark and **b** the colours of the gluon.

Particle accelerators and detectors – HL

The cyclotron

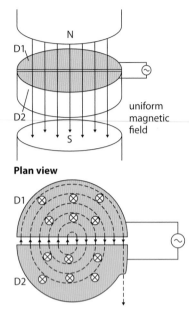

Plan view

Two hollow electrodes (called 'D's) are placed with a gap between them in a uniform magnetic field.

A source of alternating potential difference is established between the two Ds (here labelled D1 and D2).

A particle placed at the centre will follow a semi-circular path until it gets to the gap between the Ds. There it faces a potential difference that accelerates it so that it follows a semi-circular path of larger radius in the opposite D.

The potential difference between the Ds is such that a positively charged particle always sees a negative potential across the gap just as it arrives there. This means that the frequency of the alternating potential difference must be the same as the frequency of revolution of the particles. (This is explained below).

The magnetic force on a particle of charge q travelling with the velocity v is $F = qvB$ and so $qvB = m\dfrac{v^2}{r}$ $\Rightarrow r = \dfrac{mv}{qB}$, where m is the mass of the particle. The time to complete one revolution (the period) is found by using $v = \dfrac{2\pi r}{T}$. Substituting this value of v in the formula above gives $r = \dfrac{m}{qB}\dfrac{2\pi r}{T} \Rightarrow T = \dfrac{2\pi m}{qB}$. So the period of revolution is independent of the speed. This means that despite the fact that the particle is accelerating, the period is the same and only depends on the mass and charge of the particle and the magnetic field. The potential difference between the Ds must then change direction every half a period. Thus, the period of the alternating voltage source is the same as the period of revolution of the particle, i.e. $\dfrac{2\pi m}{qB}$. This is called the **cyclotron period** and its inverse, $\dfrac{qB}{2\pi m}$, is called the **cyclotron frequency**. The charged particle is therefore accelerated as it spirals in the region between the poles of the magnet. At some point additional magnetic fields placed at the edge of the magnetic field region will pull it out and direct it at a target, with which it will collide.

Just as the particle exits the cyclotron it is moving on a circle of radius R, the radius of the cyclotron itself, with the maximum speed it can attain, v_{max}. Thus, $R = \dfrac{mv_{max}}{qB} \Rightarrow v_{max} = \dfrac{qBR}{m}$ and so the maximum kinetic energy is $K_{max} = \dfrac{1}{2}mv^2_{max} = \dfrac{q^2B^2R^2}{2m}$.

Advantages of cyclotron	Disadvantages of cyclotron
• cheap, small, compact, ideal for medical research	• for fixed-target experiments only • limited energy due to limitations of magnet size

---

Test yourself **10**

A cyclotron has a radius of 0.25 m and uses a magnetic field of strength 1.4 T. It accelerates protons.
a Calculate the frequency with which the protons spiral in the cyclotron. **b** What is the kinetic energy of the protons as they leave the cyclotron?

The linear accelerator (linac) – HL

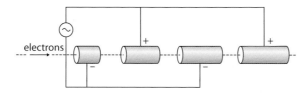

In a linac, the acceleration takes place in between the cylindrical electrodes. Electrons, for example, face a positive potential at the next electrode every time they reach the gap. The electrodes must get longer as the speed increases since the particles can then cover a longer distance in the same time.

Advantages of linac	Disadvantages of linac
• relatively 'simple' machines • synchrotron radiation is limited	• need a very long linac to achieve high energies • cannot alter the collision time once experiment starts

The synchrotron

In a synchrotron, particles follow circular paths of fixed radius. This means the magnetic fields must get stronger as the speed of the particles increases. Particles travel in bundles and another set of particles or antiparticles is made to move in the opposite direction. At the collision points, the bundles smash into each other.

Particles are accelerated by electric fields in the **radio frequency cavities** in between the gaps in the magnets.

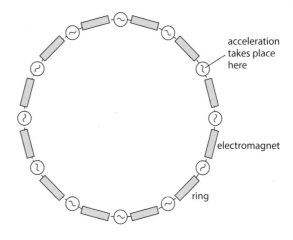

The Large Hadron Collider (LHC) at CERN accelerates protons to an energy of 7 TeV. When these collide with another beam of protons also at 7 TeV the available energy is 14 TeV, corresponding to a temperature of about 10^{16} K (see page 155). This is the temperature the Universe had 10^{-9} s after the Big Bang.

It is hoped that the LHC will discover the Higgs particle as well as **supersymmetric** particles predicted by string theories.

Advantages of synchrotron	Disadvantages of synchrotron
• very high energies can be reached • collisions are controlled	• complex machines • a very large proportion of the energy is lost to synchrotron radiation • low probability of collisions

Detectors – HL

The photomultiplier

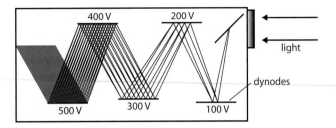

Radiation produced by particles incident on a metallic surface creates a small current (electron emission). The current is made larger by a series of dynodes of increasing potential until it is large enough to be measured. The measured current is proportional to the intensity of the radiation.

The bubble chamber

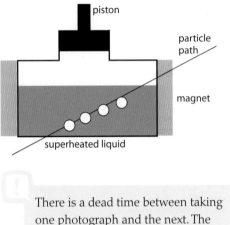

The temperature at which a liquid boils depends on pressure. In a bubble chamber a liquid is kept at a temperature just below its boiling point. The pressure is then **reduced** and the liquid just begins to boil. A charged particle moving through the liquid collides with liquid molecules and creates ions along its path. Bubbles in the liquid will **form along the path**.

A photograph thus reveals the path of the particle. (The pressure is immediately increased to prevent total boiling of the liquid.)

Magnets bend the path of the particle and measurement of the radius of the path gives information on the momentum of the particle.

> There is a dead time between taking one photograph and the next. The analysis of the photographs is very tedious and time consuming.

The (proportional) wire chamber

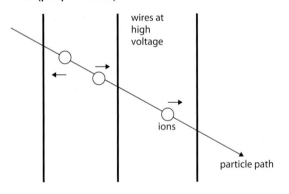

A charged particle will ionise a gas through which it passes. In the proportional wire chamber, a high potential difference is kept between wires in a fine mesh immersed in a gas. The ions and electrons produced by a charged particle travelling through the gas will **drift** towards the nearest wire, where their arrival time can be recorded with great accuracy **because their speed is accurately known**. A series of many meshes at various angles to each other can then reconstruct the path of the particle.

> The great advantage of the proportional wire chamber is that no photographs need to be taken as the data is digitised and can be analysed by computers.

Available energy – HL

According to relativity the total energy E of a particle of rest mass m consists of the rest energy and the kinetic energy: $E = mc^2 + E_K$.

Centre of mass collisions

The particles approach each other with equal and opposite momentum. Each has a total energy E. The total momentum is zero.

The total energy before collision is $2E$. All of this energy is available to produce new particles. If the collision produces a particle–antiparticle pair, the largest mass the particle can have is given by $2E = 2Mc^2 \Rightarrow M = \dfrac{E}{c^2}$

This happens when the pair is produced at rest. We have no kinetic energy and we just produce the rest energies of the pair. This is possible because the initial momentum before the collision is zero. Producing the pair at rest also has zero momentum.

Stationary target collisions

Here one particle is a stationary target. The total energy of the incoming particle is E. The total momentum is non-zero in the lab.

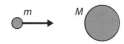

m = mass of incoming particle
M = mass of target particle

The point here is that, unlike above, **not all** of the energy E can be used to produce the rest energy of new particles. This is because we have non-zero momentum before the collision and so we must have non-zero momentum after. This means that some energy will go towards the kinetic energy of the produced particles **leaving less energy for the rest energy of the new particles**.

To just produce new particles, the total energy E of the incoming particle must satisfy $E_A^2 = 2Mc^2E + (Mc^2)^2 + (mc^2)^2$, where E_A (called the available energy) is the **sum of the rest energies of the produced particles**.

Test yourself 11

An electron of total energy E collides with an electron at rest. As a result of the collision three electrons and one positron are produced. **a** Draw a Feynman diagram for this process. **b** Calculate the minimum kinetic energy for this to happen. (Rest mass of electron = $0.511\,\text{MeV}\,c^{-2}$.)

Test yourself 12

A pion of total energy E collides with a proton at rest according to the reaction $\pi^- + p \rightarrow \Sigma^0 + K^0$. Calculate the minimum E for this to happen. (Rest masses: pion $140\,\text{MeV}\,c^{-2}$, proton $938\,\text{MeV}\,c^{-2}$, sigma $1193\,\text{MeV}\,c^{-2}$, kaon $498\,\text{MeV}\,c^{-2}$.)

More on lepton number – HL

Leptons	L_e	L_μ	L_τ
e^-	+1	0	0
ν_e	+1	0	0
μ^-	0	+1	0
ν_μ	0	+1	0
τ^-	0	0	+1
ν_τ	0	0	+1

There is a separate lepton number defined for every generation of leptons, as listed in the table. Generation lepton number is conserved. Anti-leptons have negative lepton number.

Test yourself 13

The reaction $\mu^- \rightarrow e^- + \gamma$ does not occur because conservation laws are violated. **a** Which ones? **b** What is the correct reaction equation for the decay of a muon into an electron?

Test yourself 14

A positive pion decays into an antimuon and a neutrino: $\pi^+ \rightarrow \mu^+ + \nu$. What is the type of the neutrino produced?

The experimental evidence for the standard model – HL

The first diagram shows a low-energy particle (e.g. a photon) directed at a proton. The photon will just 'see' a solid proton volume – it will not be able to probe inside the proton.

Scattering takes place from the entire proton. No quarks are seen.

The second diagram shows a high-energy particle directed at a proton. This will be able to probe inside the proton and see individual constituents in the proton – the quarks.

Scattering takes place from individual quarks.

Deep inelastic scattering experiments

These are experiments in which a large amount of energy and momentum are transferred to a nucleon.

Results of deep inelastic scattering experiments	Further evidence for the standard model
• Quarks loosely bound to each other at high energies – evidence for asymptotic freedom • Existence of three types of colour • Existence of neutral constituents inside nucleons – evidence for gluons	• Discovery of the W and Z bosons • Processes mediated by a Z boson are said to be neutral current processes. These are predicted only by the standard model, so their discovery provided strong evidence for the model.

Asymptotic freedom

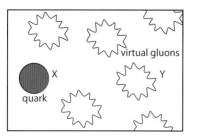

Quarks in a proton are very strongly bound to each other, hence the name 'strong interaction'. However, when a proton is probed by a particle that transfers to the proton large energy and momentum, the quarks inside the proton appear as if they are almost free. This paradoxical situation is called **asymptotic freedom**.

The origin of asymptotic freedom is the fact that **the interaction strength of the colour force is a function of the energy**.

The Higgs particle

The standard model requires the existence of just one more particle in addition to the quarks, leptons and exchange particles we have discussed so far, the Higgs particle. This may be elementary but could conceivably also be composite (of unknown constituents). It is expected that use of the LHC at CERN will answer these questions.

The standard model is a **mathematical theory based on symmetry**. The symmetry of the theory requires that the particles of the model (quarks, leptons and exchange particles) be massless. This is fine for the photon (the electromagnetic interaction has infinite range) but not for the exchange particles of the weak interaction. They must be massive. The Higgs particle achieves the trick of giving masses to some of the particles through their interactions with the Higgs, but at the same time preserving the symmetry of the theory to a sufficient degree for the theory to work.

Applications of particle physics to cosmology – HL

The Boltzmann equation

One of the biggest discoveries of 19th-century physics has been the connection between the average kinetic energy of molecules, $\overline{E}_K$, and the absolute (i.e. in degrees kelvin) temperature T:

$\overline{E}_K = \frac{3}{2}kT$ where k stands for a new constant of physics, the Boltzmann constant.

The Boltzmann constant is $k = 1.38 \times 10^{-23}\,\text{J K}^{-1}$.

Along with the speed of light c, Planck's constant h and Newton's constant of gravitation G, the Boltzmann constant is truly one of the fundamental 'numbers' of physics.

The early universe was very hot

Shortly after the Big Bang, the temperature of the universe was enormous. Going back to a time of $10^{-43}\,\text{s}$ after the Big Bang, the temperature was of order $10^{32}\,\text{K}$. (This time is perhaps the earliest we can extrapolate backwards.)

The temperature today as measured through the cosmic microwave background radiation is only 2.7 K. Boltzmann's equation, $\overline{E}_K = \frac{3}{2}kT$, is of fundamental importance in studies of cosmology and the early universe since the equation sets the order of magnitude of the energy that was available at any given temperature as the universe cooled down as it expanded.

Because we frequently use the formula $\frac{3}{2}kT = E$ to find the temperature corresponding to an amount of energy E, and vice versa, it is useful to remember that a temperature of $10^{10}\,\text{K}$ is equivalent to **approximately** 1 MeV.

$$\frac{3}{2}kT = 1\,\text{MeV}$$
$$T = \frac{2 \times 10^6 \times 1.6 \times 10^{-19}}{3 \times 1.38 \times 10^{-23}}\,\text{K} \approx 10^{10}\,\text{K}$$
$$10^{10}\,\text{K} \Leftrightarrow 1\,\text{MeV}$$

The use of $\overline{E}_K = \frac{3}{2}kT$ gives **only rough estimates**. At any given temperature the equation gives **just** the **average** energy. The particles have a **range** of energies and so there are very energetic particles even at lower temperatures.

Matter and antimatter

The very early universe contained **almost** equal numbers of particles and antiparticles. But today we see matter and not antimatter.

Theory predicts that in the very early universe there was one extra particle for every 10^9 particle–antiparticle pairs. A (virtual) photon can produce an electron–positron pair out of the vacuum if its energy is **at least** the rest energy of each particle (plus any kinetic energy they may have). Therefore the **least** amount of energy that be supplied is $2m_e c^2 = (2 \times 0.511\,\text{MeV}\,c^{-2})c^2 \approx 1\,\text{MeV}$. Using $\frac{3}{2}kT = 1\,\text{MeV} \Rightarrow T = \frac{2 \times 10^6 \times 1.6 \times 10^{-19}}{3 \times 1.38 \times 10^{-23}}\,\text{K} \approx 10^{10}\,\text{K}$. So, at temperatures of $10^{10}\,\text{K}$ and higher, photons could produce electron–positron pairs. The reverse process is always possible regardless of temperature. That is to say, electron–positron collisions produce photons at any temperature. This implies that as the temperature fell below $10^{10}\,\text{K}$, the production of pairs became impossible (because there was not enough available energy) **but the annihilation continued**. Since there was a slightly higher number of particles than antiparticles the matter that is left today is indeed matter and not antimatter.

Test yourself **15**

The nucleus of helium-4 has a binding energy of about 28 MeV. Calculate the temperature at which thermal motion would break the nucleus apart into its constituents.

➡ **Before you answer**
A quick answer is: since $1\,\text{MeV} \Leftrightarrow 10^{10}\,\text{K}$, $28\,\text{MeV} \Leftrightarrow 2.8 \times 10^{11}\,\text{K}$.

String theories – HL

These theories claim that the fundamental building blocks of matter are not point, elementary particles but tiny **strings**. The length of the strings is assumed to be very small (less than 10^{-35} m). The strings could be **open** (i.e. have two ends) or **closed** (i.e. form a loop).

The great promise of string theory was that it would provide, for the first time, a theory of quantum gravitation.

In addition, all the properties of the elementary particles would be explained in terms of strings. The idea was that the string would vibrate much like an ordinary string and 'standing waves' would be formed on the string like the harmonics on ordinary strings. What we normally call particles would then be various special modes of vibration of the string!

This would then be 'the' theory of the interactions in the universe. Unfortunately though, there are now very many possible string theories and only experiment can decide which one might describe the real world (if at all).

How are string theories so different from theories based on particles?

A particle traces out a line as it moves, whereas a closed string traces out a cylinder.

Particles and strings interact differently:

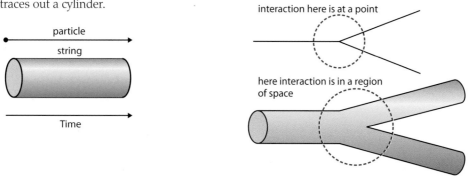

Interactions at a point are problematic because they give rise to infinite energies. For the electromagnetic, weak and strong interactions, physicists were able to solve the problem of interactions at a point (and the infinite energies they created) by a procedure called **renormalisation**. However, the same techniques failed when applied to the gravitational interaction. It was realised that interactions at a point had to be avoided. This could be done with strings.

But there is a very big price to pay by introducing strings!

String theories cannot be formulated in the ordinary four-dimensional world (three dimensions of space and one of time) in which we appear to be living. Various versions of string theories require 10, 11 or 26 dimensions of space and time. So for a theory in 10 dimensions, the extra six dimensions are supposed to be curled up into a compact, tiny space that is essentially unobservable.

Topic 1: Physics and physical measurement

1 The thermometers show two readings of the temperature of a liquid using a Celsius thermometer.

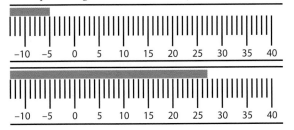

Which of the following is the best estimate of the change in temperature of the liquid?

A $32.0 \pm 1\,°C$ **B** $32 \pm 1\,°C$ **C** $32.0 \pm 0.5\,°C$ **D** $32 \pm 0.5\,°C$

2 The voltage across a resistor was measured to be 898 mV and the current through the resistor was measured to be 0.45 A. The best estimate for the resistance is

A $2.0\,\Omega$ **B** $2\,\Omega$ **C** $1996\,\Omega$ **D** $2000\,\Omega$

3 The volume of a cylinder of base radius R and height H is given by $V = \pi R^2 H$. The percentage uncertainty in the radius is 3% and the percentage uncertainty in the height is 4%. What is the percentage uncertainty in the volume?

A 7%   **B** 10%   **C** 12%   **D** 36%

4 A star has mass 10^{30} kg and it may be assumed that it is made entirely out of hydrogen. What is the order of magnitude of the number of electrons in the star?

A 10^{13} **B** 10^{27} **C** 10^{30} **D** 10^{57}

5 The distance to a star is 10^{17} m. A spacecraft travelling at $\frac{c}{100}$ where c is the speed of light will get to the star in a time of

A 10^8 s   **B** 10^{10} s   **C** 10^{12} s   **D** 10^{23} s

6 The length of rope required to go around the Earth along the equator is about 40 000 km. The **additional** length of rope required to go around the Earth at a vertical height of 1 m **above** the equator is about

A 6 m   **B** 60 m   **C** 600 m   **D** 6000 m

7 This question is about the oscillations of a cantilever.

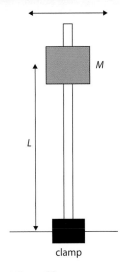

The diagram shows a thin rod clamped to a table and a mass M attached to the rod at a distance L from the base of the rod.

The mass is displaced sideways by a small amount and is then released. A student measures the period of oscillations for different values of the mass M and a fixed value of the length L.

a **i** To measure the period the student times 10 oscillations and, to get the period, divides the answer by 10. Explain why this is preferable to timing just one oscillation. [1]

ii The student repeats the procedure in **i** four times and gets the average of the four periods. Explain the advantage of doing this. [1]

b The graph shows the plotted data obtained by the student.

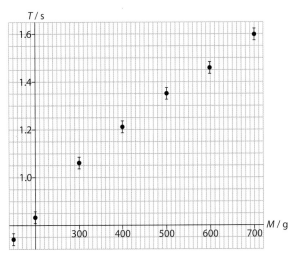

Explain why the data do not support the hypothesis that the period is proportional to the mass. [1]

c The student decides to plot T^2 against the mass, M. This results in the graph where the error bars for only the first and last data points are shown.

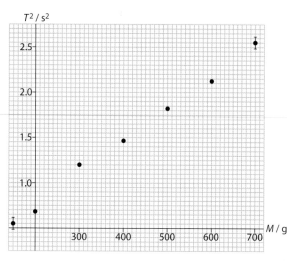

i The uncertainty in the measurement of the period is 0.02 s. Calculate the uncertainty in T^2 for the data point at $M = 400$ g. [2]

ii Copy the graph and draw the line of best fit for these data. [1]

iii Theory suggests that the relation between T (in seconds), M (in grams) and the length L of the rod (in metres) is $T = 0.12\sqrt{ML^3}$. Calculate the length L of the rod including its uncertainty. [4]

Topic 2: Mechanics

1 A body that started from rest moves on a straight line with constant acceleration. After travelling a distance d the velocity becomes v. The distance travelled from when the velocity is v until it becomes $2v$ is

A d **B** $2d$ **C** $3d$ **D** $4d$

2 A ball is dropped from rest. A second ball is dropped from rest from the same height as the first, but 1 s later. What happens to the distance between the balls when both are moving?

A stays the same   **B** keeps increasing
C keeps decreasing   **D** increases then stays constant

3 A rocket is fired vertically upwards. At the highest point it explodes. Which is a correct comparison of the momentum and the kinetic energy of the fragments immediately after the explosion compared to the rocket just before to the explosion?

	Momentum	Kinetic energy
A	same	same
B	same	different
C	different	same
D	different	different

4 Four identical balls are projected from a tower with the same speed but in different directions as shown. Which one reaches the ground with the highest speed? (Assume no air resistance.)

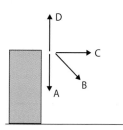

5 The diagram shows two identical containers, X and Y, connected by a very thin tube with a valve. The valve is initially closed. Container X is filled with water of depth h and mass m and container Y is empty. The valve is opened until both containers have equal quantities of water in them.

The gravitational potential energy lost by the water in this process is

A 0   **B** $\dfrac{mgh}{8}$ **C** $\dfrac{mgh}{4}$ **D** $\dfrac{mgh}{2}$

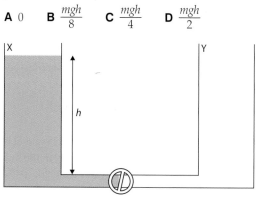

6 a A ball is thrown vertically upwards from the edge of a cliff with a speed of 20 m s^{-1}. It hits the sea below 6.0 s later.

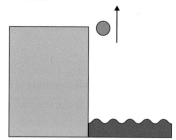

Take $g = 10$ m s^{-2}.

Calculate
i the time it takes the ball to reach its highest point. [2]
ii the maximum height reached by the ball above the cliff. [2]
iii the velocity of the ball as it hits the sea. [2]
iv the height of the cliff above the sea. [2]
v the average velocity and average speed for the motion. [2]

b Sketch graphs showing the variation with time of **i** the velocity, **ii** the speed and **iii** the displacement. [3]

7 A ball of mass 0.20 kg falling vertically collides with the ground. Just before impact its speed is 4.0 m s⁻¹. It rebounds vertically with a speed of 2.5 m s⁻¹. The ball was in contact with the floor for 0.14 s. Calculate

  a the magnitude and direction of the change in momentum of the ball. [2]

  b the magnitude of the average force the ball exerted on the ground. [2]

8 A landing module of mass 250 kg descends towards the surface of a planet. The velocity of the module at time zero is −9.0 m s⁻¹. At time zero the engine is fired for 4.5 s in order to slow down the module. The graph shows how the acceleration of the module varies with time. The module lands 5.0 s after the engine is fired.

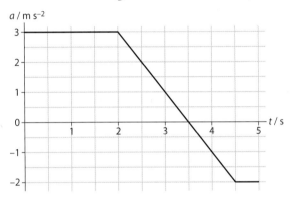

Use the graph to calculate

  a   **i**   the velocity of the landing module at 4.5 s. [2]
      ii   the acceleration of free fall on the planet. [2]
     iii   the force exerted by the engine at 1.0 s. [2]
     iv   the speed with which the landing module impacts the planet. [2]

  b The distance fallen by the landing module while the engine was on is 25 m. Calculate the power delivered to the landing module by the engine. [2]

9   **a** State Newton's second law in terms of momentum. [1]

  b A fan on a cart pushes air to the left with speed *v*.

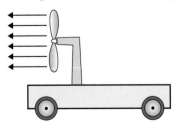

The radius of the blades of the fan is *R* and the density of air is *ρ*.

Show that the net force pushing the cart to the right is $F = \rho\pi R^2 v^2$. Ignore any resistance forces on the cart. [3]

10 A car of weight 1.2×10^4 N climbs up an incline at a constant speed of 12 m s⁻¹. The incline makes an angle 4.0° to the horizontal. A constant frictional force *f* of magnitude 600 N acts on the car in a direction opposite to the velocity.

  a Calculate the minimum power that the engine must develop. [3]

  b The frictional force stays constant but the car now accelerates from rest at 2.0 m s⁻² up the incline. Calculate the power developed after 5.0 s. [2]

11 The force on a particle of mass 0.50 kg varies with time as shown in the graph. The initial velocity is zero.

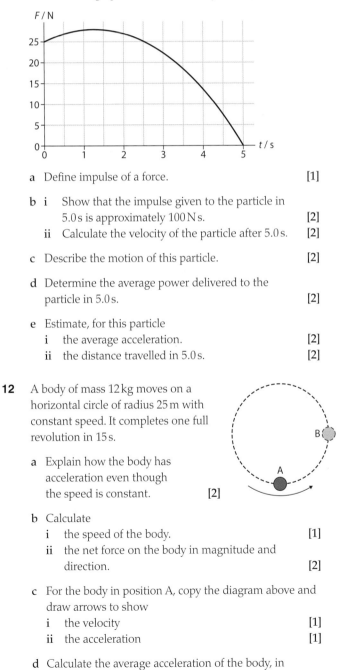

  a Define impulse of a force. [1]

  b   **i**   Show that the impulse given to the particle in 5.0 s is approximately 100 N s. [2]
     ii   Calculate the velocity of the particle after 5.0 s. [2]

  c Describe the motion of this particle. [2]

  d Determine the average power delivered to the particle in 5.0 s. [2]

  e Estimate, for this particle
     i   the average acceleration. [2]
     ii   the distance travelled in 5.0 s. [2]

12 A body of mass 12 kg moves on a horizontal circle of radius 25 m with constant speed. It completes one full revolution in 15 s.

  a Explain how the body has acceleration even though the speed is constant. [2]

  b Calculate
     i   the speed of the body. [1]
     ii   the net force on the body in magnitude and direction. [2]

  c For the body in position A, copy the diagram above and draw arrows to show
     i   the velocity [1]
     ii   the acceleration [1]

  d Calculate the average acceleration of the body, in magnitude and direction, from position A to B. [3]

Exam-style questions

Topic 3:   Thermal physics

1   Two ideal gases, X and Y, are contained at constant temperature. The mass of the atoms of X is m and that of the atoms of Y is $2m$. Which of the following is the correct value of the ratio $\dfrac{\text{average kinetic energy of molecules of Y}}{\text{average kinetic energy of molecules of X}}$?

 A 1   **B** 2   **C** 4   **D** 16

2   Two bodies have the same temperature and they are in contact. Which of the following is a correct statement?

 A   There is no flow of energy between the bodies.
 B   There is no net flow of energy between the bodies.
 C   The bodies must have the same internal energy.
 D   The bodies must have the same heat content.

3   A fixed quantity of an ideal gas is compressed at constant temperature. The reason for the pressure increase is that

 A   the molecules collide with each other more frequently.
 B   the duration of the collisions is shorter.
 C   the molecules collide with the walls more frequently.
 D   the molecules collide with the walls with a greater impact speed.

4   Energy is provided to a liquid at a rate of P joules per second. The rate of increase of temperature with time is r. The mass of the liquid is m. The specific heat capacity of the liquid is

 A $\dfrac{P}{mr}$ **B** $\dfrac{Pr}{m}$ **C** $\dfrac{mr}{P}$ **D** $\dfrac{m}{Pr}$

5   **This question is about thermal contact.**

Two bodies of equal mass and different temperatures and made of different materials are brought into thermal contact.

 a i   State what is meant by thermal contact.   [1]
 ii   State what determines the direction of energy flow between the bodies.   [1]

 b   Discuss, for each body, how the following quantities are related to each other:
 i   the change in internal energy   [1]
 ii   the change in temperature.   [2]

6   **This question is about thermal energy.**

The graph shows the variation with time of the speed of an object of mass 8.0 kg that has been dropped (from rest) from a certain height.

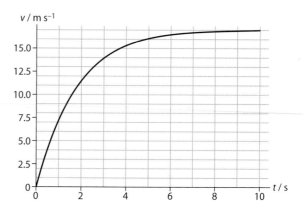

The body hits the ground 10 seconds later. The specific heat capacity of the object is 320 J kg^{-1} K^{-1}.

Use the graph to

 a i   explain why there must be air resistance forces acting on the object.   [2]
 ii   estimate the height from which the object was dropped.   [2]
 iii   calculate the speed the object would have had if there were no air resistance forces.   [2]

 b   Estimate the change in temperature of the body from the instant it was dropped to **just before impact**, listing any assumptions you make.   [4]

7   **This question is about calorimetry.**

A piece of tungsten of mass 50 g is placed over a flame for some time. The metal is then quickly transferred to a well insulated aluminium calorimeter of mass 120 g containing 300 g of water at 22 °C. After some time the temperature of the water reaches a maximum value of 31 °C.

 a   Define specific heat capacity.   [1]

 b   Calculate the temperature of the flame. You may use these values of specific heat capacity: water 4.2 × 10^3 J kg^{-1} K^{-1}; tungsten 1.3 × 10^2 J kg^{-1} K^{-1}; aluminium 9.1 × 10^2 J kg^{-1} K^{-1}.   [3]

 c   State and explain whether the actual flame temperature is higher or lower than your answer to **b**.   [2]

8 This question is about calorimetry.

   a A student claims that the kelvin temperature of a body is a measure of its internal energy. Explain why this statement is **not** correct by reference to
     i a solid melting. [2]
     ii an ice cube and an iceberg both at $0\,°C$. [2]

   b In an experiment, a heater of power $35\,W$ is used to warm $0.240\,kg$ of a liquid in an un-insulated container. The graph shows the variation with time of the temperature of the liquid.

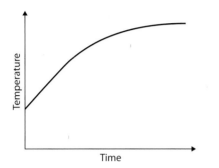

   The liquid never reaches its boiling point.
     i Suggest why the temperature of the liquid approaches a constant value. [2]
     ii After the liquid reaches a constant temperature the heater is switched off. It is measured that the temperature of the liquid decreases at a rate of $3.1\,K\,min^{-1}$.
     Use this information to estimate the specific heat capacity of the liquid. [3]

Topic 4: Oscillations and waves

1 Which of the following graphs shows the correct variation of acceleration with displacement from equilibrium in simple harmonic motion?

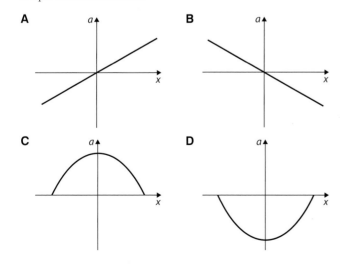

2 A particle undergoes simple harmonic oscillations with amplitude A. The total energy of the particle is E and the period of the oscillations is T. The amplitude of oscillations is reduced to $\frac{A}{2}$. The new total energy and period of the motion are

	Total energy	Period
A	$\frac{E}{2}$	T
B	$\frac{E}{4}$	$\frac{T}{2}$
C	$\frac{E}{2}$	$\frac{T}{2}$
D	$\frac{E}{4}$	T

3 The graph shows the variation with distance of the displacement, at a particular time T, of a transverse wave travelling towards the right.

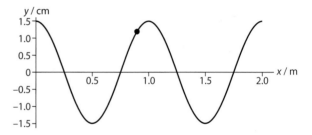

A point on the wave has been marked. The direction of the velocity of this particle at time T is

A →   **B** ←   **C** ↓   **D** ↑

4 The graph in question **3** now represents a longitudinal wave. What is the direction of velocity of the particle shown at time T?

A →   **B** ←   **C** ↓   **D** ↑

5 Consider the following waves.

    I   sound waves
    II gamma rays
    III radio waves
    IV blue light

Which of these are likely to show appreciable diffraction as they pass through an opening of size $1\,m$?

A All   **B** I only   **C** I and III   **D** II and IV

6 A wave of amplitude A, frequency f, wavelength λ and speed v enters a different medium. Which of the following lists contains gives quantities that will change as the wave enters the new medium?

A A, f, v **B** A, λ, v **C** f, λ, A **D** v, λ, f

7 This question is about simple harmonic motion.

a The graph shows the variation with displacement from equilibrium of the kinetic energy of a mass of 0.25 kg that is executing simple harmonic oscillations.

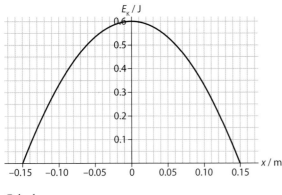

Calculate

i the period of oscillation. [3]

ii the maximum acceleration of the mass. [2]

b Copy the graph above and draw on another graph to show the variation with displacement from equilibrium of the kinetic energy of the same particle when the amplitude is reduced to 0.10 m. [2]

c A car of mass 1200 kg (including passengers) travels on a horizontal road. The effective spring constant of the shock absorbers of the car is $6.0 \times 10^4 \, \text{N m}^{-1}$.

i Calculate the frequency of vertical oscillations of the car. [2]

ii There are bumps on the road separated by 15 m. The car receives a jolt every time it goes over a bump in the road.

Explain why at a speed of about $16 \, \text{m s}^{-1}$ the ride will be especially uncomfortable. [3]

8 This question is about simple harmonic motion.

a A cart is attached to two identical springs as shown in the diagram. The other ends of the springs are attached firmly to vertical walls.

The cart is in equilibrium in the position shown. When the cart is displaced by an amount x (in metres) from its equilibrium position, the acceleration (in m s^{-2}) is given by $a = -39x$.

i State the features of this equation that imply that the oscillations will be simple harmonic. [2]

ii Determine the frequency of the oscillations. [2]

b The cart in **a** is displaced from its equilibrium position by 0.15 m and is released. The mass of the cart is 1.2 kg.

i Calculate the maximum kinetic energy of the cart. [3]

ii Draw a graph to show how the kinetic energy of the cart varies with time. [3]

iii On the graph identify one point where the cart is at its equilibrium position. Label this point E. [1]

c Describe how your graph in **b ii** would change, if at all,

i if the motion of the cart was lightly damped. [2]

ii if the motion was undamped, but the amplitude was increased from 0.15 m to 0.21 m. [2]

d The right spring is now connected to an oscillator of variable frequency.

Draw a sketch graph to show the variation with the oscillator frequency of the amplitude of oscillations of the cart assuming light damping. [3]

9 This question is about waves.

a State the difference between a longitudinal and a transverse wave. [2]

b The graph starting at (0, 4) shows the variation with distance of the displacement of a wave travelling to the right. The graph starting at (0, 0.5) shows the variation with distance of the displacement of the same wave 92 ms later.

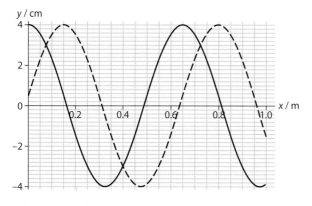

Use the graph to determine for this wave
i   the amplitude. [1]
ii the wavelength. [1]
iii the speed. [2]
iv the frequency. [2]

10 This question is about refraction.

The diagram shows wavefronts of a wave entering a medium B from a medium A.

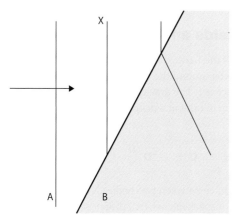

a State what is meant by the term wavefront. [2]

b i Copy the diagram precisely and draw a line to show the extension of wavefront X in medium B. [1]
  ii On your diagram draw a ray for the waves in medium B. [1]
  iii By taking measurements on the diagram, estimate the ratio $\dfrac{\text{wave speed in A}}{\text{wave speed in B}}$. [2]

11 This question is about interference.

a State the principle of superposition. [1]

b Two sources of sound, S_1 and S_2, emit identical waves towards a point P.
  i   Explain what is meant by the path difference of the waves at P. [1]
  ii Discuss the significance of the path difference for the interference of the waves at P. [2]

c The two sources of sound in b are replaced by two identical lasers. State and explain whether an interference pattern will be observed at point P. [3]

Topic 5: Electric currents

1 In the circuit shown an ammeter and a voltmeter have been **incorrectly** connected.

What is the reading of the voltmeter?

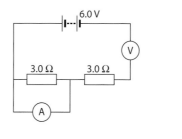

A 0 V   **B** 2.0 V   **C** 3.0 V   **D** 6.0 V

2 The resistance of a cylindrical copper wire is R. The wire is melted and then made into another cylindrical wire of double the length. The resistance of the new wire is

A $\dfrac{R}{2}$ **B** $\dfrac{R}{4}$ **C** $2R$ **D** $4R$

3 The diagram shows part of a potential divider. The potential difference across the two resistors is V.

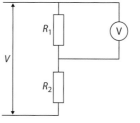

The reading of the ideal voltmeter V is

A $V\dfrac{R_1}{R_2}$ **B** $V\dfrac{R_2}{R_1}$ **C** $V\dfrac{R_1}{R_1+R_2}$ **D** $V\dfrac{R_2}{R_1+R_2}$

4 The diagram shows a circuit including a thermistor and a light-dependent resistor (LDR) connected to a battery of negligible internal resistance.

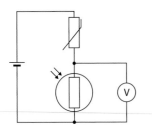

Which of the following changes in the temperature of the thermistor and the intensity of light on the LDR will **definitely** result in an increase of the reading of the voltmeter?

	Temperature	Intensity of light
A	increase	increase
B	increase	decrease
C	decrease	increase
D	decrease	decrease

5 This question is about circuits.

a A battery of internal resistance $0.80\,\Omega$ sends a current of $1.4\,A$ through an external resistor. The work required to push one electron through the external resistor is $7.2 \times 10^{-19}\,J$. Calculate the emf of the battery. **[2]**

b In this circuit the battery has negligible internal resistance.

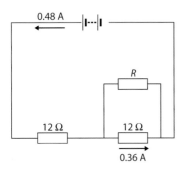

Calculate
i the emf of the battery. **[2]**
ii total power dissipated in the circuit. **[1]**
iii the value of resistance R. **[2]**

6 This question is about electric resistance.

Two devices, A and B, have voltage–current characteristics as shown in the graph.

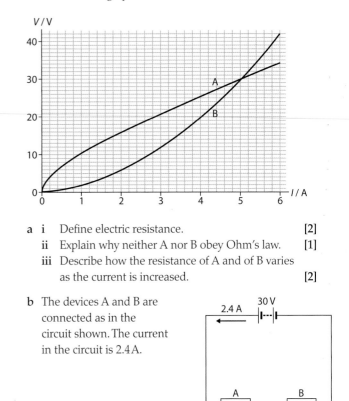

a i Define electric resistance. **[2]**
ii Explain why neither A nor B obey Ohm's law. **[1]**
iii Describe how the resistance of A and of B varies as the current is increased. **[2]**

b The devices A and B are connected as in the circuit shown. The current in the circuit is $2.4\,A$.

i State the voltage across each resistor. **[2]**
ii Calculate the power dissipated in each device. **[1]**
iii Calculate the internal resistance of the battery. **[2]**

Topic 6: Fields and forces

1 The radius of the Earth is R_E. The gravitational force on a satellite in orbit around the Earth a distance of R_E from the Earth's surface is F. The gravitational force on the same satellite when in orbit at a distance of $3R_E$ from the Earth's surface is

A $\dfrac{F}{4}$ B $\dfrac{F}{3}$ C $\dfrac{F}{9}$ D $\dfrac{4F}{9}$

2 The electric force between two bodies X and Y of electric charge q_1, q_2 respectively when a distance r apart is F. The charge q_1 on X is made four times larger. The electric force on X and Y now is

	Force on X	Force on Y
A	F	F
B	$4F$	F
C	F	$4F$
D	$4F$	$4F$

3 Three equidistant, parallel wires, X, Y and Z, carry equal currents into the page as shown. Which arrow shows the direction of the magnetic force on wire Z?

A ↑   **B** →   **C** ←   **D** ↓

4 This question is about electric fields.

a An electron is accelerated from rest by a potential difference of 120 V.

Show that the speed of the accelerated electron is $6.5 \times 10^6 \, \text{m s}^{-1}$. [2]

b The accelerated electron in **a** enters the region between two parallel oppositely charged plates.

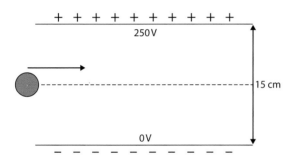

i Copy the diagram and draw an arrow to represent the force on the electron while it is within the plates. [1]

Calculate
ii the electric force on the electron while it is within the plates. [2]
iii the gravitational force on the electron. [2]
iv the ratio of the electric to the gravitational force on the electron. [1]

c It is desired to have the electron move through the plates undeflected from its original path. To do this a magnetic field will be introduced in the region between the plates.
i State and explain the direction of the magnetic field. [2]
ii Calculate the magnitude of the magnetic field strength required. [2]

5 This question is about electric fields.

Two parallel plates have a potential difference *V* across them.

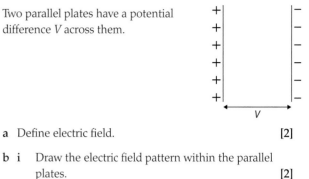

a Define electric field. [2]

b i Draw the electric field pattern within the parallel plates. [2]
ii Draw a sketch graph to show how the force on a proton within the plates varies with distance from the positive plate. [2]

c An electron is placed on the inside of the negatively charged plate and a proton on the positively charged plate.

Calculate the ratio of the kinetic energy of the electron to that of the proton when each particle arrives at the opposite plate. [3]

6 This question is about motion in a magnetic field.

A charged particle of mass $1.67 \times 10^{-27} \, \text{kg}$ and charge of magnitude $1.6 \times 10^{-19} \, \text{C}$ enters a region of magnetic field with speed $4.5 \times 10^6 \, \text{m s}^{-1}$. The magnetic field is directed out of the plane of the page and has magnitude 0.25 T. The particle exits the magnetic field region after it has completed a quarter of a circle.

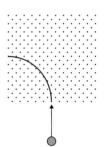

a Suggest the reason why the path of the particle in the region of the magnetic field is circular. [2]

b Determine the sign of the charge of the particle. [1]

c Explain why the speed of the particle is constant. [3]

d Calculate how much time the particle spent in the region of magnetic field. [3]

Topic 7: Atomic and nuclear physics

1 This question is about the Rutherford experiment.

a The diagram shows apparatus used in the Rutherford alpha particle scattering experiment.

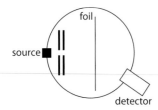

The collimating plates in front of the source ensure that the beam of alpha particles is very narrow.

Explain why
i   the beam must be very narrow. [1]
ii   the foil must be very thin. [2]

b State what the results of this experiment imply about the structure of the atom. [4]

c In the diagram below three alpha particles are approaching a nucleus of the gold isotope $^{197}_{79}$Au. The path of one of the particles is shown.

Copy the diagram and draw lines to show the paths of the other two alpha particles. [2]

d An alpha particle of initial kinetic energy E directed straight at the nucleus stops at a distance d from the centre of the nucleus. The gold nucleus is now replaced by a nucleus of a different gold isotope. An alpha particle of initial kinetic energy E is directed straight at this nucleus. State and explain any change of the distance d. [2]

2 This question is about atomic spectra.

a Outline a laboratory procedure by which an atomic emission spectrum may be observed. [3]

b Describe how the existence of atomic spectra is evidence for atomic energy levels. [2]

c The diagram shows a few atomic energy levels of a hypothetical atom.

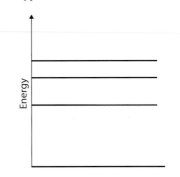

Copy the diagram and draw arrows to indicate the transition with the
i   longest wavelength. [1]
ii   shortest wavelength. [1]

3 This question is about radioactive decay.

a Radioactive decay is said to be **random** and **spontaneous**. Explain what is meant by this statement. [2]

b i   The nucleus of phosphorus-32 ($^{32}_{15}$P) decays by beta particle emission to a nucleus of sulfur (S). Write down the reaction equation for this decay. [3]
   ii The half-life of phosphorus-32 is 14.3 days. Calculate the time after which the ratio of sulfur to phosphorus atoms is 15 : 1. (You may assume that initially no sulfur atoms are present.) [2]

c The following data on atomic masses are available.

phosphorus 3.19739×10^7 u
sulfur 3.19721×10^7 u

Determine the energy released in the decay in **b**. [2]

4   This question is about fission and fusion.

a   Distinguish between fission and fusion. [2]

b   The graph shows the variation with nucleon number of the average binding energy per nucleon.

   i   Describe which region contains the most stable nuclei. [1]
   ii By reference to the binding energy curve explain why energy is released in fission and fusion. [2]

c   Use the binding energy curve to **estimate** the energy released in the fission reaction

$$^{235}_{92}U + ^{1}_{0}n \rightarrow ^{144}_{56}Ba + ^{89}_{36}Kr + 3\,^{1}_{0}n.$$ [2]

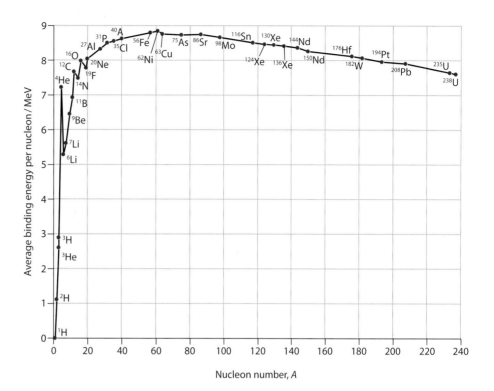

Nucleon number, A

Topic 8:   Energy, power and climate change

1   The power that can be extracted from a wind generator when the wind speed is v is P. Assuming the efficiency stays the same, the power extracted at a wind speed $2v$ is

   A $2P$ **B** $4P$ **C** $6P$ **D** $8P$

2   The percentage of electrical power that is produced through nuclear reactors worldwide is about

   A 3%   **B** 9%   **C** 18%   **D** 24%

3   Some of the solar radiation incident on the Earth is reflected back into space. Most of the reflection comes from

   A the oceans
   B the clouds
   C the greenhouse gases in the atmosphere
   D the deserts.

4   Energy density is defined as

   A the amount of energy that can be extracted from a fuel.
   B the amount of energy that can be extracted from a unit mass of fuel.
   C the amount of power that can be extracted from a fuel.
   D the amount of power that can be extracted from a unit mass of fuel.

5   This question is about a solar panel.

a   It is being considered to use a solar panel to power a pump in order to raise water from a well. The following data are available:

area of panel	$0.016\,m^2$
solar intensity at location of panel	$740\,W\,m^{-2}$
voltage output of panel	24 V
current delivered to pump	0.32 A
efficiency of pump	30%
depth of well	8.0 m

Calculate
   i   the power incident on the panel. [1]
   ii   the electric power delivered to the pump. [1]
   iii the efficiency of the solar panel. [1]
   iv   the rate, in $kg\,s^{-1}$, at which water is being raised from the well. [4]

b   Determine, based on your answer to **a**, whether this is a practical method for raising water out of the well. [2]

6 This question is about wind power.

a Derive the formula for the power generated by a wind generator $P = \frac{1}{2}\rho A v^3$ where ρ is the density of air, A the area swept by the blades of the windmill and v the speed of air. [3]

b The power required by a village is 120 kW. It is proposed to supply this power by a series of windmills. The village proposes to use windmills whose blades have a radius of 5.2 m. The average wind speed in a location near the village is 6.5 m s⁻¹ and the density of air is 1.2 kg m⁻³.

   i Calculate the number of windmills needed to supply the village with electrical power. [3]

   ii State two reasons why in practice more windmills will be needed. [2]

c A village engineer observes that the power supplied by the windmills early in the morning is greater than that at midday even though the wind speed is the same.

   Suggest an explanation of this observation. [2]

7 This question is about the Stefan–Boltzmann law.

a State the Stefan–Boltzmann law and define emissivity. [2]

b A black body of temperature T_1 is surrounded by a body X of emissivity e at a temperature T_2. The arrows in the diagram represent the power of the radiation, per unit area, radiated by the black body, reflected by body X and radiated by body X. (No radiation gets transmitted.)

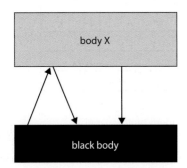

   i State an expression of each of the three intensities in terms of all or some of the symbols e, σ, T_1 and T_2. [3]

   ii Deduce, using your answer to i, that the power per unit area lost by the black body is $e\sigma(T_1^4 - T_2^4)$. [2]

   iii Hence deduce the value of the ratio $\frac{T_1}{T_2}$ given that the black body receives as much power as it emits. [1]

8 This question is about the energy balance of the Earth.

a State the Stefan–Boltzmann law. [1]

b The average distance between the Earth and the Sun is 1.5×10^{11} m. The Sun radiates a total power equal to 3.9×10^{26} W. Show that the intensity of the Sun's radiation at the position of the Earth (the solar constant S) is approximately 1400 W m⁻². [2]

c A student attempts to understand the energy balance of the Earth by making a model that ignores the greenhouse effect. The model may be described by the diagram.

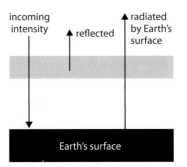

All the reflected radiation is from the atmosphere and the Earth surface may be considered to be a black body.

   i Define **albedo** and **emissivity**. [2]

   ii State two factors that affect the albedo of a planet. [2]

   iii Outline why the incoming intensity averaged over the Earth's surface is $\frac{S}{4}$. [2]

   iv Show that this model requires an Earth surface temperature of $T = \sqrt[4]{\dfrac{(1-\alpha)S}{4\sigma}}$. [3]

   v Using $\alpha = 0.30$, calculate that the equilibrium Earth temperature is 256 K. [1]

The temperature obtained in c v is too low and so the student changes the model to one in which the atmosphere absorbs long wavelength (infrared) radiation emitted by the Earth.

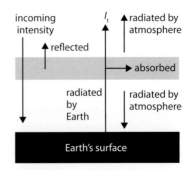

The atmosphere radiates both upwards into space as well as towards the Earth. The equilibrium temperature of the Earth is T_E and that of the atmosphere is T_A.

d The intensity of the incoming radiation at the top of the atmosphere is $\frac{S}{4}$ and the reflected intensity is $\frac{\alpha S}{4}$. The emissitivity of the atmosphere is e. Explain, briefly, why the intensity of the radiation emitted by

   i   the Earth is σT_E^4.   [1]

   ii the atmosphere towards the Earth is $e\sigma T_A^4$.   [1]

   iii Explain why the intensity labelled I_t in the diagram is equal to $(1-e)\sigma T_E^4$.   [2]

e By reference to the energy balance of the atmosphere and of the Earth surface respectively, deduce that

   i $2T_A^4 = T_E^4$ [2]

   ii $T_E = \sqrt[4]{\dfrac{(1-\alpha)S}{2\sigma(2-e)}}$ [3]

   iii Evaluate the equilibrium temperature of the Earth and of the atmosphere using $\alpha = 0.30$ and $e = 0.65$.   [2]

f The student's model is actually physically incorrect because one other source of radiation towards the Earth surface has been ignored. State this source of radiation.   [1]

g i   Outline a mechanism by which part of the radiation emitted by the Earth is absorbed by the atmosphere.   [3]

   ii Suggest why the incoming solar radiation is not affected by the mechanism you outlined in g i.   [2]

9 This question is about the temperature of Mars.

a The solar power per unit area averaged over the upper atmosphere of the Earth is about $350\,W\,m^{-2}$. The average distance between Mars and the Sun is about 1.5 times larger than the distance between the Earth and the Sun. The albedo of the Mars atmosphere is 0.15 and the surface may be assumed to radiate like a black body.

   i   Calculate the average intensity (over the whole Mars **surface**) received by Mars.   [1]

   ii Deduce that the average Mars temperature is approximately $220\,K$.   [4]

b The actual average temperature of Mars is $210\,K$. Using your answer to **a ii**, discuss whether the greenhouse effect is a significant factor in determining the average Mars temperature.   [2]

10 This question is about global warming.

a Distinguish between the greenhouse effect and the enhanced greenhouse effect.   [2]

b One of the predictions of the enhanced greenhouse effect is a rise in sea level.

   i   Define the coefficient of volume expansion of water.   [1]

   ii Calculate the expected rise in sea level in the oceans for a temperature increase of $2.5\,K$ in the average Earth temperature. You may assume that the average sea depth is $3.5\,km$ and the volume coefficient of water is $+2 \times 10^{-4}\,K^{-1}$.   [3]

c State three assumptions that were made in calculating the answer to **b ii**, apart from those that were already mentioned in question **b ii**.   [3]

d Outline why increased levels of carbon dioxide in the atmosphere are expected to lead to an increase in the Earth's average temperature.   [2]

e State one piece of experimental evidence that connects increased concentrations of carbon dioxide to increases in temperature.   [2]

Topic 9: Motion in fields

1 The diagrams show the variation with time of the horizontal and vertical components of velocity for a particle moving in two dimensions.

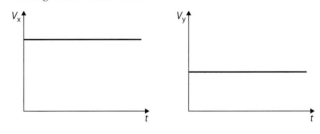

The particle must be moving in

A a circle.   **B** a parabola.
C a straight line.   **D** an ellipse.

2 A projectile is launched at some angle above the horizontal. Which of the following quantities decrease and which stay constant as the projectile moves to the highest point of its path?

	Decreases	Stays constant
A	speed	acceleration
B	total energy	vertical velocity component
C	horizontal velocity component	net force
D	kinetic energy	potential energy

3 A ball of mass m moving on a horizontal table with speed v. The ball lands a distance D from the foot of the table. Resistance forces are negligible.

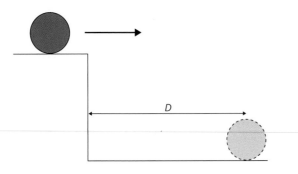

A second ball mass $2m$ moves on the table with speed $\frac{v}{2}$. The distance from the foot of the table where the second ball lands is

A D **B** $\dfrac{D}{\sqrt{2}}$ **C** $\dfrac{D}{4}$ **D** $\dfrac{D}{2}$

4 The centres of two identical spherical masses each of mass M are separated by a distance D.

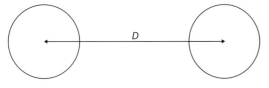

Which of the following gives the correct gravitational field strength and gravitational potential at the mid-point of the line joining their centres?

	Gravitational field	Gravitational potential
A	0	0
B	0	$-\dfrac{4GM}{D}$
C	$\dfrac{2GM}{D^2}$	0
D	$\dfrac{2GM}{D^2}$	$-\dfrac{4GM}{D}$

5 The gravitational potential at the surface of a planet is V. The gravitational potential at the surface of another planet of the same mass and eight times the density of the first is

A V **B** $2V$ **C** $4V$ **D** $8V$

6 **This question is about projectile motion.**

a A ball is projected from the edge of a cliff with a speed of $22\,\mathrm{m\,s^{-1}}$ making an angle $44°$ to the horizontal. The cliff is $35\,\mathrm{m}$ above the surface of the sea. The acceleration of free fall is $9.8\,\mathrm{m\,s^{-2}}$ and air resistance is negligible.

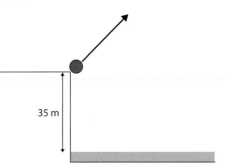

Using conservation of energy, calculate
i   the maximum height reached by the ball above the sea.   [2]
ii the speed of the ball as it impacts the water.   [2]

b Using your answer to **a** determine
i   the time it took the ball to impact the water.   [2]
ii the angle at which the ball impacts the water.   [2]

c The graph shows the path of the ball. Copy the graph and draw the path when air resistance cannot be ignored.   [3]

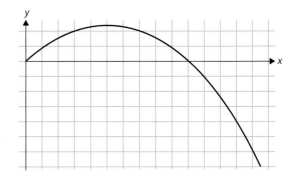

7 This question is about satellite motion.

  a A satellite orbits a planet of mass M in an orbit of radius r.

    i Show that the speed v of the satellite is given by
$$v = \sqrt{\frac{GM}{r}}.$$ [2]

    ii Use your answer to **i** to derive an expression for the kinetic energy of the satellite. [1]

    iii Hence show that the total energy of the satellite is given by $E = -\dfrac{GMm}{2r}$. [1]

  b **i** By reference to the formula for the total energy of a satellite in orbit, explain why a frictional force opposing the motion of a satellite will bring the satellite closer to the Earth. [2]

    ii Hence deduce that the satellite's kinetic energy will increase. [1]

    iii Explain where the extra kinetic energy comes from. [1]

8 This question is about gravitational potential.

The graph shows the gravitational potential of a planet and its moon as a function of the distance from the centre of the planet along a line joining their centres. The centre of the planet is at $r = 0$ and the centre of the moon at $r = d$. The centre-to-centre separation of the planet and the moon is d.

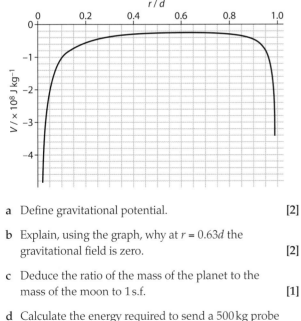

  a Define gravitational potential. [2]

  b Explain, using the graph, why at $r = 0.63d$ the gravitational field is zero. [2]

  c Deduce the ratio of the mass of the planet to the mass of the moon to 1 s.f. [1]

  d Calculate the energy required to send a 500 kg probe from the surface of the planet to the surface of the moon. [2]

  e It is required to send the probe very far away from both planet and its moon. State and explain from which point on the line joining the planet to the moon would the least energy be required for this. [2]

9 This question is about orbital motion.

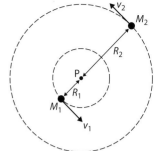

Two stars of masses M_1 and M_2 orbit a common centre P under the action of their mutual gravitational force. At a particular moment in time the stars are diametrically opposite each other as shown in the diagram.

  a By considering the force on the inner star, show that the period of the inner star is given by $T^2 = \dfrac{4\pi^2 R_1(R_1 + R_2)^2}{GM_2}$. [3]

  b Suggest why the outer star must have the same period. [2]

  c Using your answer to **a** or to **b**, determine which star has the larger mass. [2]

10 This question is about escape speed.

  a **i** Show that the escape speed from the surface of a planet of mass M and radius R is given by $v_{esc} = \sqrt{\dfrac{2GM}{R}}$. [3]

    ii Calculate the escape speed from Earth ($M = 6.0 \times 10^{24}$ kg, $R = 6.4 \times 10^6$ m). [1]

  b Voyager 2, a spacecraft launched in the late 1970s, has now left the solar system and for all practical purposes has escaped the gravitational influence of the Earth, the Sun and the other planets. The launch speed of Voyager was considerably less than the escape speed calculated in **ii**.
Explain this observation. [2]

  c A probe of mass m is launched from the surface of a planet of mass M and radius R with a speed that is half the escape speed from the planet.

Calculate the maximum distance from the planet the probe will get to. [3]

Topic 10: Thermal physics

1 An ideal gas is contained within a cylinder with a piston. The piston is moved in rapidly and the temperature of the gas increases. The reason for the increase in temperature is that

  A the molecules are colliding more frequently with each other.

  B the forces between molecules have become stronger.

  C the molecules have gained kinetic energy from the piston.

  D the intermolecular potential energy of the molecules has increased.

2 An ideal gas undergoes the change shown in the pressure–volume graph.

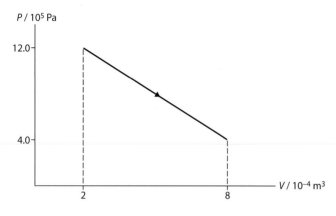

The work done by the gas is

A 24 J   **B** 48 J   **C** 240 J   **D** 480 J

3 In an isothermal compression of an ideal gas, 500 J of energy is extracted from the gas. The amount of work done on the gas is

A zero
B 500 J
C more than 500 J
D less than 500 J

4 **This question is about the first law of thermodynamics.**

The same quantity of heat is transferred into identical quantities of two ideal gases. The first gas absorbs the heat at constant volume and the second at constant pressure.

Determine in which case the temperature increase will be the largest. [3]

5 **This question is about ideal gases and thermodynamics.**

A container is filled with molecules of an ideal gas. The pressure of the gas is 9.8×10^6 Pa and the volume of the container is 3.3×10^{-3} m³. The temperature of the gas is 580 K.

a Calculate the number of molecules in the gas. [2]

b **i** The temperature of the gas is decreased at constant volume until the pressure is lowered to 5.4×10^6 Pa. Explain, in terms of molecular motion, why the pressure of the gas decreased. [3]
ii Calculate the new temperature of the gas. [2]

c The gas in **b** is now allowed to expand to a new volume at constant pressure such that the final temperature is equal to the original temperature of 580 K. The change in the internal energy of the gas during this expansion is 22 kJ.

Calculate
i the final volume of the gas. [1]
ii the work done by the gas in expanding to the final volume. [2]
iii the energy transferred. [2]

d The gas is now compressed isothermally back to its original state in **a**. The work done on the gas is 19 kJ.
i State whether energy is removed or added to the gas during the compression. [2]
ii Calculate the magnitude of the energy transferred. [2]

6 **This question is about entropy.**

a State what entropy is a measure of. [1]

A fixed quantity of liquid water at 0 °C freezes to solid ice at 0 °C.

b Explain why the entropy
i of the water decreased. [2]
ii of the surroundings increased. [2]

c Explain how your answers to **b** are consistent with the second law of thermodynamics. [2]

Topic 11:   Wave phenomena

1 Two pipes each have one closed and one open end. The length of pipe X is double the length of pipe Y. The ratio of the fundamental frequency of pipe X to that of pipe Y is

A $\frac{1}{2}$ **B** $\frac{1}{4}$ **C** 2   **D** 4

2 Which of the following is true for a standing wave?

A all points are in phase
B points within two adjacent nodes are in phase
C points within two adjacent antinodes are in phase
D the phase increases from 0 to 2π from one node to the next.

3 Coherent monochromatic light of wavelength λ is incident on a rectangular slit of width b. A diffraction pattern is observed on a screen some distance away. The angular width of the central diffraction pattern is approximately

A $\frac{\lambda}{b}$ **B** $\frac{2\lambda}{b}$ **C** $\frac{1.22\lambda}{b}$ **D** $\frac{2.44\lambda}{b}$

4 A radio telescope just manages to resolve two stars that are both emitting radio waves of wavelength 21 cm. The angular separation of the stars is 6.0×10^{-3} radians. The collecting area of the radio telescope has a diameter of about

A 0.4 m   **B** 4 m   **C** 40 m   **D** 400 m

5 Unpolarised light of intensity I_0 is incident on two polarisers whose transmission axes are parallel as shown.

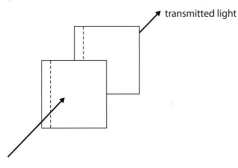

The intensity of light transmitted through the polarisers is

A I_0 **B** $\frac{I_0}{2}$ **C** $\frac{I_0}{4}$ **D** zero

6 **This question is about standing waves.**

a State two differences between a travelling (progressive) and a standing (stationary) wave. [2]

b The ends of a tight string are kept fixed.

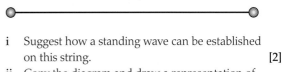

 i Suggest how a standing wave can be established on this string. [2]
 ii Copy the diagram and draw a representation of the standing wave on the string when the string vibrates at its lowest possible frequency. [1]
 iii On your copy of the diagram draw the standing wave pattern when the string vibrates at a frequency that is three times larger than the frequency in **ii**. [2]

c The frequency of the wave in **b iii** is 72 Hz and the length of the string is 1.8 m. Calculate the speed of the waves on the string. [3]

7 **This question is about the Doppler effect.**

a i State what is meant by the term **Doppler effect**. [1]
 ii By drawing an appropriate wavefront diagram illustrate the Doppler effect in the case of a source moving towards a stationary observer. [2]

b A source of sound is attached to the circumference of a horizontal disc. The disc rotates at constant speed. The source emits sound of frequency 4200 Hz as measured at the source, in all directions.

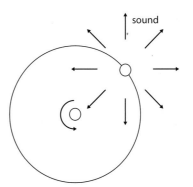

An observer at some distance from the disc measures the frequency of the sound received. The variation of the frequency with time is given by the graph. Explain the reason for the variation of frequency. [2]

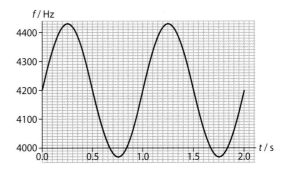

Exam-style questions

c Use the graph to determine
   i   the speed of sound given that the speed of the disc
       is $19\,\mathrm{m\,s^{-1}}$. [2]
   ii the radius of the disc. [2]

d Describe one practical application of the Doppler
   effect. [2]

8 This question is about resolution.

a State the Rayleigh criterion and illustrate your answer
   by a sketch diagram showing the variation of intensity
   with diffraction angle. [3]

b i The diameter of the pupil of a human eye is
       $3.00\,\mathrm{mm}$.
       Show that the human eye can resolve two separate
       objects in blue light of wavelength $4.80 \times 10^{-7}\,\mathrm{m}$
       provided their angular separation is at least
       $1.95 \times 10^{-4}\,\mathrm{rad}$. [2]
   ii Two objects can just be resolved in blue light. State
       and explain whether these objects can be resolved in
       red light. [3]

9 This question is about polarisation.

a State what is meant by **polarised light**. [1]

b Two polarisers whose transmission axes are
   perpendicular to each other are placed so that they
   partially overlap. The polarisers in this arrangement are
   used to view the calm surface of a lake.

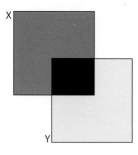

Carefully explain each of the following observations.
   i   The area of overlap is completely dark. [2]
   ii Polariser X is darker than polariser Y. [2]

c Light of intensity I_0 is incident on a polariser. The
   polariser is rotated about the direction of the incident
   light by an angle θ. On the same axes, sketch the
   intensity of the transmitted light as function of θ as
   θ varies from 0° to 360° when the incident light is
   i   unpolarised. [2]
   ii polarised. [2]

d Outline the use of polarisation in stress analysis. [4]

10 This question is about optical activity.

a State what is meant by an **optically active**
   substance. [2]

b Outline how you would investigate optical activity
   in a sugar solution. [3]

11 This question is about polarisation upon reflection.

a State what is meant by **polarised light**. [1]

b State Brewster's law. [2]

c Unpolarised light is incident from air on an air–glass
   boundary. The reflected light is transmitted through a
   polariser whose transmission axis is vertical.
   At an angle of incidence equal to 58° the transmitted
   intensity through the polariser is zero.
   i   Explain why there is an angle of incidence at
       which the transmitted light intensity is zero. [2]
   ii Determine the refractive index of the glass. [2]

Topic 12:   Electromagnetic induction

1   The diagram shows a conducting loop of wire that is partly within a region of magnetic field. The field is directed out of the page.

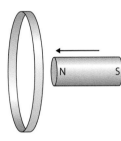

The magnitude of the field is increasing. The loop will move

A to the right
B to the left
C out of the plane of the paper
D into the plane of the paper

2   A bar magnet is moved towards a metallic ring as shown in the diagram. State and explain the direction of the induced current in the ring.   [2]

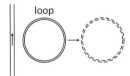

3   This question is about Faraday's law.

a   Define **magnetic flux**.   [1]

b   State Faraday's law.   [2]

c   A loop of area $6.0 \times 10^{-2}\,\mathrm{m^2}$ is moved away from a current-carrying wire.

The average field in the initial position was $5.0 \times 10^{-3}\,\mathrm{T}$ and $2.0 \times 10^{-3}\,\mathrm{T}$ in the new position. It took $0.50\,\mathrm{s}$ to move the loop. Calculate the average value of the induced emf and state the direction of the induced current.   [3]

4   This question is about Faraday's law.

A metallic wire in the form of a square loop is attached to a string that hangs from the ceiling. The string is displaced from the vertical position and released. As the loop oscillates it moves in a region of uniform magnetic field that is horizontal and directed out of the page.

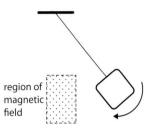

a   Explain why the oscillations of the loop will be damped.   [3]

The initial mechanical energy of the system when the wire was released was $0.26\,\mathrm{J}$ and the resistance of the wire is $0.12\,\Omega$. The oscillations die out in $4.0\,\mathrm{s}$.

b   What happens to the kinetic energy of the loop?   [1]

c   Estimate the average rms value of the current in the loop.   [3]

5   This question is about alternating current.

a   The power in the coil of a generator varies with time according to the following graph.

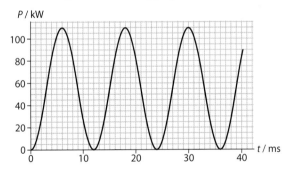

The resistance of the coil is $250\,\Omega$.
Calculate
i   the peak value of the induced emf in the coil.   [2]
ii   the rms value of the current in the coil.   [2]
iii   the period of revolution of the coil.   [2]

b   The coil is now rotated at half the period in **iii**. Copy the diagram and on the same axes draw a graph to show how the new power in the coil varies with time.   [2]

Topic 13: Quantum physics and nuclear physics

1 This question is about the photoelectric effect.

The graphs show the variation with applied voltage of the photocurrent from the **same** metal when light of low frequency and light of high frequency are incident on the metal.

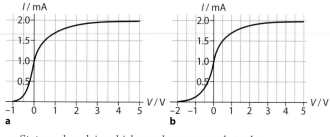

a State and explain which graph corresponds to the light of low frequency. [2]

b Explain how it may be deduced that in both cases the light has the same photon flux density (number of photons per unit area per second). [2]

c Determine which graph shows the largest light intensity. [2]

d In a photoelectric effect experiment monochromatic light of wavelength $\lambda = 4.86 \times 10^{-7}$ m is incident on a clean metal surface. The **maximum** speed of the emitted electrons is $v = 3.5 \times 10^5$ m s^{-1}.
   i Explain why not all emitted electrons have the maximum speed. [2]
   ii Calculate the work function of the surface. [2]

2 This question is about the wave nature of matter.

a State the de Broglie hypothesis. [2]

b Show that the de Broglie wavelength of an electron that has been accelerated from rest by a potential difference of 95 V is $\lambda = 1.3 \times 10^{-10}$ m. [2]

c The electrons in **b** are incident on a crystal. The diagram shows electrons scattering from atoms in the crystal that a distance d apart.

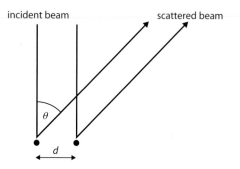

   i On a copy of the diagram draw a line to indicate the path difference between the scattered beams. [1]
   ii Show that the path difference is $d \sin \theta$. [1]
   iii A strong scattered beam is observed when $\theta = 52.9°$. The atom spacing is $d = 1.58 \times 10^{-10}$ m. Suggest how this is evidence for de Broglie's hypothesis. [4]

3 This question is about beta decay.

a State the experimental evidence in support of the existence of nuclear energy levels. [2]

b The diagram shows some of the nuclear energy levels of the nuclei of $^{12}_{5}$B and $^{12}_{6}$C.

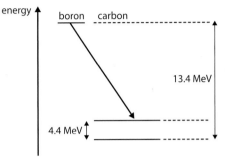

In the 1930s it was believed that the beta decay of the nucleus of $^{12}_{5}$B into $^{12}_{6}$C was described by the reaction equation $^{12}_{5}$B $\rightarrow$ $^{12}_{6}$C + e⁻. This decay is represented by the arrow.

State the expected energy Q, of the electron emitted in this decay. [1]

c In fact, the energy of the electrons emitted in this decay varies from zero up to a maximum value that is equal to Q.

  i Explain how this observation led to the prediction of the existence of a new particle. [3]

  ii State the correct reaction equation for the decay of boron into carbon. [1]

d The carbon nucleus produced in the beta decay of the nucleus of boron decays by gamma emission. Calculate the wavelength of the emitted photon. [2]

4 This question is about the uncertainty principle.

a State Heisenberg's uncertainty principle as it applies to position and momentum. [1]

b **i** The nucleus of the carbon isotope $^{14}_{6}$C has a radius of 2.9×10^{-15} m. Estimate the uncertainty in the momentum of an electron confined within a nucleus of $^{14}_{6}$C. [2]

  ii As a result of the uncertainty calculated in **i** the kinetic energy of the electron is approximately 100 MeV. By reference to the concept of binding energy, suggest whether it is possible for an electron to exist within a nucleus of $^{14}_{6}$C. [3]

c In the electron in the box model where an electron is confined within a region of linear size L, the lowest energy of the electron is $E = \dfrac{h^2}{8mL^2}$, i.e. the electron can never be at rest.

Explain how this observation is consistent with the Heisenberg uncertainty principle. [3]

5 This question is about nuclear fusion.

Two hydrogen nuclei may fuse according to the reaction $^{1}_{1}$H + $^{1}_{1}$H $\rightarrow$ $^{2}_{1}$H + e⁺ + ν provided the separation of the nuclei becomes equal to or less than 2.0×10^{-15} m. Two hydrogen nuclei approach each other along the same line with equal kinetic energies.

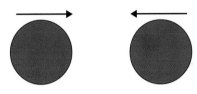

a **i** The nuclei stop when their centres are separated by a distance of 2.0×10^{-15} m. Calculate the electrical potential energy of the two nuclei. [2]

  ii Using your answer to **i** state the initial kinetic energy E_K of one of the nuclei. [1]

b The average kinetic energy of hydrogen nuclei within the Sun is $\bar{E} = 2.1 \times 10^{-23} T$ J where T is the temperature in the core of the Sun.

  i Show that the temperature for which $E_K = \bar{E}$ is about $T = 2.8 \times 10^9$ K. [1]

  ii Fusion of hydrogen does in fact take place even though the temperature in the core of the Sun is only 1.5×10^7 K. Explain how this is possible. [2]

c The binding energy per nucleon for $^{2}_{1}$H is about 1.1 MeV. Estimate the energy released in the fusion reaction $^{1}_{1}$H + $^{1}_{1}$H $\rightarrow$ $^{2}_{1}$H + e⁺ + ν, explaining your work. [3]

6 This question is about radioactive decay.

a In the context of radioactive decay, define **decay constant**. [1]

b Show that the decay constant λ and half life $T_{1/2}$ of a radioactive isotope are related by $\lambda T_{1/2} = \ln 2$. [2]

c Potassium (K-40) decays into argon (Ar-40) by beta emission. The half life of K-40 is 1.28×10^9 years. Potassium is naturally found in lava.

  i Argon is a gas. Suggest why not much argon would be found in liquid lava. [1]

  ii An old piece of solid lava is found to contain a ratio of Ar-40 to K-40 atoms of 0.15. Calculate the age of the lava rock. [4]

Topic 14: Digital technology

1 This question is about digital storage of information and the compact disk (CD).

   a Convert
      i the binary number 1101 into a decimal number   **[1]**
      ii The decimal number 14 into a binary number.   **[1]**

   b State three advantages of storing information in digital rather than analogue form.   **[3]**

   c **i** Describe how interference is used to read information stored on a compact disk (CD).   **[2]**
      ii Deduce that the pit depth on a CD track must be related to the wavelength of light used to read the CD through the relation $d = \frac{\lambda}{4}$.   **[2]**
      iii DVDs are read using shorter wavelength laser light than that used with ordinary CDs. Suggest an advantage of this.   **[2]**

   d The surface of a CD on which information is stored is the area between two concentric circles of inner and outer radii 2.3 cm and 5.9 cm respectively. The separation of two consecutive tracks is 1600 nm. The width of the track is 500 nm. Estimate the total length of the spiral track on a CD.   **[3]**

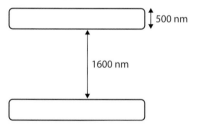

2 This question is about the charged coupled device (CCD).

   a Outline how a CCD forms the image of an object.   **[4]**

   b The collecting area of a CCD is 82 mm² and contains 12×10^6 pixels. The capacitance of a pixel is 25 pF and the quantum efficiency of the CCD is 84%.
      i Define **quantum efficiency**.   **[1]**
      ii Light of intensity 340 mW m⁻² and wavelength 520 nm is incident on a pixel of the CCD. Calculate the potential difference that will develop at the ends of the pixel after a time of 25 ms.   **[4]**

   c For the CCD in **b** calculate the smallest distance between two points on an object that can just be resolved given that the magnification of the CCD is 0.20.   **[3]**

Option A: Sight and wave phenomena

1 This question is about vision.

   a **i** Distinguish between cone and rod cells.   **[4]**
      ii Compare the distribution of cone and rod cells on the retina.   **[2]**

   b The graph shows how the response S of rod cells varies with wavelength.

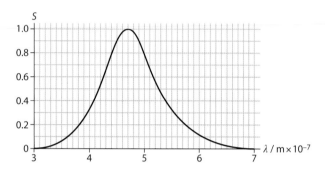

   Use the graph to explain why red objects would not clearly be seen in low-intensity light.   **[2]**

   c A rose is viewed in white light. The graph shows the relative amount of light intensity that is absorbed by the rose as a function of the wavelength of incident light.

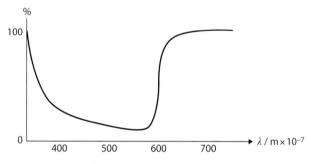

   State the colour of the rose, explaining your work.   **[3]**

2 This question is about accommodation and the eye.

   a **i** State what is meant by 'accommodation of the human eye'.   **[2]**
      ii Describe how accommodation is achieved.   **[2]**

   b The intensity of light during a bright day is 1200 W m⁻² but drops to 2.5×10^{-7} W m⁻² during a moonlit night.
      i Calculate the factor by which the pupil of the eye will change in radius in order to adjust to this change in intensity.   **[2]**
      ii Using your answer to **i** suggest whether the change of the pupil radius is the only mechanism available for this adjustment.   **[2]**

Option E: Astrophysics

1   This question is about the star Mirach (beta Andromedae).

a   Distinguish between apparent and absolute magnitude. [2]

b   The apparent magnitude of the star Mirach (beta Andromedae) is 2.06 and its absolute magnitude is –1.60. The temperature of Mirach is about 3000 K.

   i   State the spectral class of Mirach. [1]

   ii   Determine the distance to Mirach. [2]

c   i   The absolute magnitude of the Sun is 4.82. Estimate that the ratio of the luminosity of Mirach to that of the Sun is $\frac{L_M}{L_0} \approx 370$. [3]

   ii   The temperature of the Sun is 6000 K. Determine the ratio of the radius of Mirach to that of the Sun, $\frac{R_M}{R_0}$. [4]

   iii   Suggest which type of star Mirach is. [2]

d   Describe what information about a star may be deduced by a study of its spectrum. [3]

2   This question is about Cepheid stars.

a   The graph shows the variation of the apparent brightness of a Cepheid star with time.

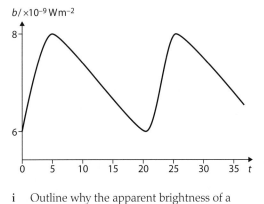

$b / \times 10^{-9}\,\mathrm{W\,m^{-2}}$

   i   Outline why the apparent brightness of a Cepheid star varies. [2]

   ii   The average luminosity, L, of a Cepheid star (in W) is related to the period of variation of apparent brightness, T (in days), by the equation $\log_{10} L = 1.13 \log_{10} T + 29.2$. Determine the distance to the Cepheid star. [3]

b   Describe what is meant by the statement **Cepheid stars are standard candles**. [3]

3   This question is about the cosmic microwave background radiation (CMBR) and the expanding Universe.

a   State what is meant by the **cosmic microwave background radiation (CMBR)**. [2]

b   Explain why the presence of the CMBR is evidence for a hot Big Bang. [2]

c   The temperature of the CMBR at present is about 2.7 K. Determine the wavelength at which most of the power of the CMBR is emitted. [2]

d   The diagram shows the expansion of the Universe if it contained no matter. The present time is indicated by P.

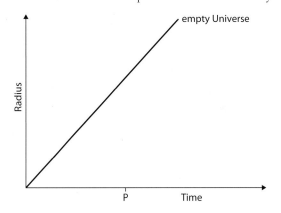

   i   Current evidence suggests that the Universe is flat. Explain what this means. [2]

   ii   Copy the diagram and draw a line to show the expected expansion of a flat Universe. [2]

   iii   It has been a very difficult process for astrophysicists to determine that the Universe is in fact flat. Suggest a reason for this. [2]

4 This question is about stellar evolution.

The HR diagram shows two main sequence stars: our Sun and another star, X.

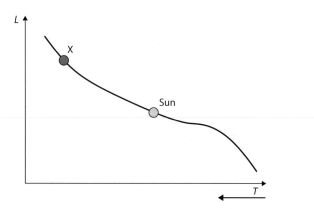

a Explain how it may be deduced that star X is more massive than the Sun. [2]

b The mass of star X is in fact about 10 times larger than that of the Sun.
Distinguish the evolution of star X from that of the Sun by reference to
i the time spent on the main sequence. [2]
ii the nuclear reactions taking place after both stars have left the main sequence. [2]
iii the likely end stage of both stars. [2]

c Describe the conditions under which the end stage of star X is the same as that of the Sun. [3]

5 This question is about Hubble's law.

a State Hubble's law. [2]

b i The wavelength of a certain spectral line in the spectrum of hydrogen is 656 nm when measured on Earth. The same line observed in the spectrum of a distant galaxy is 678 nm. The distance to the galaxy is 130 Mpc. Estimate a value for Hubble's constant. [3]
ii Using your answer to **i** estimate the age of the Universe. [2]
iii Suggest whether your estimate is an overestimate or underestimate of the true age of the Universe. [2]

Option F: Communications

1 This question is about noise and attenuation.

a The graphs show an input signal to a coaxial cable and the same signal after it has travelled a certain distance in the cable.

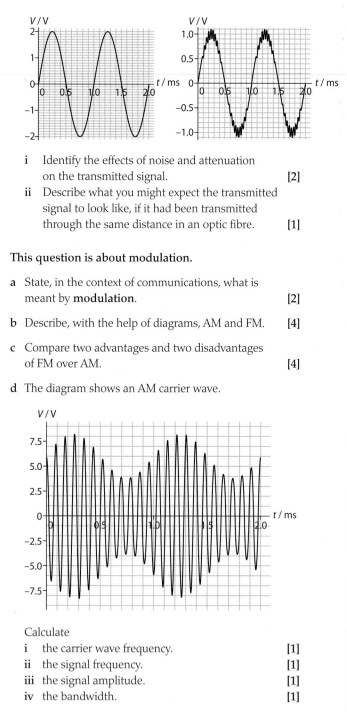

i Identify the effects of noise and attenuation on the transmitted signal. [2]
ii Describe what you might expect the transmitted signal to look like, if it had been transmitted through the same distance in an optic fibre. [1]

2 This question is about modulation.

a State, in the context of communications, what is meant by **modulation**. [2]

b Describe, with the help of diagrams, AM and FM. [4]

c Compare two advantages and two disadvantages of FM over AM. [4]

d The diagram shows an AM carrier wave.

Calculate
i the carrier wave frequency. [1]
ii the signal frequency. [1]
iii the signal amplitude. [1]
iv the bandwidth. [1]

e Draw a sketch graph of the power spectrum of the carrier wave in **d**. [2]

3 This question is about digital signals.

The diagram shows an analogue signal that has been sampled at the indicated times.

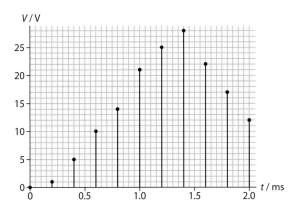

Each sample is converted into 5-bit words.

a Calculate
   i   the frequency at which the signal is being
       sampled. [1]
   ii the bit rate of transmission of the digitised signal. [1]
   iii the duration of one bit. [1]
   iv the binary equivalent of the sample taken
       at 1.0 ms. [1]

b The highest frequency contained in the signal
   is 12 kHz. Suggest whether there would be any
   advantage in increasing the sampling frequency. [2]

c A digital signal transmitted along a transmission line will
   become wider as a result of dispersion. Explain the effect
   on the maximum frequency that can be transmitted. [2]

4 This question is about optical fibres.

a State and explain two reasons for which **infrared
   laser** light is used to carry signals in an optical fibre. [4]

b A telephone call is sampled at a frequency of 8.0 kHz
   and each sample consists of eight bits. The duration of
   one bit is 1.0 ns.
   i   Calculate the time in between two consecutive
       samples. [1]
   ii Using your answer to **i**, state what is meant
       by time division multiplexing. [2]
   iii What is the largest number of additional signals
       that can be carried by this fibre? [1]
   iv In practice the number will be less than the
       number calculated in **iii**. Suggest a reason for this.[2]

c The input power in an optical fibre is 3.2 mW. The noise
   in the cable has a constant power of 6.0 μW and the
   attenuation per unit length of the fibre is 2.1 dB km^{-1}.
   It is required that the signal to noise ratio never falls
   below 18 dB. Calculate the largest distance over which
   the signal can be transmitted without amplification. [3]

5 This question is about radio and TV waves.

a A radio signal can be sent to a merchant ship on the
   other side of the Earth from the headquarters of a
   company. Explain with the help of a labelled diagram
   how sky waves can carry the signal to the ship. [2]

b i   State why a TV signal from the company's
        headquarters would not be able to reach the ship
        along the path used in **a**. [2]
   ii Suggest how a TV signal can in fact reach the ship. [1]

6 This question is about digital transmission of data.

The diagram shows blocks that might be used in the
transmission of data between a computer and a printer.

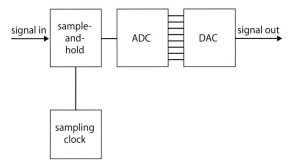

a Explain why this arrangement is not suitable for large
   distance transmission of data. [3]

b Copy and modify the block system so it is suitable for
   transmission over large distances. [2]

c A simple receiver uses the following components: **AF
   amplifier, antenna, demodulator, loudspeaker, tuned
   circuit.**

   Draw a block diagram to show how these components
   are connected. [4]

7 This question is about the operational amplifier and the mobile phone system.

The diagram shows an ideal operational amplifier operating from a ±6 V source.

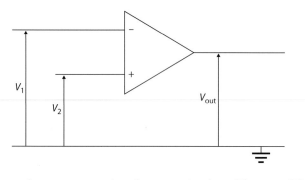

a State two properties of an operational amplifier. [2]

b State the value of the output voltage when
  i $V_1 > V_2$ [1]
  ii $V_1 < V_2$ [1]

c The first circuit is modified to the following circuit.

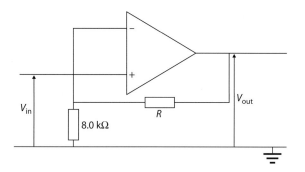

The gain of the amplifier is 21. The op–amp is still operating from a ±6.0 V source.
  i Calculate the resistance R. [1]

Calculate the value of the output voltage when
  ii $V_{in} = 0.04$ V. [1]
  iii $V_{in} = -4.0$ V. [1]

d In the mobile phone system a geographic area is divided into a number of cells. Describe what happens at the base station and in the cellular exchange of a mobile phone system when a phone is turned on. [4]

Option G: Electromagnetic waves

1 This question is about light.

a Light is described as an **electromagnetic** wave. Outline what this means. [2]

b Explain why the sky appears reddish during a sunset. [3]

c i State two differences between laser light and light emitted from an ordinary filament lamp. [2]
  ii Outline how laser light is produced. [4]

2 This question is about a simple magnifier.

a The diagram shows an object placed in front of a converging lens that is to act as a magnifier.

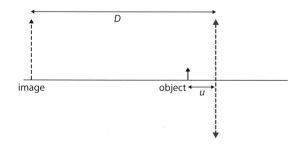

The distance of the object from the lens is u and the image is formed at the near point, a distance D from the lens.
  i State what is meant by **near point**. [1]
  ii Calculate the distance u in terms of D and f, where f is the focal length of the lens. [2]
  iii Using your answer derive an expression for the magnification of the lens. [2]

b By drawing appropriate lines on a copy of the diagram above, locate the positions of the focal points of the lens. [2]

c In a compound microscope the objective lens has a focal length of 8.0 mm and the eyepiece a focal length of 5.0 cm. The final virtual image is formed at a distance of 25 cm from the eyepiece lens. The distance between the two lenses is 22 cm. Calculate the overall magnification of the microscope. [5]

3 This question is about interference.

a Monochromatic light of wavelength 656 nm is incident normally on two very thin parallel slits.

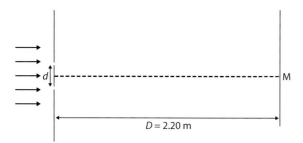

The light is observed on a screen placed far from the slits. The distance to the screen is $D = 2.20$ m and the slit separation is $d = 0.150$ mm. M is the point on the screen across from the mid-point of the slits.

  i Explain why the intensity of the light at M is a maximum. [2]

  ii Point P is the closest point to M on the screen where the light intensity is also a maximum. Calculate the distance MP. [2]

b Copy the axes below and draw a sketch graph to show the intensity distribution along the screen. [2]

c Describe the differences, if any, to the intensity pattern you drew in **b** when the slits are replaced by very many slits of the same width and separation as those in **a**. [3]

4 This question is about X-rays.

a The spectrum of X-rays produced by an X-ray tube consists of a continuous and a discrete part. Outline how each part of the spectrum is produced. [4]

b i A particular X-ray tube operates at an accelerating voltage of 28 kV. Calculate the minimum wavelength of the X-rays produced. [3]

  ii X-rays of wavelength 2.48×10^{-10} m are incident on a crystal plane. An intense beam of scattered X-rays is observed at an angle of 28.4° to the crystal plane. Determine the separation of crystal planes. [3]

5 This question is about thin film interference.

a A ray of white light is incident on a thin film of soap water that is suspended in air.

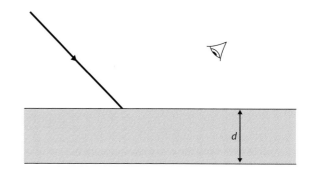

The wavelength of the light in air is λ and the refractive index of the soap water is n.

  i Copy the diagram and draw lines to show the reflected rays from the top and bottom surface of the film that enter the observer's eye. [2]

  ii Explain why there is only one point at which a phase difference occurs and label that point on the diagram using the letter P. [2]

b i Deduce that, for normal incidence, the longest wavelength for which destructive interference takes place is $\lambda = 2dn$. [3]

  ii Calculate the longest wavelength that suffers destructive interference for a soap film of refractive index 1.34 and thickness 225 nm. [1]

  iii Using your answer to **ii** explain why the film will appear coloured. [2]

Option H: Relativity

1 This question is about relativistic kinematics.

a State the two postulates of the theory of special relativity [2]

b A rocket leaves Earth with a speed of $0.60c$ towards a distant planet P. The distance between the Earth and the planet is 12 ly as measured by Earth observers.

Determine the time taken to reach P according to Earth and rocket observers. [3]

c As the rocket passes P a radio signal is sent to Earth. Determine the time taken for the signal to arrive at Earth according to Earth and rocket observers. [4]

2 This question is about relativistic kinematics.

In a thought experiment, a train of proper length 240 m is moving at $0.80c$ relative to the ground.

a Define **proper length**. [1]

b Two firework explosions take place at the front and at the back of the train. According to the clock carried by an observer at rest in the middle of the train, light from the two explosions reaches this observer at the same time.

    i Explain why the train observer may conclude that the fireworks exploded at the same time. [2]

    ii Explain why the two explosions did **not** occur at the same time according to an observer at rest on the ground and state which explosion occurred first. [4]

    iii State whether the ground observer or the train observer is right in determining the time of the explosions. [1]

The two explosions make marks on both the train and the ground.

c **i** Determine the distance between the marks made **on the train** according to train observers and according to ground observers. [3]

    ii Determine the distance between the marks made **on the ground** according to train observers and according to ground observers. [3]

3 This question is about relativistic mechanics.

a A proton is accelerated from rest to a speed of $0.980c$. Calculate the value of the accelerating potential. [3]

b Explain why the proton can never be accelerated to the speed of light. [2]

c Draw sketch graphs to show the variation with speed v of the kinetic energy of a particle according to

    i Newtonian mechanics. [1]

    ii relativistic mechanics. [1]

d Two protons are approaching each other along a straight line, each with a speed of $0.90c$ relative to a lab. Determine

    i the speed of one of the protons relative to the other. [2]

    ii the total energy of one of the protons relative to the other. [2]

    iii the total momentum of the two protons relative to the lab. [2]

4 This question is about general relativity.

a **i** State the principle of equivalence. [1]

    ii Use the principle of equivalence to deduce that a ray of light will bend towards a massive body. [3]

b A box is in free fall in a uniform gravitational field of strength g.

A red ray of light is emitted from the ceiling of the box and is received at the floor of the box. A blue ray of light is emitted from the left wall of the box from a height of 1 m above the floor.

State and explain whether

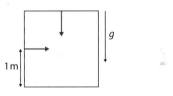

    i the frequency of the red ray of light when measured at the floor will be less than, equal to or greater than the frequency measured at the ceiling. [2]

    ii the height from the floor where the blue ray of light will hit the right wall of the box will be less than, equal to or greater than 1 m. [2]

c State how your answers to **b i** and **b ii** would change, if at all, if the box was instead accelerating in outer space in the direction shown by the arrow labelled g. [2]

5 This question is about black holes.

a Using the concept of spacetime, describe what is meant by a black hole. [2]

b Calculate the Schwarzschild radius of a black hole of mass 4.0×10^{35} kg. [1]

c A probe is stationary near the event horizon of the black hole in **b**. A signal of frequency 6.4×10^{12} Hz is emitted from the probe and is received by a spacecraft far away. The frequency measured by the spacecraft is 2.8×10^{12} Hz.

Determine the distance of the probe from the centre of the black hole. [3]

Option I: Medical physics

1 This question is about hearing.

a A student listens to music through earphones. The power of the sound delivered to one of the eardrums of the student is 150 mW. The eardrum of a student has area 58 mm².

  i Calculate the sound intensity level at the student's eardrum. [3]

  ii Comment on your answer to **i**. [1]

b The diagram shows the variation with frequency f of sound of the threshold of hearing of a young person.

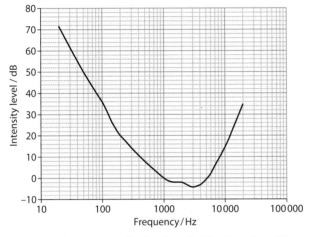

  i State what is meant by the **threshold of hearing**. [2]

  ii Determine the range of frequencies that can be heard by this person for sound of intensity $2.0 \times 10^{-10} \, W \, m^{-2}$. [3]

  ii Suggest what changes, if any, will be made to the graph as the person gets older. [2]

2 This question is about ultrasound.

a i State what is meant by **acoustic impedance**. [1]

  ii Suggest why considerations of acoustic impedance are important in ultrasound **medical imaging**. [2]

b The table gives values of acoustic impedance for air and tissue.

	Acoustic impedance / kg m⁻² s⁻¹
air	410
tissue	1.6×10^6

The reflection coefficient is given by $R = \left(\dfrac{Z_1 - Z_2}{Z_1 + Z_2} \right)^2$.

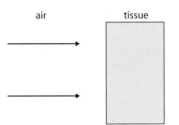

  i The intensity of ultrasound incident on tissue is I_0. Calculate the fraction of the intensity I_0 that reflects from the air–tissue boundary. [2]

  ii By reference to your answer to **i** suggest how ultrasound can be made to enter the patient's body. [2]

c The order of magnitude of the frequency of ultrasound used in medical diagnosis is 1 MHz. Suggest why such high frequencies are being used. [2]

3 This question is about X-rays.

   a Distinguish between CT scanning and X-ray imaging. [3]

   b A mono-energetic beam of X-rays of intensity I_0 is incident on tissue.

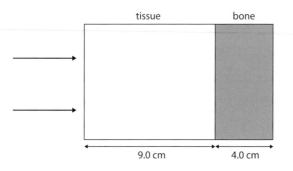

   After travelling through 9.0 cm of tissue the beam is incident on bone of thickness 4.0 cm. The attenuation coefficient for tissue is 0.14 cm^{-1} and that for bone is 0.74 cm^{-1}.

   i State what is meant by the term **attenuation coefficient**. [1]

   ii State one source of attenuation of X-rays in tissue. [1]

   iii Calculate the fraction of the X-ray intensity after the beam exits the bone. [3]

   iv Using your answer to **iii** suggest why an X-ray image of a bone fracture will be possible. [2]

   c Explain the use of an intensifying screen in X-ray imaging. [2]

4 This question is about nuclear magnetic resonance imaging and lasers.

   a Outline the principles behind nuclear magnetic resonance imaging. [5]

   b Describe **two** applications of lasers in medicine. [4]

5 This question is about radiation.

   a A radioisotope is injected into a patient in order to **monitor** the function of an organ. Suggest why it is desirable for the isotope to be a gamma emitter. [2]

   b Two radioisotopes are available for monitoring the function of an organ. The process of monitoring will last for no more than about 1 hour. Both isotopes have the same effective half-life and both are gamma emitters. Isotope X has a much shorter physical half-life than isotope Y.

   i Distinguish between the physical and effective half-life of a radioisotope. [2]

   ii Suggest why isotope X might be a better choice of radioisotope for the purpose of monitoring the function of a body organ. [2]

   c A tumour of mass 22 g is injected with a radioisotope of activity 3.6×10^7 Bq . The isotope emits gamma rays of energy 5.0×10^{-13} J. The quality factor for gamma rays is 1. Determine the dose equivalent 6 hours after injection. [3]

Option J: Particle physics

1 This question is about the Pauli principle.

   a State the difference between a fermion and a boson. [1]

   b Explain the difference between a meson and a baryon. [2]

   c Consider the spin $\frac{3}{2}$ baryon consisting of three down quarks, Δ = (ddd)

   i State the charge and strangeness of this baryon. [2]

   ii State the Pauli principle. [1]

   iii Outline how the Pauli principle applies to Δ = (ddd). [2]

2 This question is about antiparticles.

   a State the common characteristic shared by a particle and its antiparticle. [1]

   b State and explain the value of the electric charge in the case of an antiparticle that is identical to its antiparticle. [2]

   c State and explain whether the neutron is its own antiparticle. [2]

3   This question is about exchange particles.

a   The photon is said to be the exchange particle of the electromagnetic interaction. Explain what is meant by this statement. [3]

b   What can be deduced about the range of the electromagnetic interaction from the fact that the photon is massless? [2]

c i   State the names of the exchange particles of the weak interaction. [2]

   ii   Estimate the range of the weak interaction from the fact that the mass of the exchange particles is of order $100\,\mathrm{GeV}\,c^{-2}$. [2]

d   Before the discovery of the gluon it was thought that the exchange particle of the strong interaction was a massive meson.

   i   The mass of the exchanged meson is approximately $140\,\mathrm{MeV}\,c^{-2}$. Show that this gives the correct range of the strong nuclear force. [2]

   ii   The Feynman diagram shows the interaction $p+n \rightarrow p+n$ in terms of meson exchange.

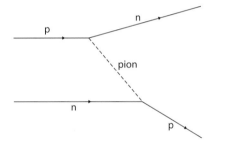

      Redraw this diagram so that the hadrons are represented with their constituent quarks and the exchange particles are gluons. [3]

4   This question is about colour.

a   A green up quark emits a gluon and becomes a blue quark. State
   i   whether the emitted gluon is a real or a virtual particle. [1]
   ii   the quark flavour of the final quark. [1]
   iii   the colour quantum numbers of the gluon. [2]

b   Explain
   i   why a baryon consisting of three red u quarks does not exist. [2]
   ii   whether a baryon consisting of a red u, a red d and a blue s quark could exist. [1]

5   This question is about Feynman diagrams.

a   Draw Feynman diagrams to represent the following reactions:
   i $e^- + e^- \rightarrow e^- + e^-$ [1]
   ii $e^- + e^+ \rightarrow \mu^- + \mu^+$ [1]
   iii $\gamma + \gamma \rightarrow \gamma + \gamma$ [1]
   iv $d \rightarrow u + e^- + \nu$ [1]
   v $\pi^0 \rightarrow \gamma + \gamma$ (take the pion to consist of a u and an anti u quark) [1]

6 HL This question is about resolution.

a   The existence of nuclei of radius of order $10^{-15}\,\mathrm{m}$ was discovered in Rutherford's classic experiment with alpha particle scattering.

   State and explain the order of magnitude of the de Broglie wavelength of the alpha particles used in the experiment. [2]

b   State and explain whether the de Broglie wavelength of photons scattering off a proton must be larger or smaller than the answer to **a** if the photon is to 'see' individual quarks in the proton. [2]

7 HL This question is about particle detectors.

a   Outline the operating principle of the bubble chamber. [3]

b   Explain how the bubble chamber may be used to measure the momentum of a particle. [2]

c   State and explain an advantage of the proportional wire chamber over the bubble chamber. [2]

8 HL This question is about the cyclotron.

a   Outline the operating principle of the cyclotron. [3]

b   A cyclotron has radius $2.0\,\mathrm{m}$ and a magnetic field of $1.5\,\mathrm{T}$.

   Show that the maximum kinetic energy a proton can be accelerated to in this cyclotron is $430\,\mathrm{MeV}$. [3]

c   The proton in **b** is incident on a stationary pion. The reaction is described by the equation $p^+ + \pi^- \rightarrow X + n^0$. (The mass of π^- is $140\,\mathrm{MeV}c^{-2}$.)
   i   The particle X is a hadron. State whether X is a meson or a baryon. [1]
   ii   State the electric charge of particle X. [1]
   iii   Calculate the largest mass particle X may have. [2]

9 HL This question is about the synchrotron.

a Describe how a particle gets accelerated in a synchrotron. [2]

b Explain why the magnets in a synchrotron are variable in strength. [2]

c In the LHC two beams of protons are circulating in opposite directions. A proton in either beam has a total energy of 7.0 TeV.

Determine the temperature that corresponds to the available energy in a collision of two protons in the LHC. [3]

10 HL This question is about deep inelastic scattering experiments.

a Describe what is meant by a deep inelastic scattering experiment. [2]

b Outline how these experiments provide evidence for
i quarks. [2]
ii gluons. [2]
iii asymptotic freedom. [2]

11 HL This question is about matter and antimatter.

a Estimate the temperature at which a photon can produce an electron–positron pair out of the vacuum. [2]

b State whether there is a limit on the temperature at which an electron–positron pair can annihilate into a photon. [1]

c Using your answers to **a** and **b** suggest why today we see predominantly matter in the Universe and not antimatter. [3]

12 HL This question is about strings.

a State two ways in which string theories differ from the standard model of particles. [2]

b String theories require more dimensions than the usual four. Assuming string theories are right, why are we not aware of the extra dimensions? [2]

The values quoted here are those usually used in calculations and problems. Fewer significant digits are often used in the text. The constants are known with a much better precision than the number of significant digits quoted here implies.

Atomic mass unit	$1u = 1.661 \times 10^{-27}$ kg $= 931.5$ MeV c^{-2}
Avogadro's constant	$N_A = 6.02 \times 10^{23}$ mol^{-1}
Boltzmann constant	$k = 1.38 \times 10^{-23}$ J K^{-1}
Coulomb constant	$\dfrac{1}{4\pi\,\varepsilon_0} = 8.99 \times 10^9$ N m^2 C^{-2}
Electric permittivity	$\varepsilon_0 = 8.85 \times 10^{-12}$ C^2 N^{-1} m^{-2}
Gravitational constant	$G = 6.67 \times 10^{-11}$ N kg^{-2} m^2
Magnetic permeability	$\mu_0 = 4\pi \times 10^{-7}$ T m A^{-1}
Magnitude of electronic charge	$e = 1.60 \times 10^{-19}$ C
Mass of the electron	$m_e = 9.11 \times 10^{-31}$ kg $= 5.49 \times 10^{-4}$ u $= 0.511$ MeV c^{-2}
Mass of the neutron	$m_n = 1.675 \times 10^{-27}$ kg $= 1.008\ 665$ u $= 940$ MeV c^{-2}
Mass of the proton	$m_p = 1.673 \times 10^{-27}$ kg $= 1.007\ 276$ u $= 938$ MeV c^{-2}
Planck constant	$h = 6.63 \times 10^{-34}$ J s
Speed of light in a vacuum	$c = 3.00 \times 10^8$ m s^{-1}
Stefan–Boltzmann constant	$\sigma = 5.67 \times 10^{-8}$ W m^{-2} K^{-4}
Universal gas constant	$R = 8.31$ J mol^{-1} K^{-1}

A few unit conversions

astronomical unit	$1AU = 1.50 \times 10^{11}$ m
atmosphere	1 atm $= 1.01 \times 10^5$ N m^{-2} $= 101$ kPa
degree	$1° = \dfrac{\pi}{180}$ rad
electronvolt	1 eV $= 1.60 \times 10^{-19}$ J
kilowatt-hour	1 kW h $= 3.60 \times 10^6$ J
light year	1 ly $= 9.46 \times 10^{15}$ m
parsec	1pc $= 3.26$ ly
radian	1 rad $= \dfrac{180°}{\pi}$

The first table gives atomic masses, including the masses of electrons, in the neutral atom. The masses are averaged over the isotopes of each element. In the case of unstable elements, numbers in brackets indicate the approximate mass of the most abundant isotope of the element in question. The masses are expressed in atomic mass units, u. The second table gives the atomic masses of a few selected isotopes.

Atomic numbers and atomic masses of the elements

Atomic number	Name and symbol	Atomic mass/u	Atomic number	Name and symbol	Atomic mass/u
1	Hydrogen, H	1.0080	30	Zinc, Zn	65.37
2	Helium, He	4.0026	31	Gallium, Ga	69.723
3	Lithium, Li	6.941	32	Germanium, Ge	72.59
4	Beryllium, Be	9.012 18	33	Arsenic, As	74.921
5	Boron, B	10.811	34	Selenium, Se	78.96
6	Carbon, C	12.000 000	35	Bromine, Br	79.91
7	Nitrogen, N	14.007	36	Krypton, Kr	83.80
8	Oxygen, O	15.999	37	Rubidium, Rb	85.467
9	Fluorine, F	18.998	38	Strontium, Sr	87.62
10	Neon, Ne	20.180	39	Yttrium, Y	88.906
11	Sodium, Na	22.999	40	Zirconium, Zr	91.224
12	Magnesium, Mg	24.31	41	Niobium, Nb	92.906
13	Aluminium, Al	26.981	42	Molybdenum, Mo	95.94
14	Silicon, Si	28.086	43	Technetium, Tc	(99)
15	Phosphorus, P	30.974	44	Ruthenium, Ru	101.07
16	Sulfur, S	32.066	45	Rhodium, Rh	102.906
17	Chlorine, Cl	35.453	46	Palladium, Pd	106.42
18	Argon, Ar	39.948	47	Silver, Ag	107.868
19	Potassium, K	39.102	48	Cadmium, Cd	112.40
20	Calcium, Ca	40.078	49	Indium, In	114.82
21	Scandium, Sc	44.956	50	Tin, Sn	118.69
22	Titanium, Ti	47.90	51	Antimony, Sb	121.75
23	Vanadium, V	50.942	52	Tellurium, Te	127.60
24	Chromium, Cr	51.996	53	Iodine, I	126.904
25	Manganese, Mn	54.938	54	Xenon, Xe	131.30
26	Iron, Fe	55.847	55	Caesium, Cs	132.91
27	Cobalt, Co	58.933	56	Barium, Ba	137.34
28	Nickel, Ni	58.71	57	Lanthanum, La	138.91
29	Copper, Cu	63.54	58	Cerium, Ce	140.12

Atomic number	Name and symbol	Atomic mass/u
59	Praseodymium, Pr	140.907
60	Neodymium, Nd	144.24
61	Promethium, Pm	(144)
62	Samarium, Sm	150.4
63	Europium, Eu	152.0
64	Gadolinium, Gd	157.25
65	Terbium, Tb	158.92
66	Dysprosium, Dy	162.50
67	Holmium, Ho	164.93
68	Erbium, Er	167.26
69	Thulium, Tm	168.93
70	Ytterbium, Yb	173.04
71	Lutetium, Lu	174.97
72	Hafnium, Hf	178.49
73	Tantalum, Ta	180.95
74	Tungsten, W	183.85
75	Rhenium, Re	186.2
76	Osmium, Os	190.2
77	Iridium, I	192.2
78	Platinum, Pt	195.09
79	Gold, Au	196.97
80	Mercury, Hg	200.59
81	Thallium, Tl	204.37

Atomic number	Name and symbol	Atomic mass/u
82	Lead, Pb	207.2
83	Bismuth, Bi	208.980
84	Polonium, Po	(210)
85	Astatine, At	(218)
86	Radon, Rn	(222)
87	Francium, Fr	(223)
88	Radium, Ra	(226)
89	Actinium, Ac	(227)
90	Thorium, Th	(232)
91	Protactinium, Pa	(231)
92	Uranium, U	(238)
93	Neptunium, Np	(239)
94	Plutonium, Pu	(239)
95	Americium, Am	(243)
96	Curium, Cm	(245)
97	Berkelium, Bk	(247)
98	Californium, Cf	(249)
99	Einsteinium, Es	(254)
100	Fermium, Fm	(253)
101	Mendelevium, Md	(255)
102	Nobelium, No	(255)
103	Lawrencium, Lr	(257)

Atomic masses of a few selected isotopes

Atomic number	Name	Atomic mass/u
1	Hydrogen, H	1.007 825
1	Deuterium, D	2.014 102
1	Tritium, T	3.016 049
2	Helium-3	3.016 029
2	Helium-4	4.002 603
3	Lithium-6	6.015 121
3	Lithium-7	7.016 003
4	Beryllium-9	9.012 182
5	Boron-10	10.012 937
5	Boron-11	11.009 305
6	Carbon-12	12.000 000
6	Carbon-13	13.003 355
6	Carbon-14	14.003 242

Atomic number	Name	Atomic mass/u
7	Nitrogen-14	14.003 074
7	Nitrogen-15	15.000 109
8	Oxygen-16	15.994 915
8	Oxygen-17	16.999 131
8	Oxygen-18	17.999 160
19	Potassium-39	38.963 708
19	Potassium-40	39.964 000
92	Uranium-232	232.037 14
92	Uranium-235	235.043 925
92	Uranium-236	236.045 563
92	Uranium-238	238.050 786
92	Uranium-239	239.054 291

Useful formulae

Property	Formula
Circumference of a circle of radius R	$2\pi R$
Area of a circle of radius R	πR^2
Surface area of a sphere of radius R	$4\pi R^2$
Volume of a sphere of radius R	$\dfrac{4\pi R^3}{3}$
Volume of a cylinder of base radius R and height h	$\pi R^2 h$

Astronomical data

Body	Mass/kg	Radius/m	Orbit radius/m (average)	Orbital period
Sun	1.99×10^{30}	6.96×10^8	–	–
Moon	7.35×10^{22}	1.74×10^6	3.84×10^8	27.3 days
Mercury	3.30×10^{23}	2.44×10^6	5.79×10^{10}	88.0 days
Venus	4.87×10^{24}	6.05×10^6	1.08×10^{11}	224.7 days
Earth	5.98×10^{24}	6.38×10^6	1.50×10^{11}	365.3 days
Mars	6.42×10^{23}	3.40×10^6	2.28×10^{11}	687.0 days
Jupiter	1.90×10^{27}	6.91×10^7	7.78×10^{11}	11.86 yr
Saturn	5.69×10^{26}	6.03×10^7	1.43×10^{12}	29.42 yr
Uranus	8.66×10^{25}	2.56×10^7	2.88×10^{12}	83.75 yr
Neptune	1.03×10^{26}	2.48×10^7	4.50×10^{12}	163.7 yr
Pluto*	1.5×10^{22}	1.15×10^6	5.92×10^{12}	248.0 yr

Luminosity of the Sun	$L = 3.9 \times 10^{26}$ W
Distance to nearest star (Proxima Centauri)	4×10^{16} m (approx. 4.3 ly)
Diameter of the Milky Way	10^{21} m (approx. 100 000 ly)
Mass of the Milky Way	4×10^{41} kg
Distance to nearest galaxy (Andromeda)	2×10^{22} m (approx. 2.3 million ly)

*Pluto has recently been downgraded into a new category of 'dwarf planet' (see Option E, Astrophysics).

Topic 1: Physics and physical measurement

1 $[\eta] = \dfrac{[F]}{[6\pi r v]} = \dfrac{\mathrm{kg\,m\,s^{-2}}}{\mathrm{m\,m\,s^{-1}}} = \mathrm{kg\,m^{-1}\,s^{-1}}$.

2 The quantity $\dfrac{Et^2}{\rho}$ has units

$\left[\dfrac{Et^2}{\rho}\right] = \dfrac{\mathrm{J\,s^2}}{\mathrm{kg\,m^{-3}}} = \dfrac{\mathrm{N\,m\,s^2}}{\mathrm{kg\,m^{-3}}} = \dfrac{\mathrm{kg\,m\,s^{-2}\,m\,s^2}}{\mathrm{kg\,m^{-3}}} = \mathrm{m^5}$ from

which the result follows. Solving for the energy we

get $E \approx \dfrac{R^5\rho}{t^2} = \dfrac{140^5 \times 1}{0.025^2} \approx 9 \times 10^{13}\,\mathrm{J}$.

3 The percentage uncertainty in the resistance is
$\dfrac{\Delta R}{R} = 4\% + 6\% = 10\%$ and so $\Delta R = \pm 10\% \times 24 = \pm 2.4\,\Omega \approx \pm 2\,\Omega$.

> Give the uncertainty to 1 s.f.

4 Since $V = a^3$ the fractional uncertainty is $3 \times 0.02 = 0.06$ or 6%.

5 The percentage uncertainty is $\dfrac{\Delta T}{T} = \dfrac{1}{2} \times (4\% + 6\%) = 5\%$.

> The common mistake is to say that the uncertainty is
> $\sqrt{(4\% + 6\%)} \approx 3\%$.

6

Equation	Constants	Variables	Gradient	Vertical intercept
$P = kT$	k	P against T	k	zero
$v = u + at$	u, a	v against t	a	u
$v^2 = 2as$	a	v^2 against s	$2a$	zero
$F = \dfrac{kq_1q_2}{r^2}$	k, q_1, q_2	F against $\dfrac{1}{r^2}$	kq_1q_2	zero
$a = -\omega^2 x$	ω^2	a against x	$-\omega^2$	zero
$V = \dfrac{kq}{r}$	k, q	V against $\dfrac{1}{r}$	kq	zero
$T^2 = \dfrac{4\pi^2}{GM}R^3$	G, M	T^2 against R^3	$\dfrac{4\pi^2}{GM}$	zero
$I = I_0 e^{-aT}$	I_0, a	$\ln I$ against T	$-a$	$\ln I_0$
$\lambda = \dfrac{h}{\sqrt{2mqV}}$	h, m, q	λ against $\dfrac{1}{\sqrt{V}}$	$\dfrac{h}{\sqrt{2mq}}$	zero
		λ^2 against $\dfrac{1}{V}$	$\dfrac{h^2}{2mq}$	zero
$F = av + bv^2$	a, b	$\dfrac{F}{v}$ against v	b	a
$E = \dfrac{1}{2}m\omega^2\sqrt{A^2 - x^2}$	m, ω^2, A	E^2 against x^2	$-\dfrac{m^2\omega^4}{4}$	$\dfrac{m^2\omega^4 A^2}{4}$
$\dfrac{1}{u} + \dfrac{1}{v} = \dfrac{1}{f}$	f	$\dfrac{1}{u}$ against $\dfrac{1}{v}$	-1	$\dfrac{1}{f}$

7 Plot $\ln d$ against $\ln h$ to get a straight line with slope 0.8 and vertical intercept $\ln c$, or d against $h^{0.8}$, or $d^{1.25}$ against h. Last two give straight lines through the origin.

8 **a** 5.344 ± 0.001

b One possibility is 67 ± 5 which is too conservative. As mentioned earlier someone may well claim to be able to read to better precision, so a better answer is 67 ± 2.

9 **a** Since r^2 is proportional to V the graph will be a straight line through the origin.

b The slope is $\dfrac{2m}{qB^2}$.

c We have that $\dfrac{\Delta r^2}{r^2} = 2\dfrac{\Delta r}{r} \Leftrightarrow \Delta r^2 = 2r\Delta r$. For the value $r = 4.5$ we thus have $r^2 = 4.5^2 = 20.2 \approx 20\,\mathrm{cm^2}$ to 2 s.f. $\Delta r^2 = 2 \times 4.5 \times 0.1 = 0.9\,\mathrm{cm^2}$ to 1 s.f. The least uncertain digit in the value of r^2 is in the units digit and so the uncertainty must express this fact. Hence the uncertainty must be rounded to the units digit i.e. $\Delta r^2 = 0.9 \approx 1\,\mathrm{cm^2}$. Hence $r^2 = 20 \pm 1\,\mathrm{cm^2}$. In the same way we can fill in the rest of the table.

Radius r/cm ± 0.1 cm	Potential difference V/V	r^2/cm^2
4.5	500	20 ± 1
4.9	600	24 ± 1
5.3	700	28 ± 1
5.7	800	32 ± 1
6.0	900	36 ± 1

In this example the absolute uncertainties in all the values of r^2 come out the same. This is not generally the case.

d & e The error bars and the line of best fit and the minimum and maximum slope lines are shown in the diagram.

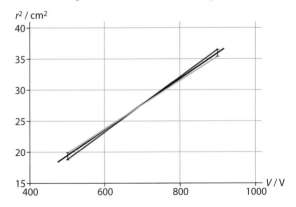

f The gradient of the line of best fit is
$$\frac{(36-20)\times 10^{-4}}{400} = 4.00\times 10^{-6}\,m^2V^{-1}.$$
The gradient of the maximum slope line is
$$\frac{(37-19)\times 10^{-4}}{400} = 4.50\times 10^{-6}\,m^2V^{-1}.$$
The gradient of the minimum slope line is
$$\frac{(35-21)\times 10^{-4}}{400} = 3.50\times 10^{-6}\,m^2V^{-1}.$$
The uncertainty in the gradient is therefore
$$\frac{4.50\times 10^{-6}-3.50\times 10^{-6}}{2} = 0.50\times 10^{-6}\approx 0.5\times 10^{-6}\,m^2V^{-1}\ \text{to 1 s.f.}$$
We therefore quote the gradient as $(4.0\pm 0.5)\times 10^{-6}\,m^2V^{-1}$.

g The slope is equal to $\frac{2m}{qB^2}$ and so
$$\frac{q}{m} = \frac{2}{B^2\times \text{slope}} = \frac{2}{(1.80\times 10^{-3})^2\times 4.0\times 10^{-6}} = 1.54\times 10^{11}\,Ckg^{-1}.$$
Let U be the uncertainty in the measured value of $\frac{q}{m}$. Then
$$\frac{U}{1.54\times 10^{11}} = \frac{0.5\times 10^{-6}}{4.0\times 10^{-6}} \Rightarrow U = 0.193\times 10^{11}\approx 0.2\times 10^{11}\,Ckg^{-1}.$$

> The uncertainty is in the first decimal place and so the measured value of $\frac{q}{m}$ must be rounded to the first decimal place. Hence we must quote $\frac{q}{m} = (1.5\pm 0.2)\times 10^{11}\,Ckg^{-1}$.

10 The speed of the boat with respect to the shore is $\sqrt{4.0^2-3.0^2}$
$= 2.646\,ms^{-1}$ and the time taken to get across is $\frac{16}{2.646} = 6.0\,s$.

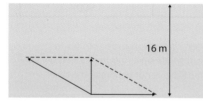

11 The mass of an apple is about 200 g so its weight is about $0.2\times 10\approx 2\,N$.

12 The number of seconds in a year is of the order $365\times 24\times 60\times 60$
$\approx 400\times 20\times 50\times 50 \approx 400\times 20\times \frac{100}{2}\times \frac{100}{2} \approx 10^2\times 20\times 10^4 \approx 2\times 10^7.$
So the distance travelled by light in a year (= a light year) is of the order $\approx 3\times 10^8\times 2\times 10^7 \approx 6\times 10^{15}\,m.$

13 The diameter of a nucleus is of the order $10^{-15}\,m$. Thus the time taken by light to cross the diameter of a nucleus is of the order
$$\frac{10^{-15}}{3\times 10^8} = 0.33\times 10^{-23}\approx 3.3\times 10^{-24}\approx 10^{-24}\,s.$$

14 You should know that the heart beats at a rate of about 70 beats per minute. Thus the interval between beats is $\frac{60}{70}\approx 1\,s.$

15 The radius of the Earth is 6400 km and so the volume of the Earth is about
$$\frac{4\pi}{3}(6.4\times 10^6)\,m^3 \approx \frac{4\times 3\times (6\times 10^6)^3}{3} \approx 4\times 6\times 40\times 10^{18} \approx 10^{21}\,m^3.$$
The volume of a grain of sand is about $1\,mm^3$ and so the number of grains of sand that can fit into the Earth is
$$\frac{2\times 10^{21}\,m^3}{1\,mm^3} \approx \frac{2\times 10^{21}\,(10^3\,mm)^3}{1\,mm^3} \approx 2\times 10^{30}\approx 10^{30}.$$

16 A glass contains about 200 g of water. The molar mass of water is 18 g per mole and so 200 g correspond to $\frac{200}{18}\approx \frac{200}{20} = 10$ moles. Each mole contains 6.02×10^{23} molecules, so the glass contains $6\times 10^{23}\times 10\approx 10^{25}$ molecules of water.

17 We know that $I\propto \frac{T^4}{d^2}$ and so the percentage increase in the intensity received would increase by $4\times 2\% + 2\times 1\% = 10\%.$

Topic 2: Mechanics

1 See the graph.

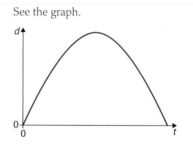

> No calculations are needed here – just use common sense about how the magnitude of the displacement changes as the particle moves.

2 The change of displacement is the vector shown in the diagram.

It has magnitude 10 m and so the average velocity is
$$\bar{v} = \frac{10}{5.0} = 2.0\,ms^{-1}$$
in the direction of the arrow.
The distance travelled is $\frac{1}{2}\times 2\pi R \approx 15.7\,m$ and so the average speed is $\frac{15.7}{5.0} = 3.1\,ms^{-1}.$

3 Use $s = \left(\frac{u+v}{2}\right)t$, to get $20 = \left(\frac{0+v}{2}\right)\times 5.0 \Rightarrow v = 8.0\,ms^{-1}$ (C).

4 **a** The acceleration at 2.0 s is the slope of the curve at this point. Drawing a tangent and finding its slope gives approximately $0.14\,ms^{-2}.$

> A common mistake would be to divide the velocity at 2.0 s by the time of 2.0 s.

b See the graph.

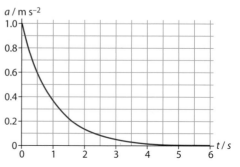

c The area under the curve is approximately 5.0 m and this is the displacement.

5 The area under the curve is the change in velocity. This is $25\,\mathrm{m\,s^{-1}}$. Since the initial velocity is zero the final velocity is then $25\,\mathrm{m\,s^{-1}}$.

6 The answer must be the same time! Explicitly, let h be the height from the floor and let t be the time to hit the floor. Let u be the downward velocity of the elevator. Then, for an observer outside, the ball will cover a distance $h+ut$ (the floor will move down a distance ut) and so $h+ut = ut + \frac{1}{2}gt^2$ (the ball has an initial velocity equal to that of the elevator) and so $h = \frac{1}{2}gt^2$, the result we would get for an elevator at rest.

It is unlikely that you would reproduce this argument in an exam – use common sense: it makes no difference whether the elevator is moving or not since an observer inside cannot know that he or she is moving! (If u is constant.)

7 See the diagram.

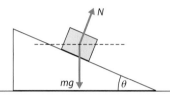

Net force on m is $mg-T$ and so $mg-T = ma$. Net force on M is T and so $T = Ma$. Thus:

$$mg-T = ma$$
$$T = Ma$$

Hence, by adding these equations,
$mg = (M+m)a$ and so
$a = \dfrac{mg}{M+m}$ and $T = \dfrac{Mmg}{M+m}$.

The advantage of considering the two bodies as one is that the net force is then mg and so right away the acceleration is $mg = (M+m)a \Rightarrow a = \dfrac{mg}{M+m}$. You now treat the bodies as separate again to find the tension.

8 The tension in **D** pulls a bigger mass and so this has the greatest tension.

9 **a** Treating the two bodies as one we see that the total mass is 20 kg and the net force 60 N so that the acceleration is $3.0\,\mathrm{m\,s^{-2}}$.
   b The net force on the 8.0 kg body is the tension in the string and so $T = ma = 8.0 \times 3.0 = 24\,\mathrm{N}$.
   c If the bodies are reversed, the acceleration will stay the same but the tension will now be $T = ma = 12 \times 3.0 = 36\,\mathrm{N}$.

No further calculations are needed for **c** – since the total mass is the same the acceleration will be the same.

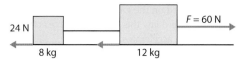

The forces are now as shown in the diagram and we have equilibrium.
Using the diagram we calculate that **d** the tension is 24 N and **e** the frictional force on the 12 kg block is $60-24 = 36\,\mathrm{N}$.

Equilibrium means the net force on each body is zero.

10 The scale exerts a force R on the girl. Hence by Newton's third law, the girl exerts a force R on the scale which is what the scale reads. The answer is **C**.

The common mistake would be to choose **B**, but scales read the force on them!

11 The forces on the block are as shown in the diagram.

We must take components along horizontal and vertical axes (because motion takes place horizontally). The vertical component of N is $N\cos\theta$ and this must equal the weight of the block, mg. The horizontal component is $N\sin\theta$ and this must equal ma. So,

$$N\sin\theta = ma$$
$$N\cos\theta = mg$$

This gives $\tan\theta = \dfrac{a}{g}$. Treating the bodies as one, we see that the net force is just F and so the acceleration is $a = \dfrac{F}{M}$ where M is the combined mass. Hence $\tan\theta = \dfrac{F}{Mg} = \dfrac{F}{W}$ as required.

It is always a good idea to choose as one of the axes the direction of motion.

12 The body is accelerating upwards so R is bigger than mg. The net force is thus $R-mg$ and so $R-mg = ma$, i.e. $R = ma+mg$.

13 **a** $\Delta p = 0.20 \times 2.5 - 0.20 \times (\underset{\text{notice the sign}}{-4.0}) = 1.3\,\mathrm{Ns}$ to the right.
   b $F = \dfrac{\Delta p}{\Delta t} = \dfrac{1.3}{0.14} = 9.3\,\mathrm{N}$.
   c If the system is just the ball the law does not apply since there is a force on the block from the wall. If the system is the ball and the wall, then it does apply. The wall must have acquired a momentum of 1.3 Ns to the left.

It all depends on what the system is taken to be.

   d The net force on the ball is now $F = R-mg$ and so $F = \dfrac{\Delta p}{\Delta t} = R-mg$ giving $R = 9.3+2.0 \approx 11\,\mathrm{N}$.

14 a The force exerted on the gases is $2.2 \times 3.0 \times 10^2 = 660 \, \text{N}$.
    b By Newton's third law this is also the force acting on the rocket and so it accelerates.
    c The initial mass of the rocket is $200 \, \text{kg}$ so the initial acceleration is $a = \dfrac{660}{200} = 3.3 \, \text{m s}^{-2}$.

15 a About $2.0 \, \text{ms}$.
    b The area is (by counting squares) about $95 \times 10^{-3} \, \text{N s}$.
    c The average force is given by $F \Delta t = 95 \times 10^{-3} \, \text{N s}$, i.e. $F = 48 \, \text{N}$.
    d The impulse is also $mv - m(-v) = 2mv$ and so $m = 5.3 \times 10^{-3} \, \text{kg}$.

16 The work is $W = Fd \cos \theta$ with $\theta = 0°$ and so
    $W = 20 \times 2\pi \times 5.0 \approx 630 \, \text{J}$.

The common mistake is to say that the work is zero because the displacement is zero.

17 Since $E_E = \dfrac{1}{2} kx^2$ to extend the spring from its natural length to an extension $2e$ would require work equal to $4W$. So to extend it from e to $2e$ requires $4W - W = 3W$, hence **C**.

18 The total momentum before the collision is
    $5.0 \times 3.0 + 7.0 \times 0 = 15 \, \text{N s}$. After the collision it is $(5.0 + 7.0) \times v$.
    Thus $12v = 15 \, \text{N s} \Rightarrow v = 1.25 \, \text{m s}^{-1}$. The total kinetic energy before the collision is $E_K = \dfrac{1}{2} 5.0 \times 3.0^2 + 0 = 22.5 \, \text{J}$. After the collision it is $E_K = \dfrac{1}{2} 12 \times 1.25^2 = 9.4 \, \text{J}$. The collision is inelastic since kinetic energy has not been conserved.

19 The change in the kinetic energy of the body is
    $\Delta E_K = 0 - 48 = -48 \, \text{J}$. The only force doing work on the body is the frictional force and $W_{\text{net}} = f \times d \times \cos 180° = -6.0 \times d$.
    Hence $-6.0 d = -48 \Rightarrow d = 8.0 \, \text{m}$.

20 The block is moving in a circle (of radius L) and so is not in equilibrium. The net force points towards the centre, i.e. upwards. This means that the tension is larger than the weight. Applying Newton's second law: $T - mg = m\dfrac{v^2}{L}$. So to find the tension we need the speed of the block. Applying conservation of energy, $\dfrac{1}{2} mv^2 = mgL$ and so $m\dfrac{v^2}{L} = 2mg$ leading, finally, to $T = 3mg$.

Equilibrium means the body moves in a straight line with constant speed – this is not the case here.

Topic 3:   Thermal physics

1   Consider a mole of lead. Its mass is $207 \, \text{g}$ ($0.207 \, \text{kg}$).
    The volume of one mole is therefore $\dfrac{0.207}{1.13 \times 10^4} = 1.83 \times 10^{-5} \, \text{m}^3$
    (density = mass/volume). Since we have one mole we have
    6.02×10^{23} molecules of lead. Thus to each molecule there
    corresponds a volume $\dfrac{1.83 \times 10^{-5}}{6.02 \times 10^{23}} = 3.04 \times 10^{-29} \, \text{m}^3$. Assuming
    this volume to be a cube, we find that the cube side is
    $a = \sqrt[3]{3.04 \times 10^{-29}} \approx 3 \times 10^{-10} \, \text{m}$ and this is also the average
    separation of the molecules (see diagram in the question).

2   The change in temperature is $10 \, \text{K}$ and the final temperature is $32 + 273 = 305 \, \text{K}$.

3   Let T be the final temperature. Then:
    thermal energy lost by aluminium is $0.080 \times 900 \times (250 - T)$.
    thermal energy gained by water and calorimeter is
    $0.75 \times 4200 \times (T - 15) + 180 \times (T - 15)$.
    By conservation of energy we have
    $0.08 \times 900 \times (250 - T) = 0.75 \times 4200 \times (T - 15) + 180 \times (T - 15)$.
    Solving for T we find $T = 20 \, °\text{C}$.

Save time by not doing any arithmetic – just put the equation in the SOLVER of your GDC.

4   a It takes $140 \, \text{s}$ to warm the paraffin from $20 \, °\text{C}$ to $48 \, °\text{C}$ and so $P = mc\dfrac{\Delta \theta}{\Delta t} = 0.120 \times 2500 \times \dfrac{28}{140} = 60 \, \text{W}$.
    b The constant temperature at which paraffin melts is $48 \, °\text{C}$.
    c It takes the paraffin $560 - 140 = 420 \, \text{s}$ to melt. The energy provided is $Q = Pt = 60 \times 420 = 25\,000 \, \text{J}$ and so the specific latent heat of fusion is $L = \dfrac{Q}{m} = \dfrac{25200}{0.120} = 2.1 \times 10^5 \, \text{J kg}^{-1}$.
    d It takes an additional $600 - 560 = 40 \, \text{s}$ to warm liquid paraffin at $48 \, °\text{C}$ to a temperature of $58 \, °\text{C}$ and so
    $P = mc\dfrac{\Delta \theta}{\Delta t} = 0.120 \times c \times \dfrac{58 - 48}{40}$
    $\Rightarrow c = \dfrac{60 \times 40}{10 \times 0.120} = 2.0 \times 10^3 \, \text{J kg}^{-1} \text{K}^{-1}$.
    e The temperature stays constant even though energy is provided because the energy is used to separate the molecules, thus increasing their intermolecular potential energy. No energy transfers into kinetic energy and so the temperature does not change.

For the non-flat sections of the graph, the gradient is $\dfrac{\Delta \theta}{\Delta t}$. Now the power supplied is P and so
$P = mc\dfrac{\Delta \theta}{\Delta t} \Rightarrow c = \dfrac{P}{m\dfrac{\Delta \theta}{\Delta t}}$.
Assuming P is constant, the larger the slope the smaller the specific heat capacity.

5   The average molecular speed stays the same since the temperature is constant. But since the volume decreases, the frequency of collisions will increase because molecules have a shorter distance to cover in between collisions. Hence the pressure increases.

6   The average molecular speed increases since the temperature increases. Hence the pressure will go up. But in addition, with a higher speed the frequency of collisions will increase as well: hence the pressure increases further.

Topic 4: Oscillations and waves

1. a Yes, since acceleration is opposite and proportional to displacement.

   b No, since acceleration is in the same direction as displacement.

   c No, since acceleration is not proportional to displacement.

2. a The graph is a straight line through the origin with negative slope so it satisfies the defining equation for SHM, i.e. $a = -\omega^2 x$.

   b From the graph, the slope is approximately
   $$\frac{-5.7 - 5.7}{15 \times 10^{-2} - (-15 \times 10^{-2})} \approx -38\,\text{s}^{-2}.$$ This equals $-\omega^2$ and so $\omega \approx 6.2\,\text{s}^{-1}$. Hence $T = \frac{2\pi}{\omega} = \frac{2\pi}{6.2} = 1.0\,\text{s}$.

   c The maximum velocity is $v = \omega x_0 \approx 6.2 \times 0.15 = 0.93\,\text{m s}^{-1}$.

3. a The maximum kinetic energy is $0.32\,\text{J}$ and so
   $$E_{\text{max}} = \frac{1}{2}m\omega^2 x_0^2 = 0.32 \Rightarrow \omega = \sqrt{\frac{2 \times 0.32}{0.25 \times (0.20)^2}} = 8.0\,\text{s}^{-1}.$$
   Hence $T = \frac{2\pi}{\omega} = \frac{2\pi}{8.0} = 0.79\,\text{s}$.

   b The maximum speed is $v_{\text{max}} = \omega x_0 = 8.0 \times 0.20 = 1.6\,\text{m s}^{-1}$.
   The maximum acceleration is $a_{\text{max}} = \omega^2 x_0 = 8.0^2 \times 0.20 \approx 13\,\text{m s}^{-2}$.

   c See graph.

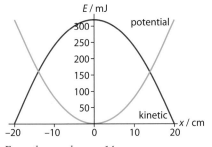

   d From the graph, $x \approx \pm 14\,\text{cm}$.

4. a The car hits a bump every $\frac{5.0}{12} = 0.417\,\text{s}$, i.e. with a frequency of $2.4\,\text{Hz}$. The natural frequency of the oscillations of the car must also be about $2.4\,\text{Hz}$ so that resonance occurs. This means that the amplitude of oscillations will be large. At a different speed, the frequency with which the bumps are hit is different from the natural frequency and so the amplitude is small.

   b $\omega = 2\pi f = 2\pi \times 2.4 \approx 15\,\text{s}^{-1}$

5. The point executes SHM and so $v = \omega\sqrt{x_0^2 - y^2}$.
   We know that $\omega = \frac{2\pi}{T} = \frac{2\pi}{4.0 \times 10^{-3}} = 1.57 \times 10^3\,\text{s}^{-1}$ and since for $x = 0.8\,\text{cm}$ $y = 0.7\,\text{cm}$, we have that
   $v = \omega x_0 = 1.57 \times 10^3 \times \sqrt{(12 \times 10^{-3})^2 - (7 \times 10^{-3})^2} \approx 15\,\text{m s}^{-1}$.
   (Notice that this is different from the speed of the wave. The period is $4.0\,\text{ms}$. The frequency is then $f = \frac{1}{4.0 \times 10^{-3}} = 250\,\text{Hz}$. The speed is $v = f\lambda = 250 \times 2.0 \times 10^{-2} = 5.0\,\text{m s}^{-1}$.)

6. a $1.33 = \frac{3.0 \times 10^8}{v} \Rightarrow v = 2.3 \times 10^8\,\text{m s}^{-1}$.

   b The frequency of light must stay the same and so
   $$\lambda_{\text{water}} = \frac{\lambda_{\text{air}}}{1.33} = 406\,\text{nm}.$$

   c Many examination questions play this trick. It is the angle between the ray and the normal that you want, i.e. $90° - 50° = 40°$, so watch out!
   Then $1 \times \sin 40° = 1.33 \sin\theta_2 \Rightarrow \sin\theta_2 \Rightarrow 0.483 \Rightarrow \theta_2 = 29°$.

7. The path difference at P is $S_2P - S_1P = 0.60\,\text{m}$ and since $\frac{S_2P - S_1P}{\lambda} = \frac{0.60}{0.30} = \underset{\text{integer}}{2}$, we will have constructive interference at P. (At a point that is equidistant from the sources, the path difference is zero and so we have constructive interference.)
   At Q, $S_2Q - S_1Q = 0.45\,\text{m}$ and since $\frac{S_2Q - S_1Q}{\lambda} = \frac{0.45}{0.30} = \underset{\text{half integer}}{1.5}$, we will have destructive interference at Q.

> You must not calculate the slope or the inverse slope.

Topic 5: Electric currents

1. When the voltage is $0.30\,\text{V}$ the current is $1.1\,\text{A}$ and so $R = \frac{V}{I} = \frac{0.30}{1.1} = 0.27\,\Omega$.

2. Using $P = \frac{V^2}{R}$ we find $R = \frac{V^2}{P} = \frac{240^2}{60} = 960\,\Omega$. The new voltage is **half** the original and so $P = \frac{60}{4} = 15\,\text{W}$.

3. a If the radius doubles the cross-sectional area increases by a factor of $2^2 = 4$ and so the resistance becomes $\frac{1}{4} \times 2 = \frac{1}{2}$ times as large, i.e. half the size.

   b Each piece will have resistance $\frac{R}{2}$. Hence the combination has resistance $\frac{R}{4}$.

4. The work required to push one electron through the resistor is $W = qV$ and so $7.2 \times 10^{-19} = 1.6 \times 10^{-19}\,V$ giving $V = 4.5\,\text{V}$. The potential difference across the internal resistor is $0.80 \times 1.4 = 1.12\,\text{V}$ and so the emf is $4.5 + 1.12 = 5.6\,\text{V}$.

5. a We have the top two resistors in series for a total of $120\,\Omega$ and this is in parallel with the bottom $60\,\Omega$ for a grand total resistance between points A and B of
   $$\frac{1}{120} + \frac{1}{60} = \frac{1}{40} \Rightarrow R_T = 40\,\Omega.$$

   b The bottom resistor must have burned out so it is effectively not there.

6. a The potential difference across the $25\,\Omega$ resistor is $25 \times 0.20 = 5.0\,\text{V}$ and this is also the p.d. across R_2.
   Hence $R_2 = \frac{5.0}{0.60} = 8.3\,\Omega$.

   b The current through R_1 is $0.80\,\text{A}$ and the p.d. across it is $12 - 5.0 = 7.0\,\text{V}$. Hence $R_1 = \frac{7.0}{0.80} = 8.8\,\Omega$.

7. a We have two resistors in series for a total of $6.0 + 6.0 = 12\,\Omega$ and this is in parallel with the bottom resistor for a total of
   $$\frac{1}{12} + \frac{1}{6.0} = \frac{3}{12} \Rightarrow R_T = 4.0\,\Omega$$ and in turn this is in series with the internal resistor for a grand total of $4.0 + 2.0 = 6.0\,\Omega$.

   b If the bottom resistor burns out the total becomes $6.0 + 6.0 + 2.0 = 14\,\Omega$.

8 **a** The lamps are in series so they take the same current. Since $P = RI^2$ it follows that lamp A has the greater resistance.

   b The lamps are in parallel so they have the same potential difference across them. Hence the convenient power formula is $P = \dfrac{V^2}{R}$. Lamp B has the smaller resistance and so the greater power.

9 The total resistance of the circuit is $\dfrac{1}{12} + \dfrac{1}{12} = \dfrac{1}{6} \Rightarrow R_T = 6.0\,\Omega$ and so the current leaving the battery is $I = \dfrac{12}{6.0} = 2.0\,\text{A}$. The current in the top $4.0\,\Omega$ resistor is then $1.0\,\text{A}$ and the p.d. across it is $4.0 \times 1.0 = 4.0\,\text{V}$. So the potential at the top end of the voltmeter is $12 - 4.0 = 8.0\,\text{V}$. Similarly, the current in the bottom $8.0\,\Omega$ resistor is $1.0\,\text{A}$ and the p.d. across it is $8.0 \times 1.0 = 8.0\,\text{V}$. So the potential at the bottom end of the voltmeter is $12 - 8.0 = 4.0\,\text{V}$. The p.d. across the voltmeter is then $4.0\,\text{V}$.

10 The total resistance of $R_1 + R_2 = 100\,\Omega$ and $R = 5.0\,\Omega$ is $\dfrac{1}{100} + \dfrac{1}{5.0} = \dfrac{21}{100} \Rightarrow R_T = 4.76\,\Omega$. This is in series with the internal resistance and so the overall total resistance of the circuit is $R_T = 2.0 + 4.8 = 6.8\,\Omega$. The current is then $I = \dfrac{12}{6.8} = 1.8\,\text{A}$ and so the reading of the voltmeter is $V = 12 - 1.8 \times 2.0 = 8.4\,\text{V}$.

11 **a** From $P = \dfrac{V^2}{R}$ we find $R = \dfrac{V^2}{P} = \dfrac{36}{12} = 3.0\,\Omega$.

   b From $P = VI$ we get $I = \dfrac{P}{V} = \dfrac{12}{6.0} = 2.0\,\text{A}$.

   c The p.d. across wire AB is $6.0\,\text{V}$ and so the p.d. across BC is also $6.0\,\text{V}$. Since the resistance of AB is double that of BC, the current in BC is double that in AB. Let x stand for the current in AB. Then, $x + 2.0 = 2x$ and so $x = 2.0\,\text{A}$. The resistance of AB is then $R_{AB} = \dfrac{6.0}{2.0} = 3.0\,\Omega$ and so $R_{AC} = 4.5\,\Omega$.

12 **a** When the temperature is increased the resistance of T will decrease. Therefore the potential difference across T will decrease as well. We can see this as follows: think of the circuit as a potential divider. Since the resistance of T is less than R and the current in T and R is the same the potential difference drops.

   b The LDR will decrease in resistance as the light gets brighter and so the answer is the same as in **a**.

Topic 6: Fields and forces

1 $20 = \dfrac{GMm}{R^2}$. Hence at the new position,

$W = \dfrac{GMm}{(2R)^2} = \dfrac{1}{4}\dfrac{GMm}{R^2} = 5.0\,\text{N}$.

2 The force on the Earth is $F = G\dfrac{Mm}{r^2}$ and so

$G\dfrac{Mm}{r^2} = \dfrac{mv^2}{r} \Rightarrow M = \dfrac{v^2 r}{G}$. The Earth moves a distance $2\pi r$ in one year and so $v = \dfrac{2\pi r}{T} = \dfrac{2\pi \times 1.5 \times 10^{11}}{365 \times 24 \times 60 \times 60} = 2.99 \times 10^4\,\text{m s}^{-1}$. Hence

$M = \dfrac{v^2 r}{G} = \dfrac{(2.99 \times 10^4)^2 \times 1.5 \times 10^{11}}{6.67 \times 10^{-11}} = 2.0 \times 10^{30}\,\text{kg}$.

3 **D:** The force will always be attractive. If Q is positive, there will be negative charges near it and positive charges further away leading to attraction. If Q is negative, it will push negative charges in the sphere away leaving positive charges nearby again leading to attraction.

4 The answer is **C**. This **comparison** type problem is best solved as follows.

EITHER: write the equation for the gravitational field strength for the Earth: $g = \dfrac{GM}{R^2}$. Do the same for the planet: $g_P = \dfrac{GM_P}{R_P^2}$.

Divide side by side: $\dfrac{g_P}{g} = \dfrac{\dfrac{GM_P}{R_P^2}}{\dfrac{GM}{R^2}} = \dfrac{M_P}{M}\dfrac{R^2}{R_P^2} = 2 \times \dfrac{1}{2^2} = \dfrac{1}{2}$.

Then $g_P = \dfrac{g}{2}$,

OR: write $g_P = \dfrac{GM_P}{R_P^2} = \dfrac{G(2M)}{(2R)^2} = \dfrac{2}{4}\dfrac{GM}{R^2} = \dfrac{1}{2}g$.

Common mistake: the denominator contains $(2R)^2$ which gives $4R^2$ and not $2R^2$.

5 The answer is **B** by considering forces on a positive charge at the centre and adding the four forces as vectors.

6 See diagram (marks for direction of arrows, normal to sphere, no lines inside conductor).

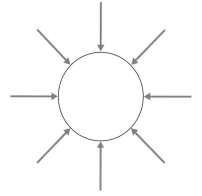

7 Applying the right hand grip rule, the answer is **D**.

Topic 7: Atomic and nuclear physics

1. **a** It must be narrow to make the determination of the scattering angle measurable.
   b It must be very thin in order to avoid absorption of the alpha particles by the foil and also in order to avoid multiple scatterings.

2. Alpha particles from a radioactive source were directed at a thin gold foil and their scattering was studied.
   Most of the alpha particles went through the gold foil essentially undeflected or suffered very small deflections. The deflection was due to the electric force of repulsion between the positive charge of the alpha particles and the positive charge of the atom. The small deflections meant that the alpha particles never got very close to the positive charge of the atom.
   Very rarely, however, alpha particles suffered large angle deflections. The force required to cause these deflections meant that the alpha particles had to get very close to the positive charge of the atom, i.e. the positive charge was located in a tiny volume. This was the nucleus of the atom that contained the atom's positive charge and most of its mass. The rest of the atom was empty space.

3. Using $\Delta E = hf$ we find $1.9 \times 1.6 \times 10^{-19} = 6.63 \times 10^{-34} \times \dfrac{3 \times 10^8}{\lambda}$ and so $\lambda = 6.5 \times 10^{-7}\,\text{m}$.

You must convert the eV into joules.

4. $\dfrac{KE_\alpha}{KE_{Pb}} = \dfrac{\dfrac{p^2}{2m_\alpha}}{\dfrac{p^2}{2m_{Pb}}} = \dfrac{m_{Pb}}{m_\alpha} = \dfrac{214}{4} = 53.5$ since the momenta are equal and opposite.

5. 12 days correspond to 3 half-lives and so the activity is $\left(\dfrac{1}{2}\right)^3 = \left(\dfrac{1}{8}\right)$ of the original.

6.

Time / min	X	Y	Y / X
0	1	0	0
2.0	$\frac{1}{2}$	$\frac{1}{2}$	1
4.0	$\frac{1}{4}$	$\frac{3}{4}$	3
6.0	$\frac{1}{8}$	$\frac{7}{8}$	7

So 6.0 minutes must go by.

7. C, there is a 50% chance of decaying in any half-life interval.

8. **a** The energy released is given by $Q = \left(M_{Po} - (M_{Pb} + M_{He})\right)c^2$.
   Now,
   $B.E._{Po} = (84m_p + 134m_n - M_{Po})c^2 \Rightarrow M_{Po}c^2 = (84m_p + 134m_n)c^2 - B.E._{Po}$
   $B.E._{Pb} = (82m_p + 132m_n - M_{Pb})c^2 \Rightarrow M_{Pb}c^2 = (82m_p + 132m_n)c^2 - B.E._{Pb}$
   $B.E._{He} = (2m_p + 2m_n - M_{He})c^2 \Rightarrow M_{He}c^2 = (2m_p + 2m_n)c^2 - B.E._{He}$
   Hence, $Q = B.E._{Pb} + B.E._{He} - B.E._{Po}$.

   This shows that the energy released is the difference between the total binding energy of the products and the binding energy of the decaying nucleus.

   b The binding energy of polonium is $218 \times 7.8 \approx 1700\,\text{MeV}$, that of helium $4 \times 7.2 \approx 29\,\text{MeV}$ and that of lead $214 \times 7.9 \approx 1690\,\text{MeV}$. The energy released is then about $29 + 1690 - 1700 = 19\,\text{MeV}$.

You must find the **total** binding energy, not just the binding energy per nucleon.

9. C: There are 11 nucleons in $^{11}_{5}\text{B}$ and so the energy is $11 \times 7.0 = 77\,\text{MeV}$.

10. The total mass on the left is $18.00567\,\text{u}$ and is **smaller** than the total on the right of 18.00696 by $0.00129\,\text{u}$. The naïve answer is that the missing energy of $0.00129 \times 931.5 = 1.20\,\text{MeV}$ must be provided by the alpha particle's kinetic energy.

Because momentum must be conserved, however, the alpha's kinetic energy must in fact be somewhat larger.

Topic 8: Energy, power and climate change

1. The power that must be provided by nuclear fission is $\dfrac{400}{0.40} = 1000\,\text{MW}$. The number of reactions per second must be $N \times 200 \times 10^6 \times 1.6 \times 10^{-19} = 1000 \times 10^6$ and so $N = \dfrac{1000 \times 10^6}{200 \times 10^6 \times 1.6 \times 10^{-19}} = 3.1 \times 10^{19}\,\text{s}^{-1}$. In a single reaction a mass of $235\,\text{u}$ or $235 \times 1.66 \times 10^{-27} = 3.9 \times 10^{-25}\,\text{kg}$ is used. Hence the mass used per second is $3.1 \times 10^{19} \times 3.9 \times 10^{-25} = 1.2 \times 10^{-5}\,\text{kg s}^{-1}$. In one year we need $1.2 \times 10^{-5} \times 365 \times 24 \times 3600 \approx 380\,\text{kg}$.

2. The rate at which thermal energy is lost is $\dfrac{\Delta Q}{\Delta t} = mc\dfrac{\Delta \theta}{\Delta t} = 220 \times 4200 \times 3.5 \times 10^{-3} = 3234\,\text{W}$. This must be provided by sunlight. If the area is A then the power supplied is $640 \times A$ and so $640A = 3234 \Rightarrow A = 5.1\,\text{m}^2$.

3. From the formula, we have simply
   $$P = \frac{1}{2}\rho A v^3 = \frac{1}{2} \times 1.2 \times \pi \times \left(\frac{12}{2}\right)^2 \times 8.0^3$$
   $$= 35\,\text{kW}.$$
   The number of windmills needed is $\dfrac{50 \times 10^3}{35} = 143$.
   This is a large number and in practice even more would be needed.

Doubling the windmill area doubles the power extracted but doubling the wind speed increases the power (in theory) by a factor of eight. Frictional and other losses (mainly turbulence) result in a smaller power increase in practice. The calculations above also assume that all the wind is actually stopped by the windmill, extracting all of the wind's kinetic energy, which is impossible – there would be no airflow in that case! In addition, the calculation assumes that the wind impacts the blades of the turbine at right angles, which is not always the case unless the windmill can be turned into the wind.

4 $\frac{P}{L} = \frac{1}{2}\rho g A^2 v = \frac{1}{2} \times 10^3 \times 9.8 \times 1.5^2 \times 4.0 = 44\,\text{kW m}^{-1}$. Hence, from a wavefront of length 5.0 m we get a power of $P = 5.0 \times 44 = 220\,\text{kW}$.

5   From $Q = AC_S\Delta T$ we have that $P = \frac{Q}{\Delta t} = \frac{AC_S\Delta T}{\Delta t}$ and so the net intensity is $I_{\text{in}} - I_{\text{out}} = \frac{P}{A} = \frac{C_S\Delta T}{\Delta t}$. Hence $\Delta T = \frac{(I_{\text{in}} - I_{\text{out}})\Delta t}{C_S}$.

Thus, $\Delta T = \frac{(800 - 0.2 \times 800) \times 2 \times 30 \times 8 \times 24 \times 3600}{8.7 \times 10^7} = 13\,\text{K}$.

The two main assumptions are that all the water is heated uniformly, and that there is no cooling of the water during the night.

6
  a   The power received by 1 square metre of the Earth's surface ($A = 1\,\text{m}^2$) is $P_{\text{in}} = (1-\alpha)\frac{S}{4}A = (1-\alpha)\frac{S}{4}$. This is because a power $\alpha\frac{S}{4}A$ has been reflected back into space. The Earth radiates power from the entire surface area of its spherical shape and so the power radiated from 1 square metre (by the Stefan–Boltzmann law) $P_{\text{out}} = \sigma T^4$. (We are using an emissivity of 1 for the Earth's surface. Of the 30% of the reflected radiation only about 4% to 5% is reflected from the surface itself and so the emissivity is about 0.96 to 0.95.) Equating the two: $(1-\alpha)\frac{S}{4} = \sigma T^4 \Rightarrow (1-\alpha)S = 4\sigma T^4$.

  b   We find $T = 4\sqrt{\frac{(1-\alpha)S}{4\sigma}}$, i.e. $T = 4\sqrt{\frac{(1-0.30) \times 1400}{4(5.67 \times 10^{-8})}} \approx 256\,\text{K}$. This temperature is $-17\,°\text{C}$.

  c   A temperature of 256 K is 32 K lower than the Earth's average temperature of 288 K and so obviously the model is wrong. One reason this model is too simple is precisely because we have not taken into account the fact that not all the power radiated by the Earth actually escapes. Some of the power is absorbed by the gases in the atmosphere and is re-radiated back down to the Earth's surface, causing further warming that we have neglected to take into account. In other words, this model neglects the **greenhouse effect**.
    Another drawback of the simple model presented above is that the model is essentially a zero-dimensional model – the Earth is treated as a point without interactions between the surface and the atmosphere (latent heat flows, thermal energy flow in oceans through currents, thermal energy transfer between the surface and the atmosphere due to temperature differences between the two, are all ignored). Realistic models must take all these factors (and many others) into account and so are very complex.

7   The total volume of water in the oceans is approximately $V = A \times 3.7 \times 10^3$ where A is the surface area of the oceans. The increase in volume is then $\Delta V = \gamma V_0 \Delta\theta = 2 \times 10^{-4} \times A \times 3.7 \times 10^3 \times 2$. This means that the sea level will increase by an amount h such that $A \times h = A \times 1.48$, i.e. $h \approx 1.5\,\text{m}$.
This answer assumes uniform heating of all the water, which is unlikely. It ignores the anomalous expansion of water (the volume decreases for temperatures in the range of 0 °C to 4 °C). It assumes that γ is constant. It ignores the cooling that would take place because with a higher temperature there would be more evaporation. Finally, the extra volume of water might cover previously dry land and so the expected increase in sea level would be less.

Topic 9:   Motion in fields

1   The body will fall a vertical distance of 12 m and so from $y = \frac{1}{2}gt^2$, $12 = \frac{1}{2} \times 9.8t^2$ giving $t = 1.56\,\text{s}$. The horizontal distance travelled in this time is then $x = vt = 15 \times 1.56 = 23\,\text{m}$.

2   Since the gravitational potential is the sum of the potentials from each mass separately and since it is negative we must choose the point that involves the largest distances from the masses, i.e. **D**.

3
  a   The gravitational potential at the mid-point is $V = -\frac{GM}{d} - \frac{GM}{d} = -\frac{2GM}{d}$ and so the work done to bring the little mass there from infinity is $W = mV = -\frac{2GMm}{d}$.

  b   The potential at the new position is $V = -\frac{GM}{3d/2} - \frac{GM}{d/2} = -\frac{8GM}{3d}$. Hence the work required is $W = m\Delta V = m\left(-\frac{8GM}{3d} - \left(-\frac{2GM}{d}\right)\right) = -\frac{2GMm}{3d}$.

4   All points on the x-axis are equidistant from a $\pm$ vertical pair of charges and so the potential due to those charges is zero. Hence the answer is **B**.

5   The field is directed from high to low potential and it gets stronger as we move to the right. This means that the equipotential lines must get closer as we move to the right. Hence the answer is **D**.

6 $E_P = \frac{9 \times 10^9 \times (1.6 \times 10^{-19})(-1.6 \times 10^{-19})}{2.0 \times 10^{-10}} = -1.2 \times 10^{-18}\,\text{J}$.

7
  a   The change in potential is 90 V and so from $\frac{1}{2}mv^2 = q\Delta V$ we get $v = \sqrt{\frac{2q\Delta V}{m}} = \sqrt{\frac{2 \times 1.6 \times 10^{-19} \times 90}{1.67 \times 10^{-27}}} = 1.3 \times 10^5\,\text{m s}^{-1}$.

  b   At infinity the potential is zero and so the change in potential is 180 V i.e. double the change in **a**. Hence $v_\infty = \sqrt{2} \times 1.3 \times 10^5 = 1.8 \times 10^5\,\text{m s}^{-1}$.

  c

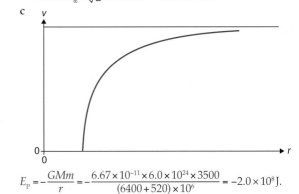

8 $E_P = -\frac{GMm}{r} = -\frac{6.67 \times 10^{-11} \times 6.0 \times 10^{24} \times 3500}{(6400 + 520) \times 10^6} = -2.0 \times 10^8\,\text{J}$.

9
  a   By drawing a tangent line at $r = 2.0 \times 10^6\,\text{m}$ and measuring its gradient we get approximately $g = 25\,\text{N kg}^{-1}$.

  b $W = m\Delta V = 350 \times (-0.5 \times 10^8 - (-2.0 \times 10^8)) = 5.2 \times 10^{10}\,\text{J}$.

  c   The additional work involves the kinetic energy of the probe when it is in orbit. This is $E_K = \frac{1}{2}mv^2 = \frac{1}{2}\frac{GMm}{r} = -\frac{1}{2}mV$ $= \frac{1}{2} \times (0.5 \times 10^8) \times 350 = 8.8 \times 10^9\,\text{J}$.

10 The launch speed is $v = \dfrac{v_{esc}}{2} = \dfrac{1}{2}\sqrt{\dfrac{2GM}{R}}$ and so by energy conservation, with r being the distance the probe gets to,
$\dfrac{1}{2}mv^2 - \dfrac{GMm}{R} = -\dfrac{GMm}{r}$ (no kinetic energy when the mass stops),
i.e. $\dfrac{1}{2} \times \dfrac{1}{4} \times \dfrac{2GMm}{R} - \dfrac{GMm}{R} = -\dfrac{GMm}{r} \Rightarrow -\dfrac{GMm}{r} = -\dfrac{3GM}{4R} \Rightarrow r = \dfrac{4R}{3}$

Topic 10: Thermal physics

1 $PV = nRT$ so $n = \dfrac{PV}{RT} = \dfrac{20 \times 10^5 \times 4.0 \times 10^{-3}}{8.31 \times 300} = 3.2$.

2 From $\dfrac{P_1 V_1}{n_1 T_1} = \dfrac{P_2 V_2}{n_2 T_2}$ we see that n and V stay the same and so $\dfrac{P_1}{T_1} = \dfrac{P_2}{T_2}$.

> Remember to always use degrees kelvin.

$\dfrac{P_1}{300_1} = \dfrac{P_2}{400} \Rightarrow P_2 = \dfrac{400}{300} \times 3.0 \times 10^5 = 4.0 \times 10^5$ Pa.

3 The answer has to be **B**. Explicitly, the pressure is $\dfrac{(2n)RT}{(2V)} = \dfrac{nRT}{V} = P$ where n and V are the number of moles and volume in one half of the container.

4 The work done is the area under the graph (a trapezium) and so (watch the axes) is
$W = \dfrac{9.0 + 12}{2} \times 10^6 \times (8.0 - 2.0) \times 10^{-3} = 6.3 \times 10^4$ J.

5 a From $\dfrac{P_1 V_1}{n_1 T_1} = \dfrac{P_2 V_2}{n_2 T_2}$ we see that $\dfrac{V_1}{T_1} = \dfrac{V_2}{T_2}$ and so
$T_2 = \dfrac{V_2}{V_1}T_1 = \dfrac{5.0 \times 10^{-3}}{2.0 \times 10^{-3}} \times 300 = 750$ K. The pressure is constant so we may calculate the work done from $W = P\Delta V = 4.0 \times 10^5 \times 3.0 \times 10^{-3} = 1.2 \times 10^3$ J.
  b From $Q = \Delta U + W$ we see that since the temperature increased, $\Delta U > 0$, and the gas expanded so $W > 0$ hence $Q > 0$. Thermal energy has been supplied to the gas.

6 a The internal energy of an ideal gas is the total random kinetic energy E_K of the molecules of the gas.
  b The absolute temperature is proportional to the **average** kinetic energy of the molecules, $T \propto \dfrac{E_K}{N}$. Therefore the internal energy is proportional to the absolute temperature (and the number of molecules), $U = E_K \propto NT$.

> You must stress that the kinetic energy referred to is random kinetic energy.

7 The piston moving rapidly in collides with molecules and the molecules rebound with a speed greater than before. The average kinetic energy of the molecules and hence the temperature increase.

8 At constant volume we have $Q = \Delta U$ since no work is being done. At constant pressure, $Q = \Delta U' + W$, with $W > 0$. Hence the change in internal energy is larger in the constant volume case ($\Delta U > \Delta U'$) and there we have the larger temperature increase.

> To decide what happens to temperature you must look at internal energy.

9 a AB is the isothermal since it is less steep than the adiabatic CA.
  b B to C because the work done is negative (on the gas) and the temperature drops so that $\Delta U < 0$. Since $Q = \Delta U + W$ we have $Q < 0$.
  c AB, because the area under the curve is greatest.

10 Applying $Q = \Delta U + W$ to the **entire cycle** we see that $\Delta U = 0$. The total work done is the area of the loop and the total thermal energy transferred is $Q_1 - Q_2$. Hence $Q_1 - Q_2 = W$ and so Q_1 is larger.

11 a The temperature at B is higher than that at A (since the pressure is constant and the volume increased). Hence $\Delta U > 0$. Work has been done **by** the gas and so $W > 0$. Hence $Q = \Delta U + W > 0$ and thermal energy has been supplied to the gas. Along CD, similarly, the temperature at D is lower that that at C (since the volume is constant and the pressure is less at D) and so $\Delta U > 0$. No work has been done (the volume is constant) and so $Q = \Delta U + W = \Delta U + 0 < 0$.
   b Along BC: $0 = \Delta U_1 + W_1 \Rightarrow \Delta U_1 = -|W_1|$.
   Along DA: $0 = \Delta U_2 + W_2 \Rightarrow \Delta U_2 = +|W_2|$. Since we do not have enough information to determine the relation between $|W_1|$ and $|W_2|$ we cannot answer the question.

12 The ice is first turned into liquid water at $0\,°C$. The liquid is more disordered than the solid ice and so the entropy of the ice has increased. The water at $0\,°C$ is now warmed to $20\,°C$ leading to more disorder and hence a further entropy increase in the water. For both the melting process and the warming process, thermal energy was provided from the warm room whose entropy therefore decreased. The overall entropy change has been an increase as demanded by the second law of thermodynamics.

Topic 11: Wave phenomena

1 The wavelength of the first harmonic is $\lambda_1 = 2L$ and that of the second is $\lambda_2 = L$. Hence $\dfrac{f_2}{f_1} = 2$.

2 The wavelength in tube X is $\lambda_X = 2L$ and that in tube Y is $\lambda_Y = 4L$.
Hence $\dfrac{f_X}{f_Y} = \dfrac{\dfrac{v}{\lambda_X}}{\dfrac{v}{\lambda_Y}} = \dfrac{\lambda_Y}{\lambda_X} = \dfrac{4L}{2L} = 2$.

3 In the first case we have the first harmonic and so $\lambda = 4L_1$.
In the second case $\lambda = \dfrac{4L_2}{3}$ i.e. $3\lambda = 4L_2$.
Subtracting, $2\lambda = 4(L_2 - L_1) = 4x = 1.20 \Rightarrow \lambda = 0.60$ m.
Thus $v = \lambda f = 0.60 \times 560 = 336 \approx 340$ m s^{-1}.

> It would have been easier to realise, through a diagram, that the distance x of the problem has to be half a wavelength.

4 The car is approaching the emitter so the frequency it receives is
$f_1 = 300 \times \dfrac{340+u}{340}$ Hz, where u is the unknown car speed.
The car now acts as an emitter of a wave of this frequency (f_1), and the original emitter will act as the new receiver. Thus the frequency received (315 Hz) is (car is approaching)
$315 = (300 \times \dfrac{340+u}{340}) \times \dfrac{340}{340-u}$ from which we find $u = 8.29\,\mathrm{m\,s^{-1}}$.

> You must feel comfortable with this type of double Doppler problems.

5 The highest frequency measured will be when the source approaches the observer and so $510 = f_S \dfrac{340}{340-v_S}$ and the lowest when it moves away so that $504 = f_S \dfrac{340}{340+v_S}$.

Hence $\dfrac{510}{504} = 1.0119 = \dfrac{f_S \dfrac{340}{340-v_S}}{f_S \dfrac{340}{340+v_S}} = \dfrac{340+v_S}{340-v_S}$.

Solving for the speed of the carousel we get
$0.0119 \times 340 = 2.0119 v_S \Rightarrow v_S = \dfrac{0.0119 \times 340}{2.0119} = 2.0\,\mathrm{m\,s^{-1}}$.

6 The received wavelength is longer than that emitted and so the galaxy moves away. The emitted frequency is
$f = \dfrac{c}{\lambda} = \dfrac{3.00 \times 10^8}{658 \times 10^{-9}} = 4.56 \times 10^{14}\,\mathrm{Hz}$; the received frequency is
$f = \dfrac{3.00 \times 10^8}{720 \times 10^{-9}} = 4.17 \times 10^{14}\,\mathrm{Hz}$ giving a shift $\Delta f = 3.9 \times 10^{13}\,\mathrm{Hz}$.
Hence using $v = \dfrac{c\Delta f}{f}$ the speed is
$v = \dfrac{3.00 \times 10^8 \times 0.39 \times 10^{14}}{4.56 \times 10^{14}} = 2.6 \times 10^7\,\mathrm{m\,s^{-1}}$.

7 Use $\theta_D \approx \dfrac{\lambda}{b}$. From the graph $\theta_D \approx 0.011\,\mathrm{rad}$ and so
$b \approx \dfrac{\lambda}{\theta_D} = \dfrac{4.8 \times 10^{-7}}{0.011} = 4.4 \times 10^{-5}\,\mathrm{m}$.

8 The angular separation of two points at the ends of the diameter of Mars is $\theta_A = \dfrac{7 \times 10^6}{7 \times 10^{10}} = 1 \times 10^{-4}\,\mathrm{rad}$. The angle of the first diffraction minimum at the eye is $\theta_D = 1.22 \dfrac{650 \times 10^{-9}}{3 \times 10^{-3}} = 3 \times 10^{-4}\,\mathrm{rad}$. The angular separation is less than this ($\theta_A < \theta_D$) and so the points are not resolved. Mars appears as a point source.

9 The intensity is reduced by a factor of 2 after going through the first polariser. There is a further reduction by $\cos^2 45°$ after transmission through the second polariser and then another $\cos^2 45°$ reduction after transmission through the third. Overall the intensity is reduced by $\dfrac{1}{2} \times \cos^2 45° \times \cos^2 45° = \dfrac{1}{2} \times \dfrac{1}{2} \times \dfrac{1}{2} = \dfrac{1}{8}$.

10 From Snell's law, $1.33 \times \sin\theta = 1.00 \times \sin(90° - \theta) = 1.00 \times \cos\theta$.
Hence, $\tan\theta = \dfrac{1.00}{1.33}$ and so $\theta = 36.9°$.

Topic 12:   Electromagnetic induction

1 The flux is decreasing and so there is an induced current. As explained earlier in the topic, the current is counterclockwise. Then there is a magnetic force on the rod directed to the left and so the velocity decreases. The loss in kinetic energy of the rod gets transformed into the electrical energy that lights up the lamp.

2 The device is probably a coil. When the switch is closed, the current in the coil induces an emf. By Lenz's law this emf has the opposite sign to the battery's emf and so the current takes time to rise to its final constant value. Since the constant final current is 1.0 A the resistance of D must be $R = \dfrac{12}{1.0} = 12\,\Omega$.

3 a

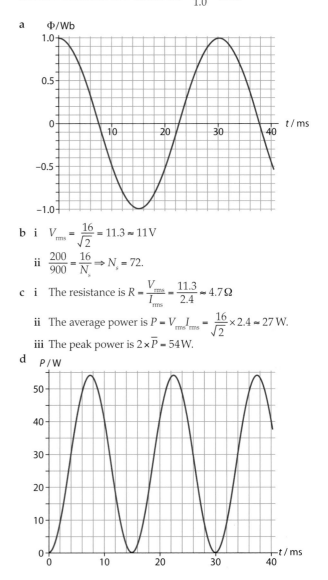

b i $V_{rms} = \dfrac{16}{\sqrt{2}} = 11.3 \approx 11\,\mathrm{V}$

   ii $\dfrac{200}{900} = \dfrac{16}{N_s} \Rightarrow N_s = 72$.

c i The resistance is $R = \dfrac{V_{rms}}{I_{rms}} = \dfrac{11.3}{2.4} \approx 4.7\,\Omega$

   ii The average power is $P = V_{rms} I_{rms} = \dfrac{16}{\sqrt{2}} \times 2.4 \approx 27\,\mathrm{W}$.

   iii The peak power is $2 \times \overline{P} = 54\,\mathrm{W}$.

d

Topic 13: Quantum physics and nuclear physics

1 **a** At the threshold frequency, $E_K = 0$ and so

$$hf = \phi \Rightarrow f = \frac{1.8 \times 1.6 \times 10^{-19}}{6.6 \times 10^{-34}} = 4.4 \times 10^{14}\,\text{Hz}.$$

    b The kinetic energy of the emitted electrons is

$$E_K = hf - \phi = 6.6 \times 10^{-34} \times \frac{3.0 \times 10^8}{4.8 \times 10^{-7}} - 1.8 \times 1.6 \times 10^{-19} = 1.2 \times 10^{-19}\,\text{J}.$$

> Notice finding frequency from wavelength and conversion of eV to J.

    Hence, from $E_K = \frac{1}{2}mv^2$ we find $v = \sqrt{\dfrac{2 \times 1.2 \times 10^{-19}}{9.1 \times 10^{-31}}} = 1.7 \times 10^7\,\text{m s}^{-1}$.

2 From $E_K = hf - \phi$, and $E_K = qV$ we find $qV = hf - \phi \Rightarrow V = \dfrac{h}{q} - \dfrac{\phi}{q}$.

    Hence the vertical intercept is $-\dfrac{\phi}{q}$ and so $-\dfrac{\phi}{q} = -4.0\,\text{V}$ giving

    $\phi = 4.0\,\text{eV} = 4.0 \times 1.6 \times 10^{-19} = 6.4 \times 10^{-19}\,\text{J}$. The slope of the

    graph equals $\dfrac{h}{q}$ and is measured to be 4.25×10^{-15}.

    Hence $h = 4.25 \times 10^{-15} \times 1.6 \times 10^{-19} = 6.8 \times 10^{-34}\,\text{J s}$.

> Notice that if we plot V on the vertical axis the gradient is $\dfrac{h}{q}$.

3 The kinetic energy of the accelerated electron is $E_K = \dfrac{p^2}{2m}$

    and equals the work done in moving through the
potential difference i.e. qV. Hence $p = \sqrt{2mqV}$ and so

$$\lambda = \frac{h}{\sqrt{2mqV}} = \frac{6.6 \times 10^{-34}}{\sqrt{2 \times 9.1 \times 10^{-31} \times 1.6 \times 10^{-19} \times 250}} = 7.7 \times 10^{-11}\,\text{m}.$$

> Notice that $\lambda \propto \dfrac{1}{\sqrt{V}}$: this is convenient for Paper **1** questions.

4 To resolve something the wavelength used must of the same order of magnitude as the size of the object to be resolved. The de Broglie wavelength of the electrons used in an electron microscope is much smaller than visible light and so can resolve very small objects.

> It is important to stress the connection between wavelength and ability to resolve.

5 **a** A wavefunction is a mathematical function which, when squared and multiplied by small volume element, gives the probability of finding a particle within that volume element.

    b **i** The wavelength is $\lambda = \dfrac{1.0 \times 10^{-10}}{2} = 0.5 \times 10^{-10}\,\text{m}$. The

          momentum is therefore $p = \dfrac{h}{\lambda} = \dfrac{6.63 \times 10^{-34}}{0.5 \times 10^{-10}} = 1.3 \times 10^{-23}\,\text{N s}$.

      ii The kinetic energy is $E_K = \dfrac{p^2}{2m}$ and so equal to

          $\dfrac{(1.3 \times 10^{-23})^2}{2 \times 9.1 \times 10^{-31}} = 9.3 \times 10^{-17}\,\text{J}$.

    c Any point where the wavefunction is zero.

6 The uncertainty in the position of the electron is of order $\Delta x \approx 10^{-10}\,\text{m}$ and so the uncertainty in the momentum is $\Delta p \approx \dfrac{h}{4\pi\Delta x} = \dfrac{6.6 \times 10^{-34}}{4\pi \times 10^{-10}} \approx 5 \times 10^{-25}\,\text{N s}.$

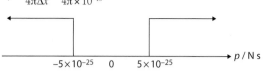

> It is important that you understand the logic of the diagram.

    Now the momentum will be measured to be $p_0 \pm \Delta p$. The least magnitude of p_0 is 0 and so the least possible magnitude of the momentum of the electron is $5 \times 10^{-25}\,\text{N s}$. The energy of the electron is then at least:

$$E_K \approx \frac{(5 \times 10^{-25})^2}{2 \times 9 \times 10^{-31}} \approx 3 \times 10^{-20}\,\text{J} \approx \frac{3 \times 10^{-20}}{1.6 \times 10^{-19}} \approx 2\,\text{eV}.$$

7 **a** The measurement must be completed in less than $0.1\,\text{N s}$ i.e.

      $\Delta t \approx 10^{-10}\,\text{s}$. Then $\Delta E \approx \dfrac{h}{4\pi\Delta t} = \dfrac{6.6 \times 10^{-34}}{4\pi \times 10^{-10}} \approx 5 \times 10^{-25}\,\text{J}$.

    b The energy difference between levels is not precisely known because of the uncertainty in **a**. Hence there will be a range of wavelengths for a given transition rather than a strictly monochromatic photon.

8 After acceleration the kinetic energy of the proton is eV and this is all converted to electrical potential energy when it just stops

    on the nuclear surface. Hence $eV = \dfrac{ke(42e)}{R}$ where R is the radius

    of the nucleus. The radius is $R \approx 1.2 \times 10^{-15} \times 96^{1/3} = 5.5 \times 10^{-15}\,\text{m}$.

    Hence, $V = \dfrac{ke(42e)}{eR} = \dfrac{8.99 \times 10^9 \times 42 \times 1.6 \times 10^{-19}}{5.5 \times 10^{-15}} \approx 11\,\text{MV}$.

> It is crucial that you realise the conversion KE to electric energy.

9 From the hint we see that the number in front of $\dfrac{m}{q}$ is the ratio $\dfrac{A}{n}$

    where A and n are integers – the charge of the atoms may be ne. Mass numbers 35 and 37 are both possible for either $n = 1$ or $n = 2$ and so the answer is **D**.

10 **a** The experimental evidence is the fact that energies of alpha and gamma particles in radioactive decay are discrete.

    b The alpha particle ends in an excited state of uranium. When the uranium returns to its ground state photons will be emitted.

11 $\dfrac{E_{\text{atom}}}{E_{\text{nucleus}}} = 10^{-6} = \dfrac{m_n L_n^{\,2}}{m_e L_a^{\,2}}$ so that $\dfrac{L_a}{L_n} = \sqrt{10^6 \dfrac{m_n}{m_e}} \approx \sqrt{10^6 \times 2000} \approx 10^4$.

12 The initial activity is given by $A_0 = \lambda N_0$. The number of moles of

    strontium is $\dfrac{50}{90} = 0.56$ and so the number of strontium nuclei in

    the sample is $N_0 = 0.56 \times 6.02 \times 10^{23} = 3.3 \times 10^{23}$. Hence $\dfrac{\ln 2}{T_{1/2}} N_0$

    $= 2.5 \times 10^{14}$ and so $T_{1/2} = \dfrac{\ln 2 \times 3.3 \times 10^{23}}{2.5 \times 10^{14}} = 9.14 \times 10^8\,\text{s} \approx 29\,\text{yr}$.

> It is important that you remember that the formula for the initial activity and that you can find the initial number of nuclei present.

13 The decay constant is $\lambda = \dfrac{\ln 2}{2.45} = 0.283 \, \text{min}^{-1}$.

Thus $A = A_0 e^{-\lambda t} = A_0 e^{-0.283 \times 1.0} = A_0 0.753$, i.e. about 75% of the original activity.

> You will not gain any marks if you do not use the radioactive decay formula.

14 $N_X = N_0 e^{-\lambda t}$ $\quad$ $N_Y = N_0 - N_0 e^{-\lambda t}$

$\dfrac{N_X}{N_Y} = \dfrac{N_0 e^{-\lambda t}}{N_0 - N_0 e^{-\lambda t}} = \dfrac{e^{-\lambda t}}{1 - e^{-\lambda t}} = \dfrac{1}{4}$

Hence $4e^{-\lambda t} = 1 - e^{-\lambda t} \Rightarrow 5e^{-\lambda t} = 1 \Rightarrow e^{-\lambda t} = \dfrac{1}{5} \Rightarrow \lambda t = \ln 5$

$t = \dfrac{\ln 5}{\lambda} = \dfrac{\ln 5}{\ln 2} \times 2.0 = 4.6 \, \text{min}$.

> You will not gain any marks if you do not use the radioactive decay formula.

15 For X we go to half the initial activity and find a time of 0.35 min. For Y we must wait until most of X has decayed away so that no new Y nuclei are produced. Looking at how long it takes for the activity to halve (after 2.5 min) we find a Y half-life of about 0.65 min.

Topic 14: Digital technology

1 We put the appropriate power of 2 under each digit starting with 0 on the right: 10101.

$$10101 \rightarrow \underline{1} \times 2^4 + \underline{0} \times 2^3 + \underline{1} \times 2^2 + \underline{0} \times 2^1 + \underline{1} \times 2^0 \rightarrow 16 + 0 + 4 + 0 + 1 = 21$$

2 With 5 bits we can have at most $2^5 = 32$ numbers. These are the numbers from 0 to 31.

3 The number of bits imprinted on the CD is
$44100 \times 32 \times 74 \times 60 = 6.27 \times 10^9$ bits
Since 1 byte = 8 bits this corresponds to
$\dfrac{6.27 \times 10^9}{8} = 780 \times 10^6$ bytes = 780 Mbytes.

4 The charge in 30 ms is $2.0 \times 10^8 \times 30 \times 10^{-3} \times 1.6 \times 10^{-19} = 9.6 \times 10^{-13} \, \text{C}$
and so $V = \dfrac{Q}{C} = \dfrac{9.6 \times 10^{-13}}{25 \times 10^{-12}} = 38 \, \text{mV}$.

5 **a** The collecting area of the CCD is
$30 \times 30 = 9.0 \times 10^2 \, \text{mm}^2 = 9.0 \times 10^2 \times 10^{-6} \, \text{m}^2 = 9.0 \times 10^{-4} \, \text{m}^2$.

The area of one pixel is then $\dfrac{9.0 \times 10^{-4}}{2.0 \times 10^6} = 4.5 \times 10^{-10} \, \text{m}^2$.

The power incident on a pixel is
$P = 6.8 \times 10^{-4} \times 4.5 \times 10^{-10} = 3.1 \times 10^{-13} \, \text{W}$. The energy deposited in 25 ms is then $E = 3.1 \times 10^{-13} \times 25 \times 10^{-3} = 7.8 \times 10^{-15} \, \text{J}$.
The energy of one photon is
$E = \dfrac{hc}{\lambda} = \dfrac{6.63 \times 10^{-34} \times 3.0 \times 10^8}{5.0 \times 10^{-7}} = 4.0 \times 10^{-19} \, \text{J}$ and so the number
of photons per pixel is $\dfrac{7.8 \times 10^{-15}}{4.0 \times 10^{-19}} = 195 \times 10^2 \approx 2 \times 10^4$.

b The number of electrons is therefore $0.80 \times 2 \times 10^4 = 1.6 \times 10^4$.
The charge of this number of electrons is
$1.6 \times 10^4 \times 2.6 \times 10^{-19} = 2.6 \times 10^{-15} \, \text{C}$. The potential difference is
$V = \dfrac{Q}{C} = \dfrac{2.6 \times 10^{-15}}{22 \times 10^{-12}} = 0.12 \, \text{mV}$.

c The area of one pixel is $4.5 \times 10^{-10} \, \text{m}^2$ and so the length of a pixel is $\sqrt{4.5 \times 10^{-10}} = 2.1 \times 10^{-5} \, \text{m}$. The images of the two points are a distance $1.4 \times 0.025 \, \text{mm} = 3.5 \times 10^{-5} \, \text{m}$ apart. This is not larger than two pixel lengths and so the points are not resolved.

Option A: Sight and wave phenomena

1 Since the intensity of light is low, vision takes place mainly through the rods. The highest concentration of the rods is away from the principal axis so by looking a bit sideways at the object, light falls on the rods.

2 In low-intensity light vision is through rods. Rods are more sensitive for blue than red and so the blue paper will be more clearly seen.

3 In bright sunlight cones are being used and they are sensitive to colour so red appears clearly. In low-intensity light, the rods are used and these are **not** sensitive to colour.

4 Yellow is a secondary colour obtained when red mixes with green. Adding blue leads to white colour.

5 A yellow filter subtracts its complementary colour, i.e. blue. The transmitted light has a colour given by
$W - B = (B + G + R) - B = G + R = Y$, i.e. yellow, as expected of a yellow filter.

6 The filters subtract in turn blue and then green. Thus the transmitted colour is $W - B - G = (B + G + R) - B - G = R$, i.e. red.

Option E: Astrophysics

1 The Sun will become invisible when its apparent magnitude becomes about 6. This is a difference of $6 - (-27) = 33$ magnitudes. Thus the apparent brightness of the Sun will decrease by a factor of $(2.512)^{33} \approx 1.6 \times 10^{13}$. The distance must then increase by a factor of $\sqrt{1.6 \times 10^{13}} = 4 \times 10^6$, i.e. to a distance of
$4 \times 10^6 \times 1.5 \times 10^{11} = 6 \times 10^{17} \, \text{m} = \dfrac{6 \times 10^{17}}{9.46 \times 10^{15}} = 63 \, \text{ly}$.

2 The ratio $(2.512)^{M_B - M_A} \approx (2.512)^{15.99} \approx 2.5 \times 10^6$ gives the ratio of the apparent brightness of the two stars when both are viewed from 10 pc away. Since the distance is the same, this ratio is also the

ratio of luminosities: $\dfrac{b_1}{b_2} = \dfrac{\frac{L_1}{4\pi d^2}}{\frac{L_2}{4\pi d^2}} = \dfrac{L_1}{L_2}$.

3 The star appears dimmer when seen from 10 pc (since 4.8 is **less** bright than 3.2). Thus its distance is less than 10 pc.

4 Vega is a distance $d = 10 \times 10^{\frac{0.03 - 0.58}{5}} = 7.8 \, \text{pc}$ from the Earth.

5 The wavelength is found from $\lambda_0 = \dfrac{2.9 \times 10^{-3}}{3000} = 9.7 \times 10^{-7} \, \text{m}$ and so will appear reddish. (The peak wavelength is in the infrared but the left side of the black body curve is mainly over red wavelengths.)

6 a Achernar and EG129 have the same temperature but Achernar has a much higher luminosity so it must have a very large area: approximately,
$$\frac{L_A}{L_E} \approx \frac{10^3}{10^{-4}} = \frac{\sigma A_A T^4}{\sigma A_E T^4} = \frac{A_A}{A_E} \Rightarrow \frac{A_A}{A_E} \approx 10^7 \Rightarrow \frac{R_A}{R_E} \approx 3 \times 10^3.$$

b Achernar and Ceti have the same luminosity but Ceti is much cooler. This means that Ceti has a much larger area than Achernar: approximately,
$$\frac{L_C}{L_A} \approx 1 = \frac{\sigma A_C T_C^4}{\sigma A_A T_C^4} = \frac{A_C (3 \times 10^3)^4}{A_A (2 \times 10^4)^4} \Rightarrow \frac{A_C}{A_A} \approx 2 \times 10^3 \Rightarrow \frac{R_C}{R_A} \approx 40.$$
This means that stars near Ceti (i.e. **red giants**) are huge followed by stars around Achernar (**blue giants**). Stars in the **white dwarf** region of EG129 are very small (typically the size of the Earth).

7 A main sequence star with a temperature of 10 000 K has a luminosity that is about 80 times that of the Sun (from the HR diagram). Hence $d = \sqrt{\frac{L}{4\pi b}} = \sqrt{\frac{80 \times 3.9 \times 10^{26}}{4\pi \times 4.4 \times 10^{-10}}} = 2.4 \times 10^{18}$ m.

8 The first is the existence of background radiation. This is radiation that existed when the universe was very young. As the universe expanded, the original high temperature fell and so the peak wavelength of this radiation shifted to its present low value of about 3 K.
The second piece of evidence is the expansion of the universe according to Hubble's law. If the distance between galaxies is getting larger then in the past the distance must have been smaller, indicating a violent start of the universe from a small region.

9 According to the **standard** Big Bang model, comparing the actual density of the universe to the critical density allows a prediction of whether the universe will continue its expansion forever (open universe $\rho < \rho_c$), halt the expansion and re-collapse (closed universe $\rho > \rho_c$) or continue the expansion forever at a rate that will stop at infinity (flat universe $\rho = \rho_c$).

10 If it were, its luminosity should have been between $50^3 = 125\,000$ and $50^4 = 6\,250\,000$ times larger than the luminosity of the Sun. So this star is **not** a main sequence star.

11 From $\frac{\Delta\lambda}{\lambda_0} = \frac{v}{c}$ the speed of the galaxy is
$$\frac{689.1 - 656.3}{656.3} = \frac{v}{c} \Rightarrow v = 1.5 \times 10^4\,\text{km s}^{-1}.$$
From $v = Hd$, $1.5 \times 10^4 = 72d \Rightarrow d = 210\,\text{Mpc}.$

12 a $T = \frac{1}{H} = \frac{1}{72\,\text{km s}^{-1}\,\text{Mpc}^{-1}} = \frac{\text{Mpc}}{72 \times 10^3\,\text{m}}$ s
$$= \frac{10^6 \times 3.09 \times 10^{16}\,\text{m}}{72 \times 10^3\,\text{m}}\,\text{s} = 4.29 \times 10^{17}\,\text{s}$$
$$= \frac{4.29 \times 10^{17}}{365 \times 24 \times 60 \times 60} = 13.6\,\text{billion years}.$$

b This estimate is based on a **constant** rate of expansion based on its **present** value. In the past the universe expanded faster and so the universe is younger than the estimate in **a**.

Option F: Communications

1 a There are four full waves in a time interval of 0.1 ms. Hence the carrier period is $\frac{1}{4} = 0.25$ ms. The frequency is therefore $\frac{0.10}{0.25} = 40$ kHz.

b The period of the information signal (we look at the envelope from peak to peak) is $0.305 - 0.055 = 0.25$ ms. The frequency is then $\frac{1}{0.25} = 4.0$ kHz.

c The bandwidth is twice the information signal frequency and so is 8.0 kHz.

d The maximum value of the modulated signal is 2.0 mV and the minimum value is 1.0 mV. Hence the information signal amplitude is $\frac{2.0 - 1.0}{2} = 0.50$ mV.

2 a The amplitude of the FM modulated signal is 12 V, the same as the carrier.

b The lowest frequency is $f_C - kA_S = 600 - 20 \times 2.0 = 560$ kHz and the highest is $f_C + kA_S = 600 + 20 \times 2.0 = 640$ kHz.

c $\beta = \frac{40}{8.0} = 5.0$

3 Applying the formula gives $\beta = \frac{75}{15} = 5$ and bandwidth $= 2(75 + 15) = 180$ kHz. (This is larger by 150 kHz compared to an AM transmission containing the same audio information.)

4 We put the appropriate power of 2 under each digit starting with 0 on the right: 10101.
$$\begin{array}{ccccc} 4 & 3 & 2 & 1 & 0 \end{array}$$
$10101 \rightarrow \underline{1} \times 2^4 + \underline{0} \times 2^3 + \underline{1} \times 2^2 + \underline{0} \times 2^1 + \underline{1} \times 2^0 \rightarrow 16 + 0 + 4 + 0 + 1 = 21$
and
$25 = \underline{1} \times 2^4 + \underline{1} \times 2^3 + \underline{0} \times 2^2 + \underline{0} \times 2^1 + \underline{1} \times 2^0$
$25_2 = 11001$

5 With 5 bits we can have at most $2^5 = 32$ numbers. These are the numbers from 0 to 31.

6 a The samples are taken every 0.50 ms and so the sampling frequency is $\frac{1}{0.50\,\text{ms}} = 2.0$ kHz.

b The smallest difference between any two samples is 0.1 V. The samples range from 0 V to 2.0 V and so we need $\frac{2.0 - 0}{0.1} = 20$ quantisation levels. With 4 bits we can have $2^4 = 16$ and this is not enough. With 5 we can have $2^5 = 32$ which is plenty. So we need 5 bits per sample.

c The bit rate is $2000 \times 5 = 10\,000\,\text{bit s}^{-1} = 10\,\text{kbit s}^{-1}$

d From the first graph we see that the signal shows variation within 0.07 ms. So a better sampling frequency would be $\frac{1}{0.07\,\text{ms}} \approx 14$ kHz. Similarly, the signal varies by as little as 0.05 mV so we need $\frac{2.0 - 0}{0.05} = 40$ quantization levels. So we need six bits per sample $(2^6 > 40)$.
Answers using other similar values are also acceptable.

7 The bit rate is $8000 \times 8 = 64\,000\,\text{bit s}^{-1} = 64\,\text{kbit s}^{-1}$. The duration of one bit is then $\frac{1}{64\,000} = 1.6 \times 10^{-5}\,\text{s} = 16\,\mu\text{s}$. The total number of bits generated is $64 \times 12 \times 60 \approx 46$ Mbit or 5.7 Mbyte.

8 The bandwidth is $3.0 \times 10^3 - 50 = 2950$ Hz and this is also the bit rate, $2.95 \approx 3.0\,\text{kbit s}^{-1}$.

9 From Snell's law, $1.33 \times \sin\theta_C = 1.00 \times \sin 90°$,
$\sin\theta_C = \frac{1.00}{1.33}$, $\theta_C = \arcsin\frac{1.00}{1.33} = 48.8°$.

10 $-16 = 10\log\frac{P_{final}}{P_{initial}} \Rightarrow -1.6 = \log\frac{P_{final}}{8.0} \Rightarrow \frac{P_{final}}{8.0} = 10^{-1.6} \approx \frac{1}{40}$.

So $P_{final} \approx \frac{1}{40}P_{initial} \Rightarrow P_{final} = \frac{8.0}{40}$ mW = 0.20 mW.

11 The **loss** is $3.0 \times 12 = 36$ dB. Then $-36 = 10\log\frac{P_{out}}{P_{in}}$,

$\frac{P_{out}}{P_{in}} = 10^{-3.6}$, $P_{out} \approx 180 \times 2.51 \times 10^{-4} = 0.045$ mW.

12 $G = 10\log\frac{P_{out}}{P_{in}}$, $\frac{P_{out}}{P_{in}} = 10^{\frac{G}{10}}$, $P_{out} = P_{in}10^{\frac{G}{10}} = 0.25 \times 10^{\frac{6.8}{10}} = 1.2$ mW.

13 The total power loss without any amplifiers would have been $-4.0 \times 400 = -1600$ dB. The net gain of the amplifiers must then be $+1600$ dB and so we need $\frac{1600}{20} = 80$ amplifiers.

14 **a** The attenuation after a distance of 3.0 km is $3.0 \times 14 = 42$ dB. The power is then found from

$-42 = 10\log\left(\frac{P}{200}\right)$, $\log\left(\frac{P}{200}\right) = -4.2$,

$\frac{P}{200} = 10^{-4.2} \approx 6.3 \times 10^{-5}$, $P = 0.013$ mW.

b Attenuation in coaxial cables is very frequency dependent. There is much more attenuation at higher frequencies.

15 **a** The power is distributed uniformly over a sphere of radius d. The power **per unit sphere area** is therefore $\frac{P}{4\pi d^2}$ and so the power collected by the antenna is

$\frac{P}{4\pi d^2} \times A = \frac{28 \times 10^6}{4\pi(10^5)^2} \times 1.2 = 0.27$ mW.

b The power loss in dB is $10\log\frac{0.27 \times 10^{-3}}{28 \times 10^6} = -110$ dB. This corresponds to a specific attenuation of $\frac{110}{100} = 1.1$ dB km^{-1}.

16 **a** The gain is $G = -\frac{R_F}{R} = -\frac{80}{16} = -5$.

b $V_0 = GV_{in} = -5 \times (-0.60) = +3.0$ V.

c $9.0 = -5 \times V_{in} \Rightarrow V_{in} = -1.8$ V. Since $V_{in} = -2.0$ V < -1.80 V the output will saturate at $+9.0$ V.

d The potential difference at the ends of resistor R is $1.2 - 0 = 1.2$ V. Hence the current through this resistor is $\frac{1.2}{16 \times 10^3} = 75\,\mu$A. This is also the current in R_F since the op–amp takes no current.

e The output will saturate when the input exceeds 1.8 V. The input is 1.8 V at times (approximately) 0.1 s and 0.4 s. Hence we have this graph.

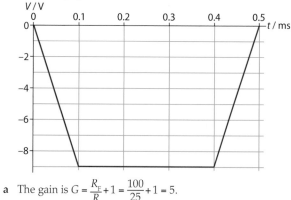

17 **a** The gain is $G = \frac{R_F}{R} + 1 = \frac{100}{25} + 1 = 5$.

b $V_0 = GV_{in} = 5 \times (-0.50) = -4.5$ V.

c $6.0 = 5 \times V_{in} \Rightarrow V_{in} = 1.2$ V. Since $V_{in} = 3.0$ V > 1.20 V the output will saturate at $+6.0$ V.

Option G: Electromagnetic waves

1 $\frac{1}{v} = \frac{1}{f} - \frac{1}{u} = \frac{1}{6.0} - \frac{1}{8.0} = \frac{1}{24.0} \Rightarrow v = 24.0$ cm. $M = -\frac{24.0}{8.0} = -3.0$.

The image is real, upside down and of height 9.0 cm.

2

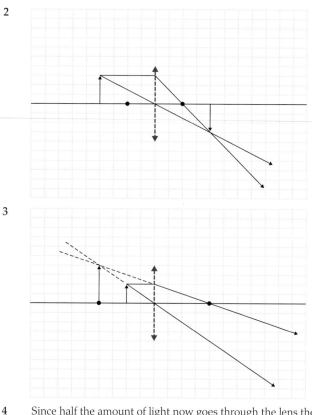

3

4 Since half the amount of light now goes through the lens the image formed will be half as bright.

5 Draw the dotted line (line 1) from the top of the image through the centre of the second lens. Extend this line backwards until it intersects the screen. This locates the image. Now draw line 2, parallel to the principal axis from the top of the image. Join the point where it intersects the eyepiece (3) with the top of the final image. Extend this forward until it intersects the principal axis. This the focal point.

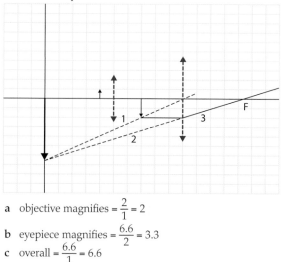

a objective magnifies $= \frac{2}{1} = 2$

b eyepiece magnifies $= \frac{6.6}{2} = 3.3$

c overall $= \frac{6.6}{1} = 6.6$

6 We must draw a construction line from the top of the image in the objective through the centre of the eyepiece. The rest of the rays upon refraction in the eyepiece must emerge parallel to the construction line.

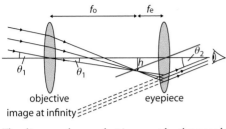

7 The diagram shows what is meant by the angular width of the central maximum. It is the angle subtended at the midpoint of the slits by the distance between the centres of the first minima on either side of the central maximum, i.e. 2θ.

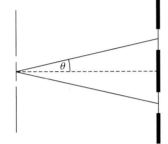

Since $d\sin\theta = (0+\frac{1}{2})\lambda$, we find

$\sin\theta = \frac{\lambda}{2d} = \frac{656\times10^{-9}}{2\times0.125\times10^{-3}} = 2.624\times10^{-3}$.

This is small and so $\theta \approx \sin\theta = 2.624\times10^{-3}\,\text{rad}$. So the angular width is $2\theta = 5.25\times10^{-3}\,\text{rad}$.

8 The energy gets redistributed in the interference pattern. The energy that would appear at the minimum appears at the maximum.

9 At the minima there will not be complete cancellation any more and so the fringes there will not be completely dark. At the maxima the amplitude will be less than before and so these fringes will not be as bright.

10 The separation of two consecutive slits is

$d = \frac{1}{600}\,\text{mm} = 1.67\times10^{-6}\,\text{m}$.

a In the first-order maximum, $n = 1$ and so

$d\sin\theta_1 = \lambda_1 \Rightarrow \sin\theta_1 \approx \theta_1 = \frac{589\times10^{-9}}{1.67\times10^{-6}} = 3.534\times10^{-4}\,\text{rad}$

and $d\sin\theta_2 = \lambda_2 \Rightarrow \sin\theta_2 \approx \theta_2 = \frac{589.6\times10^{-9}}{1.67\times10^{-6}} = 3.538\times10^{-4}\,\text{rad}$.

The difference is $\Delta\theta = (3.538 - 3.534)\times10^{-4} = 4\times10^{-7}\,\text{rad}$.

b In the second-order maximum, $n = 2$ and so, similarly, $\Delta\theta = 8\times10^{-7}\,\text{rad}$.

11 $\lambda = \frac{hc}{eV} = \frac{6.63\times10^{-34}\times3.0\times10^{8}}{1.6\times10^{-19}\times25\times10^{3}} = 5.0\times10^{-11}\,\text{m}$.

12 $2d\sin\theta = 1\times\lambda \Rightarrow d = \frac{\lambda}{2\sin\theta} = \frac{3.80\times10^{11}}{2\sin25.3°} = 4.45\times10^{-11}\,\text{m}$.

13 The wavelength in the soap film that undergoes destructive interference is $\lambda = 2d \Rightarrow \lambda = 2\times0.26\times10^{-6} = 5.2\times10^{-7}\,\text{m}$. This corresponds to a wavelength in air of $\lambda_{\text{air}} = \lambda n = 5.2\times10^{-7}\times1.33 = 6.9\times10^{-7}\,\text{m}$ which corresponds to red. The reflected light is missing red and so appears cyan.

14 $\tan\theta = \frac{\Delta d}{\Delta x} = \frac{260\times10^{-9}}{1.5\times10^{-4}} = 1.7\times10^{-3}$.

So $D = L\tan\theta = 5.0\times10^{-2}\times1.7\times10^{-3} = 8.5\times10^{-5}\,\text{m}$.

Option H: Relativity

1 Light will cover the distance $\Delta x = 6\times10^{8} - 3\times10^{8} = 3\times10^{8}\,\text{m}$ in a time of $\frac{\Delta x}{c} = \frac{3\times10^{8}}{3\times10^{8}} = 1\,\text{s}$. The event 'lightning strikes' thus occurred at $t = 3-1 = 2\,\text{s}$, at position $x = 3\times10^{8}\,\text{m}$. **All** observers in frame S agree that these are the coordinates of the event 'lightning strikes'.

> The time of an event is not the time that you see it unless you are at the position of the event.

2 **a** One half-life has gone by, i.e. 12 minutes.

b The interval of 12 minutes in **a** is the proper time interval between the two events for the rocket observer. So the interval is time interval $= \gamma\times$ proper time interval $= \frac{5}{3}\times12 = 20\,\text{min}$ for the lab observer.

c For the lab observer the half-life is 20 min and so he will also measure $\frac{N_0}{2}$ nuclei of the radioactive material in the container.

3 The gamma factor for a speed of $0.80c$ is $\gamma = \frac{1}{\sqrt{1-0.80^2}} = \frac{5}{3}$.

a The time is simply $\frac{40\,\text{ly}}{0.80c} = \frac{40\,\text{y}}{0.80} = 50\,\text{y}$.

> Remember that $\frac{1\,\text{ly}}{c} = 1\,\text{y}$.

b We provide two solutions: according to the spacecraft, the distance separating it and the planet is length contracted to $\frac{40\,\text{ly}}{\gamma} = \frac{40\,\text{y}}{5/3} = 24\,\text{ly}$. Hence the time for the planet to arrive at the spacecraft is $\frac{24\,\text{ly}}{0.80c} = \frac{24\,\text{y}}{0.80} = 30\,\text{y}$. OR: the time interval between leaving Earth and arriving at the planet is a proper time interval for the spacecraft observers. Therefore, proper $\Delta t' = \frac{\Delta t}{\gamma} = \frac{50}{5/3} = 30\,\text{y}$.

c For Earth the time is $\frac{40\,\text{ly}}{c} = 40\,\text{y}$.

d Let T be the time for the signal to arrive at Earth according to spacecraft clocks. According to the spacecraft the Earth is moving away at $0.80c$. The signal (moving at speed c) has to cover the distance originally separating the Earth and the spacecraft (24 ly according to spacecraft observers) plus the additional distance that the Earth will move away in time T (i.e. $0.80cT$). Therefore, $cT = 24 + 0.80cT \Rightarrow T = \frac{24}{0.20} = 120\,\text{y}$.

4 Light from the lightning strikes arrives at G at the same time (according to G). Observer R measures that light arrives at G at the same time as well since the arrivals occur at the same point in space. But according to R, G is moving away from the light from the right building. The light from both buildings travels at the same speed c according to R. For light to arrive at the same time, the signal from the right building must have been emitted first according to the R.

> Notice the logic of the argument and the detail required in the answer.

5 Take the ground as frame S and A as frame S'.
Then $v = 0.80c$, $u = -0.40c$ and we need to find u':

$$u' = \frac{u-v}{1-\frac{uv}{c^2}} = \frac{-0.40c-0.80c}{1-\frac{(-0.40c)(0.80c)}{c^2}} = \frac{-1.20c}{1+0.32} = -0.91c.$$

The speed of B relative to A is $0.91c$ directed to the left.

6 The total energy is $E = \sqrt{938^2+2800^2} = 2953\,\text{MeV}$. Hence the gamma factor is $\gamma = \frac{2953}{938} = 3.148$.

So $\frac{1}{\sqrt{1-\frac{v^2}{c^2}}} = 3.148$, $1-\frac{v^2}{c^2} = \frac{1}{3.148^2} \Rightarrow \frac{v}{c} = \sqrt{1-\frac{1}{3.148^2}} = 0.948.$

7 The gamma factor is $\frac{1}{\sqrt{1-0.98^2}} = 5.025$ and so the total energy after acceleration is $E = \gamma mc^2 = 5.025 \times 0.511 = 2.568\,\text{MeV}$. The kinetic energy therefore is $E_K = (2.568-0.511) = 2.057\,\text{MeV}$ and thus the voltage is $V = 2.057 \approx 2.06\,\text{MV}$.

8 The gamma factor is $\frac{1}{\sqrt{1-0.95^2}} = 3.203$. The total energy is thus $E = \gamma mc^2 = 3.203 \times 938 = 3004\,\text{MeV}$ and so the kinetic energy is $E_K = (3004-938) = 2066\,\text{MeV}$.

9 Use $E^2 = (mc^2)^2 + p^2c^2$ to get
$540^2 = 106^2 + p^2c^2 \Rightarrow p = 529 \approx 530\,\text{MeV}c^{-1}$.

10 Since $E = \gamma mc^2$ the gamma factor is $\gamma = \frac{6500}{1800} = 3.61$. Hence

$\frac{1}{\sqrt{1-\frac{v^2}{c^2}}} = 3.61$, so $1-\frac{v^2}{c^2} = \frac{1}{3.61^2} \Rightarrow \frac{v^2}{c^2} = 0.923 \Rightarrow \frac{v}{c} = 0.961.$

11 From $p = \gamma mv$ we find $\frac{p_\phi}{p_\eta} = \frac{\gamma_\phi(2m)v}{\gamma_\eta m(2v)} = \frac{\gamma_\phi}{\gamma_\eta} < 1$, i.e. the η meson has the greater momentum.

12 **a** Combining $E = \gamma mc^2$ and $p = \gamma mv$ we find
$p = \frac{\gamma mc^2 v}{c^2} = \frac{Ev}{c^2} \Rightarrow v = \frac{pc^2}{E}$. For a massless particle,

$E = pc$ and so $v = \frac{pc^2}{pc} = c$.

b $v = \frac{(640\,\text{MeV}c^{-1})c^2}{654\,\text{MeV}} = 0.979c.$

c $mc^2 = \sqrt{E^2-p^2c^2} = \sqrt{654^2-640^2} = 135\,\text{MeV}$, $m = 135\,\text{MeV}c^{-2}$.

13 Before acceleration, $E_0 = mc^2$. After acceleration, $E = \gamma mc^2$. Hence the change is $\Delta E = \gamma mc^2 - mc^2 = (\gamma-1)mc^2$ and this equals $qV = 3.2 \times 10^9\,\text{eV} = 3200\,\text{MeV}$. So, $(\gamma-1) = \frac{3200}{938} \Rightarrow \gamma = 4.41$.

Hence $4.41 = \frac{1}{\sqrt{1-\frac{v^2}{c^2}}} \Rightarrow \frac{v}{c} = \sqrt{1-\frac{1}{4.41^2}} = 0.97$.

And $p = \gamma mv = 4.41 \times 938 \times 0.97 = 4.0 \times 10^3\,\text{MeV}c^{-1}$. This is also expressed as $p = 4.0\,\text{GeV}c^{-1}$.

14 The best way to proceed is to find the total energy of the proton through $E^2 = (mc^2) + p^2c^2$, i.e. $E = \sqrt{0.938^2 + 2.40^2} = 2.58\,\text{GeV}$. Then use $E = \gamma mc^2$ to find $\gamma = \frac{2.58}{0.938} = 2.75$ and finally

$2.75 = \frac{1}{\sqrt{1-\frac{v^2}{c^2}}} \Rightarrow \frac{v}{c} = \sqrt{1-\frac{1}{2.75^2}} = 0.93$.

> Notice the change of the proton rest energy from $938\,\text{MeV}$ to $0.938\,\text{GeV}$. This method is preferable to solving for v from $p = \gamma mv$.

15 The Ψ is at rest so its momentum is zero. Therefore the muon and antimuon have equal and opposite momenta. Let the magnitude of the momentum of the muon be p. Conservation of energy states that

$$3100 = 2\sqrt{106^2 + p^2c^2}$$
$$3100^2 = 4(106^2 + p^2c^2)$$
$$p^2c^2 = \left(\frac{3100^2}{4} - 106^2\right)$$
$$p = 1.55 \times 10^3\,\text{MeV}c^{-1} = 1.55\,\text{GeV}c^{-1}$$

16 By the equivalence principle, the situation is equivalent to a rocket at rest on the surface of a massive body. In this case we know that the ray of light will bend towards the massive body and so the ray will follow a curved, downward path. It will therefore hit the opposite side of the rocket at a height less than h.

> You **must** refer to the equivalence principle.

17 Working backwards from the previous example, the situation is equivalent to a rocket accelerating in outer space with acceleration $9.8\,\text{ms}^{-2}$. The time for light to cross the distance of $300\,\text{m}$ is $t = \frac{s}{c} = \frac{300}{3 \times 10^8} = 10^{-6}\,\text{s}$. In this time the light has moved down a distance $x = \frac{1}{2}at^2 = \frac{1}{2} \times 9.8 \times (10^{-6})^2 \approx 5 \times 10^{-12}\,\text{m}(!)$.

18 The situation is equivalent to a rocket at rest on the surface of a massive object. Hence the ray of light is climbing up a gravitational field and so the frequency will get smaller by the gravitational redshift effect.

19 Newton would claim the path of the planet is due to the gravitational force between the Sun and the planet. Einstein would claim the path is due to the curved spacetime: the planet follows a geodesic, i.e. a path of least length, in the curved spacetime around the massive Sun.

> This is an 'explain' question. There has to be some detail.

20 We have that $5 = \dfrac{1}{\sqrt{1-\dfrac{R_s}{r}}}$ and so $r = \dfrac{25}{24}R_S = 5.2 \times 10^8\,\text{m}$.

Hence $h = \dfrac{25}{24}R_S - R_S = \dfrac{R_S}{24} = 22 \times 10^7\,\text{m}$.

> The question refers to height so we must remember to subtract the radius in the end.

Option I: Medical physics

1 No, because the response of the ear is not linear.
In the first case the sensation of loudness would increase by $10\log\left(\dfrac{2\times10^{-6}}{1\times10^{-6}}\right) = 3.0\,\text{dB}$ and in the second by $10\log\left(\dfrac{3\times10^{-6}}{2\times10^{-6}}\right) = 1.7\,\text{dB}$.

2 The original level was $IL_1 = 10\log\left(\dfrac{10^{-10}}{10^{-12}}\right) = 10\log 10^2 = 20\,\text{dB}$.
The new sound intensity level is
$IL_2 = 10\log\left(\dfrac{10^{-8}}{10^{-12}}\right) = 10\log 10^4 = 40\,\text{dB}$. The increase is thus 20 dB.

> It would have been quicker to say
> $\Delta IL = 10\log\left(\dfrac{10^{-8}}{10^{-10}}\right) = 10\log 10^2 = 20\,\text{dB}$.

3 The intensity from one machine is found from
$95\,\text{dB} = 10\log\left(\dfrac{I}{10^{-12}}\right) \Rightarrow \dfrac{I}{10^{-12}} = 1.0\times10^{9.5} \Rightarrow I = 0.0316\,\text{W m}^{-2}$.
The intensity at 102 dB is
$102\,\text{dB} = 10\log\left(\dfrac{I}{10^{-12}}\right) \Rightarrow \dfrac{I}{10^{-12}} = 1.0\times10^{10.2} \Rightarrow I = 0.158\,\text{W m}^{-2}$.
The number of machines is therefore $\dfrac{0.158}{0.0316} \approx 5$.

4 $I = I_0 e^{-\mu x} = I_0 e^{-0.52\times1.2} = 0.54 I_0$.

5 The photoelectric effect is more useful since we need to have a contrast between, for example, tissue and bone that have different atomic numbers.

6 a μ is the probability per unit length that a particular X-ray photon will be absorbed.
   b No significant change is expected. The low-energy photons would be absorbed and would not contribute to making the image.
   c The attenuation coefficient at 50 keV is 1.5 mm^{-1} and so $I = I_0 e^{-\mu x} = I_0 e^{-1.5\times2.2} = 0.037 I_0$.

7 The transducer acts as both emitter and receiver. The emissions must stop so that the reflected ultrasound may be detected.

8 The charge in 1 kg is $6.9\times10^{-3}\,\text{C}$ corresponding to $\dfrac{6.9\times10^{-3}}{1.6\times10^{-19}} = 4.3125\times10^{16}$ elementary charges. This requires an energy of $4.3125\times10^{16}\times40\times1.6\times10^{-19} = 276\times10^{-3}\,\text{J}$. The dose equivalent is thus $1\times276\times10^{-3}\,\text{Sv} \approx 280\,\text{mSv}$.

9 a Gamma emitters are preferable because the gamma rays are not easily absorbed by the body and so can be detected.
   b The energy absorbed is $380\times10^6\times140\times10^3\times1.6\times10^{-19} = 8.51\times10^{-6}\,\text{J}$. The absorbed dose is thus $D = \dfrac{8.51\times10^{-6}}{70} = 1.22\times10^{-7}\,\text{Gy}$ and since the quality factor for gamma rays is 1, the dose equivalent is $1.22\times10^{-7}\,\text{Sv}$.

10 The activity is $A = A_0 e^{-\lambda_E t}$ where the effective decay constant is $\lambda_E = \lambda_P + \lambda_B = \dfrac{\ln 2}{2} + \dfrac{\ln 2}{4}$.
Hence, after 6 days $A = A_0 e^{-\left(\frac{\ln2}{2}+\frac{\ln2}{4}\right)\times4} = A_0 e^{-3\ln2} = \dfrac{A_0}{8}$.

11 Let A be the initial activity in the $10\,\text{cm}^3$ of albumen and V the volume of blood in the patient.
Then, $120 = A\dfrac{5}{V+10}$, $125 = A\dfrac{5}{5000+10}$. We may neglect the 10 in the denominators so that $120 = A\dfrac{5}{V}$ and $125 = A\dfrac{5}{5000}$.
Hence $\dfrac{125}{120} = \dfrac{A\dfrac{5}{5000}}{A\dfrac{5}{V}} = \dfrac{V}{5000}$ and so $V = 5200\,\text{cm}^3$.

Option J: Particle physics

1 No, because the kaon has non-zero strangeness quantum number.

2 a $p \rightarrow e^- + \gamma$ baryon number
   b $p \rightarrow \pi^- + \pi^+$ electric charge, baryon number
   c $n \rightarrow p + e^-$ lepton number
   d $e^- + e^+ \rightarrow \gamma$ momentum
   e $e^+ \rightarrow \mu^+ + \nu_\mu$ energy, lepton number
   f $p \rightarrow n + e^+ + \nu_e$ energy (but can occur within a nucleus where the required energy is provided by the binding energy of the nucleus)

3 a Strangeness is violated here since $S = -1$ on the left hand side of the reaction equation but $S = 0$ on the right. Hence the decay must be a weak interaction process.
   b A possible diagram is shown.

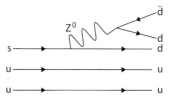

4

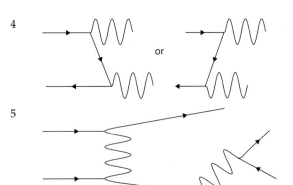

or

5

6

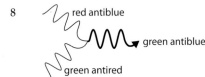

7 $R \approx \dfrac{6.6 \times 10^{-34}}{4\pi \times \left(\dfrac{80 \times 10^{9}}{(3 \times 10^{8})^{2}} \times 1.6 \times 10^{-19}\right) \times 3 \times 10^{8}}$ m $= 10^{-18}$ m.

(Notice the conversion of mass from $GeV\,c^{-2}$ to kg.)

8

red antiblue

green antiblue

green antired

9 **a** The red quark will have the same flavour as the original quark, i.e. strange.
b The gluon colours will be green antired.

10 **a** $f = \dfrac{qB}{2\pi m}$ and so $f = \dfrac{1.6 \times 10^{-19} \times 1.4}{2\pi \times 1.67 \times 10^{-27}} = 21$ MHz.

b $K_{max} = \dfrac{q^{2}B^{2}R^{2}}{2m} = \dfrac{(1.6 \times 10^{-19} \times 1.4 \times 0.25)^{2}}{2 \times 1.67 \times 10^{-27}}$

$= 9.39 \times 10^{-13}$ J $= \dfrac{9.39 \times 10^{-13}}{1.6 \times 10^{-19}}$ eV ≈ 5.9 MeV.

11 **a**

b Here, $m = M = m_{e}$ and $E_{A} = 4m_{e}c^{2}$.
Hence $16(m_{e}c^{2})^{2} = 2m_{e}c^{2}\,E + (m_{e}c^{2})^{2} + (m_{e}c^{2})^{2}$ giving $E = 7m_{e}c^{2}$.
Thus $E_{K} = E - m_{e}c^{2} = 6m_{e}c^{2} = 3.1$ MeV.

Notice that the total rest energy in the final state is $4m_{e}c^{2}$ and $2m_{e}c^{2}$ in the initial. The kinetic energy supplied is much more than the difference $4m_{e}c^{2} - 2m_{e}c^{2} = 2m_{e}c^{2}$ because the particles produced must have kinetic energy.

12 $E_{A} = 1193 + 498 = 1691$ MeV.
Hence $1691^{2} = 2 \times 938E + (140)^{2} + (938)^{2}$ giving $E = 1045$ MeV.

13 **a** The reaction violates both muon and electron lepton number conservation. $L_{\mu} = +1$ on the left and 0 on the right and $L_{e} = +1$ on the right and 0 on the left.
b The correct reaction is $\mu^{-} \rightarrow e^{-} + \overline{\nu}_{\mu} + \nu_{e}$.

14 To conserve lepton number it has to be a muon neutrino.

15 The energy needed to break apart the nucleus of helium into its constituents is 28 MeV. The average kinetic energy at a temperature T is $\overline{E}_{K} = \dfrac{3}{2}kT$ and so equating the two gives

$\dfrac{3}{2}kT = 28$ MeV $\Rightarrow T = \dfrac{2 \times 28 \times 10^{6} \times 1.6 \times 10^{-19}}{3 \times 1.38 \times 10^{-23}}$ K $\approx 2 \times 10^{11}$ K.

A more accurate estimate than the one presented here gives a temperature closer to $T \approx 10^{10}$ K. This is the time of **nucleosynthesis**, the time when protons and neutrons combined to form nuclei for the first time. The Universe then was only a few minutes old.